FIRST EDITION

# INDIAN SOCIETY (GS-1) & SOCIAL JUSTICE (GS-2)

**ARIHANT PUBLICATIONS (INDIA) LIMITED**

All Rights Reserved

卐 **© Author**

No part of this publication may be re-produced, stored in a retrieval system or by any means, electronic, mechanical, photocopying, recording, scanning, web or otherwise without the written permission of the publisher. Arihant has obtained all the information in this book from the sources believed to be reliable and true. However, Arihant or its editors or authors or illustrators don't take any responsibility for the absolute accuracy of any information published and the damage or loss suffered thereupon.

*All disputes subject to Meerut (UP) jurisdiction only.*

卐 **Administrative & Production Offices**

**Regd. Office**

'Ramchhaya' 4577/15, Agarwal Road, Darya Ganj, New Delhi -110002
Tele: 011- 47630600, 43518550

卐 **Head Office**

Kalindi, TP Nagar, Meerut (UP) - 250002
Tel: 0121-7156203, 7156204

卐 **Sales & Support Offices**

Agra, Ahmedabad, Bengaluru, Bareilly, Chennai, Delhi, Guwahati, Hyderabad, Jaipur, Jhansi, Kolkata, Lucknow, Nagpur & Pune.

卐 **PRICE** ₹ 325.00

**PO No :** TXT-59-T064053-03-25

Published by Arihant Publications (India) Ltd.

For further information about the books published by Arihant, log on to www.arihantbooks.com or e-mail at info@arihantbooks.com

Follow us on    

# Few Words
## to the Budding UPSC Aspirants

**UPSC Mains Exam** is the most crucial stage on your path to becoming a civil servant. But conquering it isn't a walk in the park - it's a strategic game. You need the right arsenal (effective study materials) and honed tactics (answer writing skills) to succeed. **PULSE Mains Series** equips you for every challenge, a one-stop solution for your Mains preparation.

Forget about sifting through mountains of irrelevant information. **PULSE Mains books** are meticulously organized, packed with dynamic analysis and updated with the latest developments.

These books provide only exam-relevant content and removing the cluttered content available in the market, thus bringing time-optimised notes for the students.

Following are the salient features of Pulse Mains books:

- **Comprehensive and Exam-oriented content** covering all relevant topics in depth.
- **Content Enrichment with the help of current examples,** data & facts, case studies and supreme court judgements.
- **Innovative exam-ready frameworks** (PESTEL, Stakeholder, Life-cycle, etc) to meet evolving answer writing demands.
- **Visually appealing presentation by incorporating flowcharts,** timelines, mindmaps, hand-drawn diagrams, tables and maps.
- **Integration of PYQs** at the end of each chapter to align the content with the recent exam trends.
- **Easy for multiple revision of the syllabus** which can help in improving the Mains score.

On behalf of MentorsHut, I would like to express our deepest gratitude to each and every student for placing your trust in Pulse Books. **Thanks to your incredible support, Pulse Books have become best-sellers!**

We are also incredibly thankful to **Arihant Publications** for partnering with us and providing the opportunity to develop the PULSE series for the UPSC Mains examination.

The creation of these masterpiece Mains books wouldn't have been possible without the tireless, combined efforts of the entire MentorsHut family, who dedicated thousands of hours to the project. Our sincere thanks go to **Vishal Singh, Shefali, Ashutosh Bansal, Tarun Sahu, Shadab Ahmad, Avinish Kumar and Vishal Anand for their exceptional contributions.** Their creativity in content presentation, clear handwriting and unwavering support for each other were instrumental in this success.

We also want to express my **deepest gratitude to my daughter, Prisha Mangtani.** While we poured our heart into these books, we know the sacrifices this meant for you. You are truly special!

We at MentorsHut are dedicated to continuous improvement. While we believe Pulse Books represent our best effort, we recognize the possibility of human error. We welcome any suggestions for improvement to the content. Please feel free to share your thoughts at info@mentorshut.com

**Amit Mangtani,**
**CA Shalini Wadhwani**
**Founders, MentorsHut**

# Let's Begin Our Journey

**Note**: The book covers current developments till May 2024. Recent current developments and some peripheral issues will be given as Value Addition Material (Online). Scan the QR Code to get access of current issues.

CHAPTER 01

# Salient Features of Indian Society

## CONCEPT OF SOCIETY

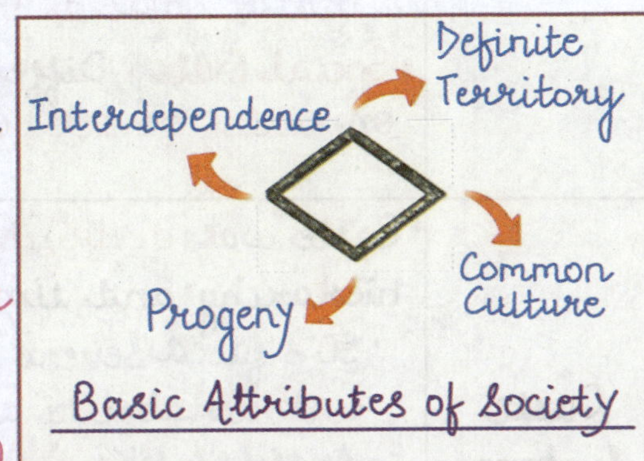

Basic Attributes of Society

- **About Society:** It is a dynamic system of interconnected social relationships that creates a shared sense of identity and purpose among its members.
  - It forms a structure that guides behaviour and is more important than the individual people involved.
- **Characteristics:** Society isn't just about physical proximity or shared needs; it's about the mental state of its members who recognise their independence.

## INDIAN SOCIETY ON THE EVE OF INDEPENDENCE

| | |
|---|---|
| Health | • Health Infrastructure was extremely underdeveloped.<br>• India had 7400 hospitals with a bed population ratio of 0·24 per 1,000 population.<br>• Alarming health indicators:<br>• Life expectancy was around 32 years<br>• Birth rate stood at 48 per thousand individuals, whereas death rate was 40 per thousand.<br>• Infant morality rate was high at 146 per 1000 in 1951. |

| | |
|---|---|
| | · Rampant spread of tuberculosis, and Cholera.<br>· Nutrition and Sanitation : Widespread Malnutrition + Limited access to clean water + Limited sanitation facilities → contributing to poor health outcome. |
| Education | · Literacy Rates (1951): Only 18.3% of the population was literate.<br>· Female literacy was even lower around 8%.<br>· Poor Enrollment Ratio due to widespread poverty and high cost of education. Ex:<br>· Primary Enrollment Rate : 43%, with a high dropout rate.<br>· Middle School Enrolment Ratio : 13%<br>· High School Enrolment Ratio : 5.3%<br>· Gender Disparity : Female employment rate was much lower than Male employment rate.<br>· At primary level schools only 15% women were teachers and this ratio stood at 16% in terms of middle and High School.<br>· Social Evils : Differential and unequal access to education based on caste, gender, and region. |
| Caste System | · Caste was deeply entrenched in Indian society, dictating social hierarchy and limiting social mobility.<br>· SC's faced Severe discrimination, Exploitation → subjected to untouchability and social exclusion.<br>· Articles like 15(4), 17, 46 and 338 of Indian Constitution puts a constitutional checks and provide a safeguard to them.<br>· Economic Disparities : Caste based division of labour.<br>· Upper castes dominated land ownership and skilled professions, while lower castes were relegated to menial jobs. |
| Class Inequality | · Skewed Land ownership : According to FAO, 53% of land was held by 7% of the landowners, whereas 28% of landowners with submarginal and marginal holdings owned about 6%.<br>· Poverty : Almost 70% of population lived in poverty with subsistence agriculture and limited opportunities. |
| Religion | · Religious Demography (1951 Census) : Hindus comprised 84.1%, Sikhs were 1.9%, Muslims 9.8% in the and Christians were 2.28%.<br>· Communal Tension : Partition triggered large-scale riots and displacement. |

| | |
|---|---|
| Ethnicity | • Ethnic Diversity : A significant population of Adivasis (indigenous tribal people) faced marginalisation and exploitation.<br>• Constitution of India with enactment of Articles like Article 15(4), 16(4), 46 and Article 338A puts a constitutional check and provides a safeguard to them.<br>• Regional Disparities : Ethnic, linguistic diversity corresponded with regional disparities → regionalism and demands for autonomy.<br>• Ex : Languages become ground for state reorganisation (Andhra Pradesh became first state to reorganise on basis of it). |
| Status of Women | • Social Status : Women's status in society was low + pervasive patriarchy and gender discrimination.<br>• Practices like child marriage, dowry, and purdah were common.<br>• Women have limited property rights.<br>• Education and Employment : Womens were largely confined to domestic sphere → limited acess to education + healthcare → poor participation in formal workforce. |

## SALIENT FEATURES OF INDIAN SOCIETY

➤ **Unity in Diversity** : India is a vibrant mosaic of cultures, languages, and ethnicities. India encompasses Dravidian, Indo-European, and Tibeto-Burman language families.

➤ **Multiculturalism** : There exist two school of thought defining India's Multiculturalism as :

- Salad Bowl describes a heterogenous society where different cultures are brought together as ingredients of salad but individual flavour is retained instead of merging into a single homogenous culture.
- Ex : Dosa in Chennai, Bihu in Assam, Bengali in West Bengal justify how Indian society preserved distinction.
- Melting point advocates that people of various cultures melt together deserting their individual culture → fully assimilated into pre-dominant society.
- Ex : Bollywood blends regional styles of music and dance, Sarees in modern fabrics → highlights fusion of differentiation

➤ **Accommodative Society** : India has retained its core identity while embracing External influences like British Mughals etc.

- Ex : Architectural styles like the Taj Mahal blending Persian and Mughal elements
- Ex : Unique blend of Indian spices with European culinary traditions.

➤ **Caste System:** A hierarchical social structure based on birth, occupation and social status, has been a defining feature of Indian Society for centuries.

➤ **Cultural Lag:** Period of delay or adjustment that occurs when non-material culture (beliefs, values, norms, and social practices) struggles to keep pace with changes in material culture (technology and inventions).
Ex:

- **Social media and Privacy:** The rapid rise of social media has outpaced the development of social norms and laws around data privacy.
- **Dual Burden of Work** on women is resulted of a mismatch between pace of change peripheral values to core values.

➤ **Joint Family System:** A.M. Shah observe that this concept of "jointness" continues to some extent in modern India, with multiple generations sometimes sharing a household.

- Ex: Economic Survey 2018 highlights that Child Sex Ratio is declining due to Patrilocality and Patrilineality.

Patrilocality refers to a social system where a married couple resides with or near the husband's family after marriage.
Patrilineality is a Kinship system where descent and inheritance are traced through the father's line.

➤ **Family Values:** Elders are seen as repositories of wisdom and experience → Customary to seek their advice on important matters.

➤ **Patriarchy:** Indian culture is patriarchal, with clear expectations for each gender.

- Ex: Son-Meta Preference, Gender Pay Gap and Glass ceilings.

➤ **Religions Harmony:** India is a land of diverse religious faiths, including Hinduism, Buddhism, Jainism, Sikhism, Christianity, Islam etc.

- Ex: Sarva Dharma Sambhava → Kumbh Mela (welcomes people from all faiths).

➤ Spirituality is central to live of many Indians, shaping their values, rituals, and daily practices.

- Ex: Yoga, meditation, and pilgrimages.

➤ **Co-existence of Individualism and collectivism:**

- **Individualism** emphasised on personal achievements and self-expression, prioritisation of own goals and aspirations.
- Ex: Younger generation making career choices on personal interests and talents

- **Collectivism** is a social, cultural, and political principle that prioritise the group over individual interests.
  - Ex: Strong family bonds, communal decision-making, shared responsibilities and an emphasis on social harmony and cohesion is its manifestation.

# SOCIAL INSTITUTION

## The Kinship:

**About:** Kinship system can be defined as a "the customary system of statuses and roles that governs the behaviour of people who are related to each other though marriage or descent from a common ancestor."

**Kinship Groups of North India**

- Kinship Groups
  - Clan & lineage group
  - Patrilineage
  - Caste & Subcaste
  - Fictive kin

## Types of Kinship

| Basis of Comparison | Affinal Kinship | Consanguineous Kinship |
|---|---|---|
| Basis of Relationship | Marriage | Blood relation |
| Shared Ancestor | No | Yes (common ancestor) |
| Examples | Spouse (husband-wife), in-laws (parents-in-law, siblings-in-law). | Parents, siblings, grandparents, aunts, uncles, cousins (all blood relaties) |
| Permanence | Not permanent; ends with divorce or death of spouse | Permanent; blood ties cannot be broken |
| Choice | Relationship is chosen through marriage | Relationship is not chosen; determined by birth |
| Strength of Bond | Varies depending on the relationship | Generally strong due to shared history and blood ties. |

## Functional Role of Kinship

| Kinship Type | Functional Role |
|---|---|
| Consanguineous Kinship | • Socialization and Nature: Provides a primary socialisation while raising children and inulcating cultural values.<br>• Economic Cooperation. Family members work together to share resources and provide economic support. • Ex: It becomes crucial in times of emergency like a pandemic. |

| | |
|---|---|
| | • Emotional Support : Offers a network of love, affection, and security.<br>• Social Identity : Provides a sense of belonging and connection to a larger group. |
| Affinal Kinship | • Alliance Formation : Creates bonds between families, fostering social cohesion and reducing conflicts<br>• Kin Network Expansion : Expands social networks and access to resources through in-laws<br>• Social Integration : Helps integrate spouses into a new family and community<br>• Child Rearing Support : In-laws can provide additional support for raising children. |

## FAMILY

**About:** A family is a social group made up of individuals connected by adoption, marriage, and blood relationships, having common residence working together economically, engaging in sexual activity, and procreating.

» It also involves prohibition of sexual relationship between members of family excluding affines (Martial relations).

### Types of Indian Families:

**On basis of Marriage**

- **Monogamous Family** : A family with only one husband and one wife, and their children
- **Polygamous Family** : A family structure where one person is married to multiple spouses simultaneously. There are main types :
  - **Polygyny** : One man with multiples wives.
  - **Polyandry** : One woman with multiple husband

**On basis of Residence**

- **Patrilocal family** : A family where the couples resides with husband's family after marriage. Wife moves in → husbands's family.
- **Matrilocal Family** : A family where the couple resides with wife's family after marriage. The husband moves in → wife's family.
- **Neolocal Family** : A family where the couples establishes a new households after marriage, independent of both the husband's and wife families.

- On basis of Descent
  - Patrilineal Family: A family system where ancestry is traced throught the father' side.
    - Children inherit property, titles, and family names from their father's lineage.
  - Matrilineal Family: A family system where descent is traced through the mother's side.
    - Children inherit property, titles, and family names from their mother's lineage
- On basis of Composition
  - Nuclear Family: The traditional family unit consisting of parents and their children.
  - Joint Family: An extended family unit comprise of three or more generation → includes parents, children, grandparents, aunts, uncles, or cousins, all living in the same households.

## Characteristics of Family:

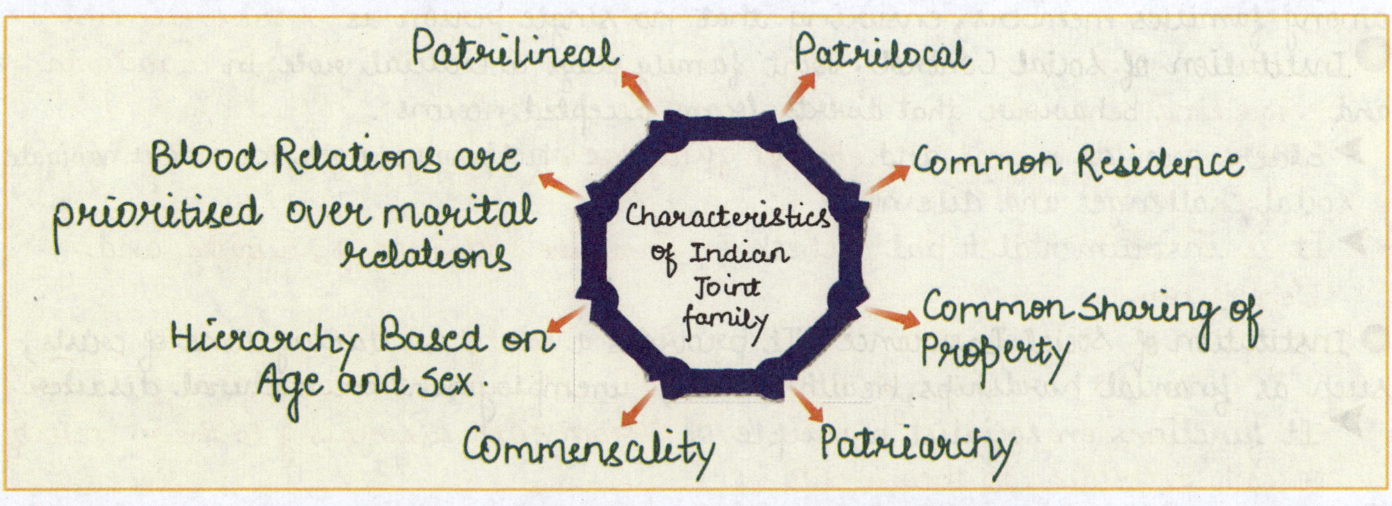


- Universal Unit: Families exist in all societies, fulfilling vital functions for individuals and society at large.
- Emotional Core: Families provide love, support, and a sense of belonging. Members offer care, protection, and are willing to make sacrifices for each other's well-being
- Socialisation and Norms: Families transmit social norm and expectations, shaping behaviour through interactions governed by social and legal guidelines.
- Safe Haven: A stable home environment is crucial for families, especially for raising children.
- Kinship Systems: Families have their own Kinship structures (patrilineal or matrilineal) that shape identity and social connections.

→ Change and Evolutions : Family structures and functions are not static → subjected to, social, economic, and technological shifts.

→ Commensality is the social glue that binds families together during shared meals led interactions.

## Functions of Joint Family :

- Institution of Primary Socialisation : Joint family act as first school for children responsible for including basic norms, values and behaviours expected by society.
  - ➤ Family members guided their behaviour and development → Instills fundamental values like respect for elders, communal living, and cooperation.
- Cultural Transmission : Joint families are custodians of cultural heritage, ensuring that traditions, customs and rituals are preserved and passed down through generations.
  - ➤ Celebration of festivals, religious beliefs and practices are taught and observed collectively → strengthening the family's social fabric and spiritual connectivity.
- Effective Division of Labour : Household chores and responsibilities are distributed among families members, ensuring that no single person is overburdened.
- Institution of Social Control : Joint family plays a crucial role in monitoring and correcting behaviour that diverts from accepted norms.
  - ➤ Elders provide moral and ethical guidance, helping younger members navigate social challenges and dilemmas.
  - ➤ It is instrumental to put a check on Juvenile Deliquency, Suicide and Depression.
- Institution of Social Insurance : It provides a safety net during time of crisis, such as financial hardships, health issues, unemployment or natural disaster.
  - ➤ It functions on socialist principle of "From each according to their ability, to each according to their needs."
- Economic Cooperation : Joint families pool their financial resources, land, assets, allowing for better economic stability and investment in shared goals.
- Assertiveness of Collectivism : Joint family fosters a strong sense of collective identity and belonging, prioritising family unity and solidarity over individualism

## Dysfunction of Joint family

- Limited Privacy : Multiple generations living under one roof → individuals have little personal space → lead to feelings of suffocation and lack of privacy
- Absence of Individualism : Emphasis on collective wellbeing → suppress individual ambition and personal desires.
  - ➤ Absence or little room for individual autonomy hinder personal growth and self-expression.

- **Low Standard of Living:** Resource pooling sometimes leads to insufficient allocation, resulting in a lower standard of living for all members.
- **Assertiveness of Patriarchy:** With decision making power concentrated in the hands of male members → marginalisation of women and restricting their roles to domestic sphere.
- **Status of Women:** Patriarchal norms can restrict women's autonomy, mobility and choices, reinforcing gender stereatypes and discrimination.
- **Disguised Unemployment:** Joint families characterised by hidden form of unemployment → some members appear busy but effective productivity is significantly low.
- **Self Alienation:** Overemphasis on collective identity may lead to self-alienation, where individuals feel disconnected from their personal identity and aspirations
- **Reproduction of Social Labour:** It perpetuates traditional gender roles and labour division, which can hinder progress towards more equitable labour distribution.
  - It taught preservations of status quo i.e never to question the authority → create a workforce which is socially fit.
- **Arena of Conflict:** This short premise witnesses interpersonal conflicts over issues like resource allocation, decision-making, and personal behaviours.

## Life Cycle of Joint Family

Joint family root as the basic social unit, it witnessed a shift towards nuclear families due to modernization. Yet, a new trend emerges- the reintegration of families, seeking a balance between tradition and contemporary needs

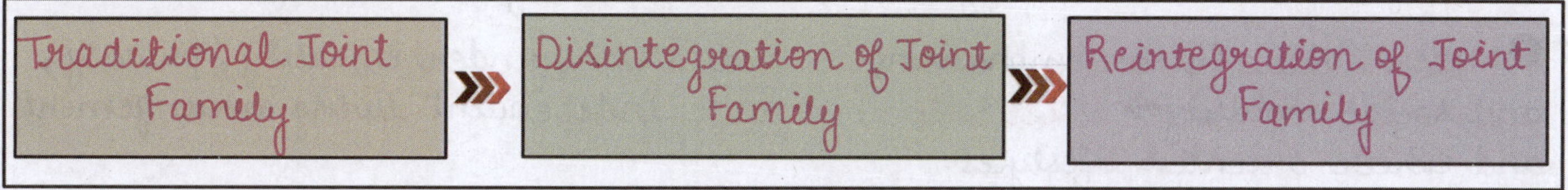


## Factors Responsible for Disintegration of Joint Family:

- **Urbanization and Industrialization:** Urban migration leads to nuclear families as it is challenging to accommodate large joint families in cities.
  - According to Census 2011, urban population increased from 27.7% in 2001 to 31.2% in 2011.
- **Employment Opportunities:** Urban employment grew at a faster rate than rural employment, driving young adults to cities where nuclear family structures are more practical.

- **Higher Education:** As per AISHE India's Gross Enrolment Ratio (GER) in higher education, increased to 28.4% in 2021-22.
  - It requires young people to move to urban centres or abroad, leading to the separation from joint families.
- **Changing Aspirations:** Increased literacy rate i.e 74.04% → fostered new aspirations among youth to pursue individual and lifestyles.
- **Individualism:** Centre for the Study of Developing Societies (CSDS) survey shows a shift in attitudes among younger generations, with a growing preference for nuclear families to ensure privacy and personal freedom.
- **Changing Social Norms:** Census 2011 indicates an increase in nuclear families from 51.7 in 2001 to 52.1.
- **Women's Employment:** As per PLFS 2022-23, Female labour force participation (FLPR) in India stood at 37%
  - This shift challenges traditional roles of women in family → led to formation of nuclear families to balance work and home responsibilities.
- **Media and Communication:** The proliferation of smartphones and internet access exposes individuals to global lifestyles, promoting the nuclear family model.
- **Inheritance Laws:** Hindu Succession (Amendment) Act 2005 → grants equal inheritance right to daughters, encourages nuclear families as women increasingly seek their share of property independently
- **Housing Policies:** Urban housing schemes like Pradhan Mantri Awas Yojana (PMAY) focus on smaller housing units, better suited for nuclear families.
- **Modern Value System** emphasising individualism, gender equality, privacy, and social mobility → collectively encourage independent living arrangements and career-oriented lifestyles.
- **Better Infrastructure** including affordable urban housing, efficient transportation, quality healthcare, advanced educational facilities + life-style appliances facilitates practical aspects of independent living.

### Factors Aids Re-integration of Joint Family:

- **Chain migration** is a process where migrants sponsor close family members to join them in a destination → creating a series of linked migrations.

- **Cost of Living:** Rising costs of living can make joint family living more economically viable, as resources and expenses can be shared among multiple family members.
- Functional Jointness is still retained due to physical and financial obligation.
  - Families still retained joint family ethics and norms like participation in functions and ceremonies.
- **Counter Migration:** Economic sustainability in urban area has the potential to send back the people to native places → reinforcement of joint family structure.
- **Elderly Care:** Presence of elderly family members requiring care and support can encourage formation of joint families, as multiple generations can share caregiving responsibilities.
- **Child Rearing:** Joint families offer built-in childcare support, which can be especially beneficial for working parents who need assistance with raising children.
  - It become instrument in society where maids were accused of child abuse.
- **Work from Home/Hybrid Culture:** Increasing acceptance of remote work allow family members to live together without being constrained by job location, making joint family living more feasible.
- **Industrialization:** With increased wages it provides an economic basis to sustain a joint family.

## Emergent form of Family

- **Nuclear Families with extended ties:** Principal family unit consisting of parents and their children → maintain close relationship with extended family members grandparents, aunts, uncles, cousins.
  - Transportation and communication technology (whatsapp group and family group calls and social media) allow families to maintain strong bonds despite physical distance.
- **Single Parent Household:** Family unit with one parent raising children.
  - Secularisation of Marriage, De-stigmatization of divorce, widowhood, choosing single parenthood through adoption or assisted reproduction.
- **Female Headed Household:** A family unit where a woman is the primary caregiver and financial provider for the children, with or without a male partner present.

- Increased women's workforce participation and financial independence.

- **Cohabitation/Live-In:** A couple who share a living space and a committed relationship, but are not married.
- **Dual Career Family:** A family where both partners pursue professional careers outside the home.
  - Increased educational attainment and career aspirations for both men and women.
- **Conjugal Symmetrical Family:** A family where both partners share household chores, childcare responsibilities, and decision-making equally.
  - Shifting gender roles and greater emphasis on gender equality within families → Equal status in Marital Relation.

# MARRIAGE

- According to Haston and Hanks, "Marriage is the approved social pattern whereby two or more persons of opposite sex establish a family".
- According to Nuntberg, "Marriage consists of the rules and regulations which define the rights, duties and privileges of husband and wife."

## Charactcristics of Marriage:

- **Commitment and Partnership:** Marriage is a special bond between two people, traditionally of opposite gender, built on shared rights and responsibilities.
- **Foundation of Family:** Marriage act as the building block for families. The relationships between spouses from the core structure of this family unit.
- **Cultural and Religious Variations:** The concept of marriage can differ greatly across culture and religions.
  - In Islam, it's seen as a contract, while Hinduism views it as a sacred ceremony.
- **Legal Agreement:** Marriage is a legal contract that stipulates rights and obligations of each partner.
  - This contract can cover aspects like property rights, alimony and inheritance.
- **Intimacy and Procreation:** Marriage provides a framework for intimate relationships and is often seen as a foundation for having and raising children.
  - It foster love, cooperation, and emotional support within the family.
- **Legitimization of Children:** Marriage provides a socially approved context for bearing and raising children.
  - It legitimises offspring and often assigns parental rights and duties.

- **Socially Sanctioned Intimacy:** Marriage establishes exclusive and socially acceptable sexual rights between partners.
  - It regulates sexual behaviour and promotes sexual fidelity within the union.
- **Universality with Variations:** Marriage is a nearly universal concept, through customs, religious beliefs and practices surrounding it differ greatly between societies.
- **Symbolic Traditions:** Many cultures have symbolic traditions associated with marriage, such as rings, wedding attire, decorations, or specific markings.

## Types of Marriage:

01 On Basis of Number of spouse

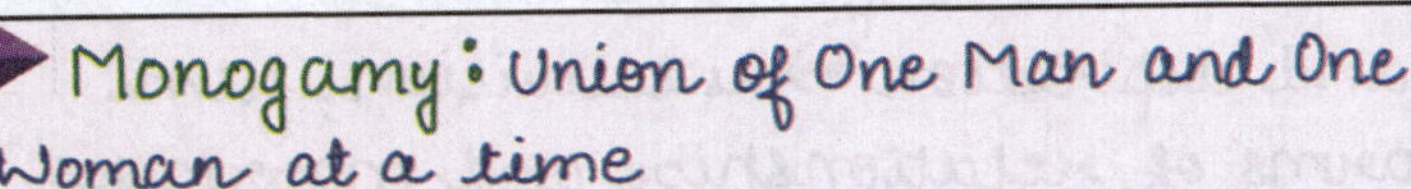

- **Monogamy:** Union of One Man and One Woman at a time
  - **Serial Monogamy:** Individuals can remarry after the death or divorce of their previous spouse, but only have one spouse at a time.
  - **Non-Serial Monogamy:** Concept of remarriage is strictly prohibited.

- **Polygamy:** A form of marriage where multiple partners are involved at same time.
  - **Polygyny:** A man simultaneously marries multiple wives.
    - Ex: Islam permits this type of marriage subjected to specific terms and conditions.
  - **Polyandry:** A woman marries multiple men simultaneously.
    - Ex: Todas tribe of Nilgiri Hills practise it.

02 On Basis of Spouse Selection

- **Endogamy:** Marriage within a specific social group, such as caste, tribe, or religion.
  - Ex: Traditional Indian arranged marriages.

- **Exogamy:** Marriage outside of one's own social group, sometimes to form alliances with other groups
  - Ex: Marrying someone from a different caste in India i.e. Inter Caste Marriage.

## Structural and Functional Changes in Marriage Institution:

### Force of Change

- **Employment:** Women, gaining financial independence through employment → their economic dependency within marriage has diminished.
- **Globalisation:** Economic liberalisation and globalisation have introduced new values and lifestyles, impacting traditional marriage structures.
- **Higher Education:** Increased access to higher education, especially for women → led to shift in marriage age, partner selection and expectations within marriage.
  - It fosters awareness and aspirations, leading individuals to prioritize personal growth and career over traditional marital roles.
- **Individualism:** Modern societies emphasise individualism and personal freedom.
  - Individuals seek marital relationships based on mutual compatibility and love rather than solely on familial arrangements.
- **Media** influences public perceptions and aspiration → as television, films and the internet, partrays diverse forms of relationships and marriages.
- **Online Dating:** Advent of online datings apps and websites has revolutionised the way people find partners.
  - Ex: Jeevansathi.com made it easier to connect with patential spouses based on shared interests and compatibility.
- **Marriage Laws:** Legal reforms, such as the legalization of same-sex marriage have made it easier for individuals to exit-unhappy marriages.
  - It leads to changes in the stability and dynamics of marital relationships.
- **Migration:** Internal and international migration for work, education, or better living → altered traditional family structures and marriage patterns.
- **Women's Right Movements:** Advocacy for women's rights and gender equality has challenged traditional gender role within marriage.
- **Feminist Perspectives** have influenced societal views on marriage, advocating for partnerships based on equality and mutual respect.

### Displacement by Forces

- **Secularization of Marriage:** Traditional focus of fulfilling one's religious "dharma" of marriage shifted towards "life-long companionship."
- **Evolution of Marriage Forms:** Legal restrictions on traditional polygamy polygyny through Hindu Marriage Act 1955 made → Monogamous marriage as dominant form.

**Shifting Nuptiality Pattern:**

- **Legal Minimums:** The legal age for marriage in India is currently 21 for men and 18 for women.
- **Delayed Marriages:** The average age of marriage has risen significantly.

**Increase in Divorce:** Relaxed legislative process + Financial Independence of women + De-stigmatization of divorce + Secularization of Marriage Institution → Upward trend in divorce.

- 0.3% of women and men aged 15-49 are divorced. 11% of women aged 45-49 are widowed, compared with 1% of men.

**Legal Recognition to Live-In:** Supreme Court in S. Khushboo vs. Kanniammal & Anr. recognised live-in relationship as a right protected under Article 21 (Right to Life and Liberty).

- The court also clarified that children born out of such relationships have legal rights and can inherit property.

## Divorce: A Shield became Weapon

- **False Dowry cases:** In India, Section 498 A of IPC (dealing with cruelty by husband or relatives) is heavily misused as observed by the Supreme court → to file false cases, impacting accused's life severely even before the matter is legally resolved.
- **Vexatious litigation** to harass or intimidate the other party, often as a form of revenge.
- **Alimony and Maintenance:** Individuals seeking divorce primarily to gain financial benefits through alimony or maintenance, exploiting the other partner financially.
- **Property Disputes:** Divorce Proceedings can be used to claim or deny property and assets, often unfairly benefitting one party over the other.
- **Child Custody** battles often meet allegations of neglect or abuse fabricated to gain an advantage, affecting child's well-being and estranged parent's relationship with them.
- **Gaslighting:** Psychological manipulation where one party may attempt to make other doubt their sanity, memories, or perceptions during the divorce process.

# CASTE SYSTEM

**About:** Caste System is defined as a system of social stratification, consisting of hierarchically arranged, closed, endogamous strata where membership is ascriptive, contract is restricted and mobility is theoretically impossible.

Stratification is differential access to political, social and economic resources due to hierarchical arrangement.

**Features of Caste System:**

- **Birth Ascription:** Caste is assigned at birth, determining an individual's social position for life.
  - Dalit IPS officer Sunil Kumar Dhanwanta had to take police protection to carry out his pre-wedding ceremony called Bindori on a horse.
- **Fluid Nature:** SECC 2011 recorded 46,73,034 caste categories, sub-castes, surnames, gotras, and clan name → Increase from 4,147 Castes recorded in the 1931 census.
- **Hierarchical Structure:** Caste system establishes a rigid social hierarchy, with Brahmins positioned at tops dictates social interactions and opportunities.
  - Historically and even today Brahmins have easy access to educational and religious institutions as compared to dalits.
- **Endogamy:** Marriage strictly within one's caste or sub-caste is essential for upholding the caste system and preserving its social order.
  - Census (2011): Intercaste marriage in India stands as low as 5.82%.
- **Privileges and Disabilities:** Different caste groups face varying degrees of social restrictions (civil and religious disabilities) to maintain nations of purity and pollution.
  - Commensality (a practice of together dining) is not allowed between upper caste and lower caste.
- **Occupational Division of Labour:** Occupation of every caste is predetermined by Birth and every caste is supposed to treat their occupation as religion.
- **The Practice of Untouchability:** Extreme form of social exclusion → isolates a group considered "impure" by forcing them to live on the fringes of society and denying them basic rights.
- **Manifestation Beyond Hinduism:** Pew Research Centre 2021 survey, Indian Christian disproportionally identify with lower castes (74%), including 57% with Scheduled Caste (SC) or Scheduled Tribes (ST).

## Transformation of Caste

Caste system faces a growing challenge from forces like industrialization, urbanization, and embrace of modern values are eroding its rigid structure, propelling the nation towards a more equitable and inclusive social landscape.

- Industrialization: Industries require a skilled workforce → opened doors for lower castes → challenged the traditional occupational division of Labour.
- Urbanisation: Urban cities are characterised by Anonymity and Heterogeneity, promoting a secular pattern of living → challenging the concept of pollution and purity.
- Modern Value System: Increased access to education promotes ideas of equality, rationality, scientific temper and individual merit, challenging caste-based discrimination.
- Reservation Policy: Affirmative action policies provide quotas in education and government jobs, political institutions for historically disadvantaged castes.
    - According to Central governments data of 19 ministries, SC's comprise 15.34%, ST's 6.18% and OBC 17.5% in October 2021.
    - According to AISHE 2021-2022
        - SC student enrolment is 15.3% of the total enrolment. SC female enrolment is 47.9% of total SC enrolment.
        - ST student enrolment is 6.3% of total enrolment. ST female enrolment is 49.7% of total ST enrolment.
        - OBC enrolment is 37.8% of total enrolment with female enrolment 47.9% of total OBC enrolment.
    - Although, the benefit of reservation is not equally reaped by all → lead to emergence of class with caste. Ex: Creamy Layer in OBCs.

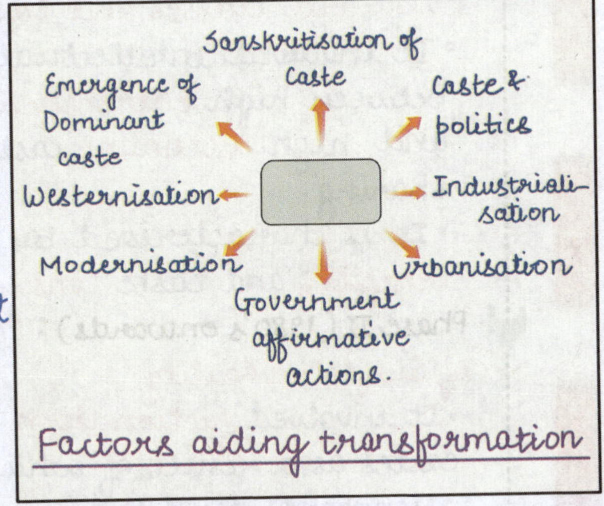

Factors aiding transformation

- Land Reforms (redistribution of landholdings) have empowered low castes who were traditionally landless labourers.
- Modern Avatar of Caste: Vertical Arrangement based on stigma → emergence of horizontal competition for backward classes without any stigma.
- Universal Adult Franchise (Art. 326) gives a political voice to all castes, regardless of social standing.
    - Caste has been displaced from religious domain but it has entered in consciousness of people especially during electoral politics.

**Attitudinal and Societal Changes:**

- Commensality had been changed because of the rise of urbanisation and restaurant culture.
- Inter-Caste marriages have increased in recent years.

## Politics and Caste

### Pre-Independence Phase:

- Christian Missionaries spread the message of Christianity as a reform movement against dogmatic practice of caste.
- Emergence of Educated middle class like Jyotirao Phule, E.V. Ramaswamy Naicker (Periyar) and B.R. Ambedkar who worked for caste emancipation.
  - Ex: Establishment of Satyashodhak Samaj to promote education and social equality for all, especially women and Dalits.
  - Establishment of Self-Respect Movement, promoting self-respect and social equality for all, especially Shudras and Dalits.

### Post-Independence Phase

**Phase I (Independence to 1980's):** Mobilisation and assertion of backward classes and Dalits

- It involved intellectuals, and antagonism and resentment between high entrenched castes like Reddy in Andhra Pradesh and high ascendant castes-Jats in Haryana over benefits and power sharing.
- It is characterised by power structure, distribution of economic benefits, and caste consciousness.

**Phase II (1980's onwards):** Politicization of caste - Objective Realisation of Subjective Reality

- It involved factionalism and fragmentation within the competing castes as a result of which multi-caste and multi-factional alignments developed.
- **Characteristics Features:**
  - Caste-Centric Parties to represent specific caste groups. Ex: Bahujan Samaj Party primarily represent Dalits.
  - Caste Alliances: Mainstream political parties like Rashtriya Janata Dal, have formed alliances with smaller, caste-based parties such as Lok Janshakti Party.
  - Reservation Politics to attract votes. Ex: UPA government announced Jat reservation in 2014 before general election.
  - Political Mobilisation around caste identity to unify voters under a common cause or grievance. Ex: Samajwadi Party in Uttar Pradesh.

## Caste Based Associations

**Caste-based Marriage associations** help members find suitable partners within their caste or sub-caste, catering to the prevalence of endogamy in Indian Society.

**Caste-based political Associations** mobilise voters and advocate for their political interest.
Ex: Harijan Sevak Sangh, Maratha Kranti Morcha, Bhim Sena.

**Caste-based economic associations** offer financial assistance to members through scholarships, loans, or microfinance initiatives to support business ventures.
- Ex: Dalit Indian Chamber of Commerce & Industry, National Scheduled Caste Finance and Development Corporation.
- It facilitates professional networking among members, share business opportunities, and potentially offers skill development programs.

**Caste-based educational** associations like Vaishya Education Society enhance access to education and support social mobility for marginalised groups.
- These Association aids in process of Inclusive growth by widening political representation, social upliftment and keeps representatives accountable.

## Reservation Policy in India

➤ **About:** It is an affirmative instrument through which a certain proportion of seats are reserved for people belonging to Socially and Educationally Backward communities.

➤ **Rationale:** Equality of opportunity to discriminated section i.e to correct historical injustice and give effect to the redistributive agenda of government

### The Mandal Commission

- In 1990, the Union government announced that Other Backward Classes (OBCs) would get 27 percent reservation in jobs in central government services and public sector units (under Article 16(4) of the constitution).
- The Creamy layer criterion was invoked by Supreme Court in the ruling called the 'Indira Sawhney Judgement' (1992).
- The decision was based on Mandal Commission Report (1980).
- The education quota came into force in 2006 (under Article 15(4) of the constitution).

## Constitutional provisions related to reservation

- Reservation in educational institution has been provided in Article 15(4) while reservation in posts and services has been provided in Article 16(4), 16(4A) and 16(4B) of the Constitution.
- Article 46 of the constitution provides that the State shall promote with speial care the educational and economic interests of the weaker sections of the society and, of the SCs and STs and shall protect them from social injustice and all forms of exploitation.
- Article 243 D provides reservation of Seats for Schedule Caste and Schedule Tribes in Panchayats.
- Article 330 provides reservations of Seats for Schedule Caste and Schedule Tribes in the House of the People.
- Article 332 provides reservation of seats for Schedule Caste and Schedule Tribes in Legislative Assemblies of the States.

### Debates of Reservation

| Arguments in Favour of Reservation | Argument Against Reservation |
|---|---|
| 01 Instrumental in upliftment of weaker section → social Empowernment. | 01 Merit is compromised and administrative efficiency is in question. |
| 02 Inclusive Growth: To reduce the potential difference between have's & havenat's. | 02 Widened Social Cleavages: It has generated resentments among forward or non-reserved castes. |
| 03 Spirit of Equality: Meritocracy is meaningless without equality of opportunity. | 03 Class within Caste: Benefits of reservation was only reaped by creamy section of backwards only → created nation of Elite Caste. |
| 04 Social Justice: It is a political necessity to provide representation to all sections | 04 Politicization of Caste: Now it has become an instrument of vote bank politics. |
| 05 Reduce Social Unrest and National Cohesion → prepare a fabric for reaping demographic dividends. | 05 It has further strengthened Caste Consciousness. |

### Way Forward:

- **New Yardsticks:** To determine backwardness of caste. Ex: NALSA Judgement 2014, advocated for OBC status to Transgenders.
- **De-reservation:** On the basis of Social Mapping → to address the issue of bogus beneficiary.

- Introduction of Creamy Layer in SCs and STs.
- Overhauling of Education System: Increase ambit of Right to Education till secondary education
- Perception Management: To acknowledge that "Reservations is means, not an end"

## Why is Dominant Castes Demanding Reservation?

M.N. Srinivas, a prominent Indian sociologist, introduced concept of "Dominant Caste." He identified key characteristics that define a dominant caste:

- Traditional Authority: Dominant castes have a historical legacy of authority and power that has been passed down through generations.
  Example: Legacy of Maratha Empire has provided the Marathas (in Maharashtra) with a sense of pride and presence of traditional authority.
- Population Size: It constitutes a substantial portion of local population. This numerical advantage translates to significant influence in both social and political spheres.
  - Ex: Numerical advantage of Jats in Punjab and Haryana allows them to exert substantial influence in social matters like marriage alliances and village customs.
- Economic Control: They hold power over crucial economic resources, like land and wealth.
  - Ex: Reddy Community in Andhra Pradesh influence prices, access to credit, and employment opportunities within the region.
- Political Power: They hold sway over local administrative bodies, granting them significant political influence that can sometimes extend beyond regional politics.
  - Ex: Maravar Caste has a long history of dominance in village councils and district-level politics in Tamil Nadu.
- Ritual Standing: May or May not at highest in ritual hierarchy, but dominant castes typically hold a higher status, allowing them to claim authority within the community.
  - Ex: Yadav Caste in Uttar Pradesh and Bihar, may not be ranked at the very top of traditional caste system, but they hold a respectable position.

## Demand for Reservation

- Shifting Economics Landscape: Agrarian Distress forced dominant caste to search for alternate economic opportunities.

- They didn't reap the benefits of education in contrast to affirmative action where other castes have benefitted from reservations in education and government jobs → upward economic mobility.

Upper caste couldn't complete in private jobs due to lack of quality education

Dominate Caste
Feeling of relative deprivation: as unable to compete with lower caste due to reservation

Lower Caste

- Shrinking Employment:
  - In private sector it is shrinking because of the increase of automation and Artifical Intelligence
  - Contractual Nature of Government Jobs: According to Indian Staffing Federation, 43% of total government workforce is contractual or temporary in nature.
- Perception of Stagnation: Dominant caste might be considered "socially upward", they might feel economically stagnant or even declining compared to their past prosperity.
- Relative Deprivation: Dominant castes might feel disadvantaged relative to other who have seen significant progress due to reservations.
- Lower Education Levels: Some dominant caste might have lower literacy and education rates. They argue that reservations can help improve their educational attainment and compete in the job market.

## DALIT CAPITALISM

Dalit capitalism (Coined by Chandra Bhan Prasad) is a strategy of encouraging economic empowerment and upward social mobility for Dalits through entreprenurship and participation in the capitalist marketplace.

### Key Aspect of Dalit Capitalism

- Focus on Occupational Mobility to move Dalits away from traditional menial occupations associated with their caste → towards diverse business venture and professions.
- Building Self-Reliance to become economically independent and challenge the social and economic exclusion they have historically faced.

### Dalit Capitalism: A Panacea or Mirage?

- Demographic Transformation: It helps in transforming Job seekers to Job giver. Hence government is taking a proactive role to promote dalit capitalism.
  - Ex: Margin Money Scheme for SC/ST Entrepenures provides a subsidy for setting up new businesses in the manufacturing and service sector.

▶ National Schedule Caste Finance and Development Corporation (NSFDC) offers specifically to SCs financial aid, loan guarantees, equity support, and skill development programs for SCs enterpeneures.

▶ Dalit Indian Chamber of Commerce and Industry established in 2005 for economic empowerment of Dalits through self-help and enterpreneurship.

➡ Inadequate Skilled Education: Because of rigid caste system, still majority of lower caste people lack skilled and technical education → unable to reap benefits of true capitalism.

➡ Potential for Class Inequality: Capitalism is exploitative and promotes inequality → Dalit capitalism has hidden potential of Intra-Caste inequalities.

➡ Skewed Targets: Dalit capitalism deviates from emancipation of the poorest of poor.

▶ It does not focus on issue of social justice, social inclusion and the dignity of caste.

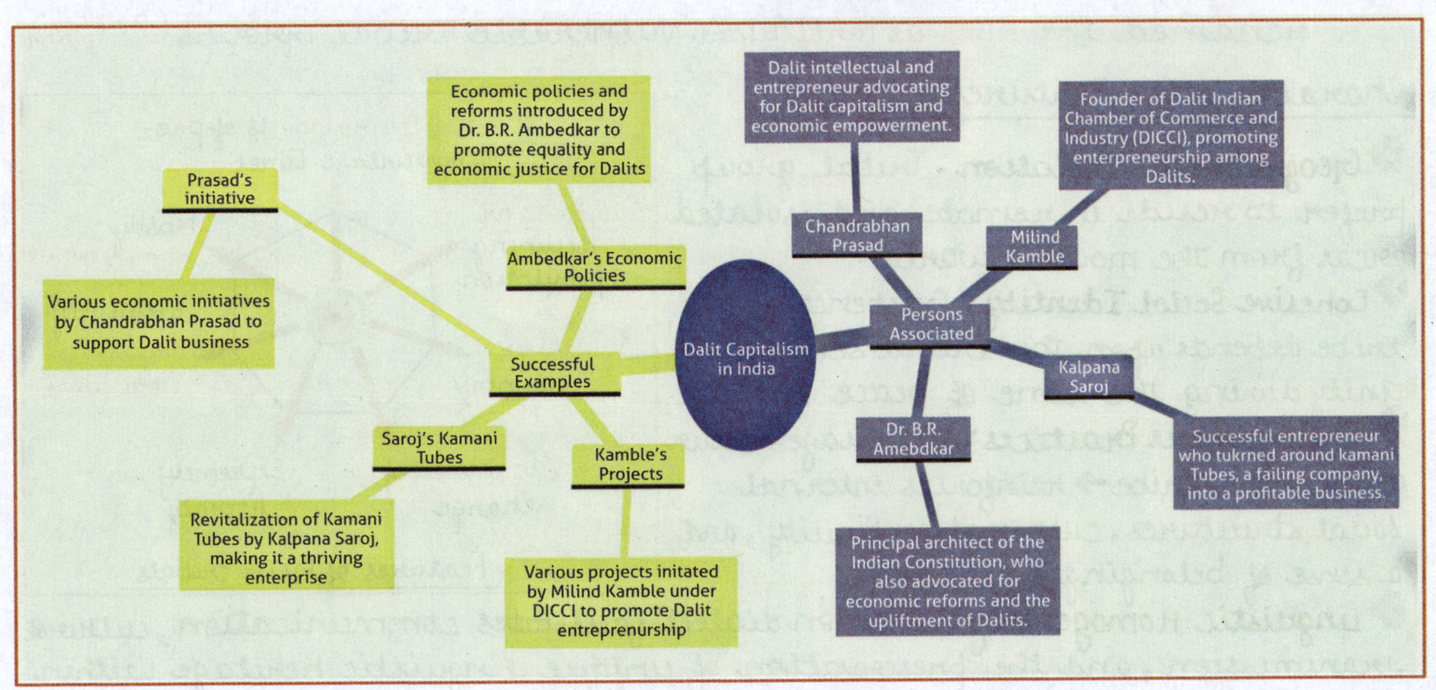

# TRIBAL COMMUNITIES

**About:** Tribe is a social division made up of families connected by socio-economic, and ancestral ties as well as by common culture and dialect. The Indian Constitution recognizes tribal communities as "Scheduled Tribes" under Schedule V of the Constitution.

## Current Status and Facts:

- Census 2011: STs constitute 8.6% of entire population of India.
  - Madhya Pradesh has highest tribal population.
- Dhebar Commission, 1973 created Primitive Tribal Group (PTGs) as a separate category, who are less developed among the tribal groups.
  - In 2006, the Government of India renamed the PTGs as Particularly Vulnerable Tribal Groups (PVTGs).

**Figure 1: State/UT's share of scheduled tribes(ST) to total ST population of India**

Other State/UTs, 4%; West Bengal, 5%; Uttar Pradesh, 1%; Tripura, 1%; Rajasthan, 9%; Odisha, 9%; Nagaland, 2%; Mizoram, 1%; Meghalaya, 2%; Maharashtra, 10%; Andhra Pradesh, 5%; Assam, 4%; Bihar, 1%; Chattisgarh, 8%; Gujarat, 9%; Jammu and Kashmir, 1%; Jharkhand, 8%; Karnataka, 4%; Madhaya Pradesh, 15%

## Characteristics Features of Tribes

- **Geographical Isolation:** Tribal group prefer to reside in remote and isolated areas from the modern world.
- **Cohesive Social Identity:** Existence of a tribe depends upon the tribal sense of unity during the time of peace and war.
- **Endogamous Practices:** Marriages occur within the tribe → reinforces internal social structures, cultural continuity, and a sense of belonging.

Level of technology is of pre-agriculture times
Mostly homogenous
Relatively physically isolated
Extremely low literacy
Slow rate of change
Subsistence economy
Stagnant or declining population

Features of PVTG tribals

- **Linguistic Homogeneity:** Common dialect facilitates communication, cultural transmission, and the preservation of unique linguistic heritage within the tribe.
- Kinship-Based Social Organisation forms bedrock of social organisation in Indian tribes
- **Relative Egalitarianism:** In constrast to caste system, tribal societies in India tend to exhibit a more egalitarian structure.
  - Ex: Sex Ratio of STs stand at 990 in contrast to 945 in SCs.
- **Autonomous Political System:** Indian tribes posses distinct political

systems led by a designated chief or council to protect tribe's interests

- Ex: Schedule VI of constitution provides 10 Autonomous District Councils in Assam, Meghalaya, Mizoram, and Tripura.

## Issues Confronting Tribal Consolidation:

- **Pre Independence: Phase of Systematic Disempowerment**
  - **Loss of Land and Livelihoods:** Colonial land policies and commercial forestry disrupted tribal self-sufficiency and traditional ways of life.
    - Ex: Indian Forest Act of 1878 restricted access to forest, tradionally used for hunting, gathering, and shifting cultivation.
  - **Debt Traps and Exploitation:** The introduction of a cash economy facilitated the exploitation of tribals by moneylenders and traders.
    - Ex: Unfair trade practices + high-interest loans + exploitation → vicious cycle of Debt Trap.
  - **Forced Labour and Displacement:** Infrastructure projects and resource extraction often relied on forced labour from tribal communities.
  - **Missionary Activity:** Missionary endeavours aimed to provide education to facilitate conversion → challenged tribal culture and social fabric.
- **Post-Independence:**
  - After debate on integrating, assimilating, or isolating tribal communities, the Indian government adopted the 'Panchsheel' approach.

## Tribal Panchsheel Policy

Nehru's five pronged strategy aimed to balance development with cultural preservation, marking a shift towards a more inclusive and respectful approach for tribal consolidation.

- **Self Determination:** People should develop along the line of their own genius and the imposition of alien values should be avoided.
- **Land Rights Protection:** Tribal right in land and forest should be respected → preventing alienation without informed consent.
- **Resource Management:** Tribal communities should have control over the natural resources in their areas.
- **Linguistic Preservation:** Panchsheel advocated development and use of tribal languages in education and administration.
- **Cultural Respect:** Tribal culture should be preserved and promoted

## Provision taken to Materialise Vision of Panchsheel:

**Constitutional Provision:**

- Article 15(4) has special provision for advancement of STs also.
- Article 29 talks about protection of interests of minorities which also include STs
- Article 46: "The state promotes, with special care, the educational and economic interests of weaker section of the people, and in particular, of the schedule caste and Schedule tribes."
- Article 164: Provides for a minister of Tribal Affairs in Jharkhand, Odisha, Chhattisgarh and Madhya Pradesh
- Article 243: Reservation of seats in Panchayats.
- Schedule V & VI to promote self-governance and protect the rights of tribal communities.
- Article 338 A gives powers to National Commission for Schedule Tribes to oversee implementation of various safeguards provided to Scheduled Tribes (STs).

**Legal Provisions:**

- The Andaman and Nicobar (Protection of Aboriginal Tribes) Regulation, 1956.
- Foreigner Restricted Area Order, 1963: Andaman & Nicobar Islands are a "Restricted Area" in which foreigners with a restricted area permit (RAP) can stay.
- SC/ST Prevention of Atrocities Act, 1989: To prohibit discrimination, and hate crimes and prevent atrocities against SC and ST.
- The Provisions of the Panchayats (Extention to the Scheduled Areas) Act, 1996 extends Scheduled Areas of India under the purview of the national frame-work of Panchayat → [detailed discussion has been done under Polity Main Pulse].
- The Scheduled Tribes and other Traditional Forest Dwellers (Recognition of Forest Rights) Act, 2006 Forest Right Act recognizes four Key rights for forest dwellers:
  01. Title Rights: Ownership of land being cultivated by family, up to 4 hectares
  02. Use Rights: Access to minor forest products and grazing areas.
  03. Relief and Developments Rights: Participation in protecting and managing community forest resources
  04. Forest Management Rights: Participation in protecting and managing community forest resources.

## Government Schemes:

→ Eklavya Model Residential School to impart quality education to tribal students of classes 6 to 12th.

→ Stand-Up India Scheme (2016): Provide SC/ST/Women with a loan between Rs 10 lakhs to Rs 1 crore to promote entrepreneurship among them.

→ Van Dhan Scheme (2018): 10 SHGs of 30 tribal gathereres will be formed + will be assisted with working capital to add value to products collected from jungle.

→ PM Janjatiya Vikas Scheme (2021) seeks to achieve livelihood-driven tribal development in the next five years through formation of Van Dhan groups.

→ PM-JANAM (15th November 2023) launched on Janjatiya Gaurav Diwas, focuses on 11 critical intervention through 9 ministries to improve the socio-economic welfare of PVTGs.

## Issues/Challenges present in Tribal Society:

➤ Social Stigmatization: Tribals are often stereotyped as being "Adivasi" (and equated with poverty, illiteracy, and lack of development.

➤ Persistent Poverty and Exploitation: A substantial portion of tribal population remains trapped in poverty cycles, lacking access to critical resources and economic opportunities.

- Ex: According to Tribal Health Report, 2013 → In India, 40.6% of the ST population lived below poverty line.

➤ Encroachment of Traditional assets: Jal, Jangal, Zameen was encroached by both government and private entities.

- Ex: Hasdeo Deforestation will impact the livelihoods of 700 indigenous families in district of northern Chhattisgarh.

➤ Violence: NCRB, 2022 data highlights → Crime against Scheduled Tribes (STs) has increased by 14.3% over 2021.

- Surge in Rape and Assault on Tribal women have been observed

➤ Health Concerns: Tribes suffer from anaemia, malaria, gastro-intestinal disorders, micronutrient deficiency and skin diseases.

- 65% of tribal women in the 15-49 years age group suffer from anaemia.
- Tribal population accounts for 50% of deaths from Malaria nationwide

➤ Educational Backwardness: ST student enrollment is 6.3% of the total enrollment and ST female enrollment is 49.5% of total STs enrollment.

➤ Shifting Cultivation is becoming unsustainable due to environmental degradation and declining land productivity.

- **Unorganized Minor Forest Produce Trade** leading to low returns for tribals and high wastage.
  - Ex: It highlight failure of TRIFED → established to promote making development for the tribal people.
- **Erosion of Cultural Identity**: Pressures towards assimilation threatens the unique cultural identity of tribal communities.
  - Ex: Hinduization of scheduled tribes in North India.
- **Outdated Lists of PVTGs**: Current list was prepared by Anthropological Survey of India in 1970s, might not reflect current situation of some communities.

| Reason for Poor State of Tribes | Way Forward |
|---|---|
| Weak Execution of provisions and policies. | Gram Sabha power needs to be increased with Land alienation. |
| Misappropriation or underutilisation of funds. | Unused land should be acquired and used for tribal rehabilitation. |
| Ineffective functioning of Tribal Advisory Council. | Appoint a judicial Commission to investigate Naxal cases registered against tribals. |
| Absence of awareness among tribes about their rights and entitlements | Implementation of Panchsheel Policy in letter and spirit. |
| Government tilt towards development policies over displacement concern. | Imposing penalty on officials for delayed implementation of FRA and PESA. |
| Emergence of Class within Tribes → result of unequal impact of affirmative action. | Adoption of 4A approach with respect to infrastructure → Availability, Accessibility, Awareness and Affordability. |
| One Size fit approach fails to deliver the actual ground result. | Adherence to Piecemeal engineering approach → focuses on achieving social change through incremental, peaceful, and, iterative improvement → based on credible and updated data. |
| Bureaucratic and Political Apathy marginalised the tribal people from mainstream development and society. | |

# MANIFESTATION OF UNITY AND DIVERSITY

Unity refers to a sense of oneness, it is a bond which holds members of a society together, it can either based on uniformity or differences.

## Bonds of Unity in Diversity

- **Geopolitical Factors:** First bond of unity is found in geo-political integration. India is known for its geographical unity marked by Himalayas in North and Indian Ocean in South.
  - Amidst geographical unity India stands politically united → reflected by Common Political culture, Single Constitution, Single Citizenship.
- **Geo-Cultural Unity:** Geographical distribution of Temples, Mosques & Church along with religious significance acts as a source of unity.
  - It was reflected in network of Shrines & Sacred places and their unifying force in terms of Social Cohesion.
- **Cultural Factors:**
  - Inter-Religious Unity: Earning religious merit by visiting various religious institutions is a unifying thread among different religious sects like Hinduism, Islam, Christianity.
  - Intra-Religious Unity: Various sects, cults and castes in every religion be it Hinduism or Islam are unified by teachings of Holy Scriptures.
  - Linguistic Unity: Amidst linguistic Diversity of India → Sanskrit act as a Bridge language whereas English and Hindi acts as unifying thread.
- **Other Unifying Factors:**
  - Defence Culture: Indian Armed forces comprise personnel from various states, religions and communities, exemplifying unity in diversity through their shared commitment to national security.
  - Corporate Culture: Corporations in India employ people from different regions, languages & backgrounds, promoting inclusivity & mutual respect.
    - Companies undertake CSR activities that benefit diverse communities, fostering a sense of unity through shared social goals.
  - All India Services: Services like Indian Administrative Service, Indian Police Service, Indian Forest Service recruit individuals from all over the country & assign them to different states, promoting national integration.

• Sports: Indian sports team bring together players & fans from all over the country, fostering a sense of national pride and unity.

• Indian cinema produces films that are popular nationwide, reflecting & celebrating country's diversity while promoting a shared cultural identity.

# MANIFESTATION OF DIVERSITY IN UNITY

• Diversity refers to "differing from each other" and composed of distinct qualities, elements, or characteristics. Religions, races, dialects, art forms and culture all coexist in united India.

• This multilingual, multiracial, multicultural, multi religious, & multiethnic nation has maintained its unity in the face of foreign invasions.

• India's beauty lies in its ability to unite its diverse population.

## Various Forms of Diversity in India

- Geographical Diversity: India is a vast country with an area of about 3.2 lakh Square kilometer.
  - the diverse topography consists of dry deserts, evergreen forests, snowy Himalayas along the coast, and fertile plains.
- Religious Diversity: India is a multi-religious country consisting of Hindus (79.9%), Muslims (14.2%), Christian (2.32%), Sikhs (1.7%), Buddhist (0.6%) and Jains (0.41%).
- Language: India is called a 'Veritable tower of Babel' & according to A.R. Desai, "India presents a spectacle of Museum of tongues."
  - The Census 2011 identified about 122 languages.
- Cultural Diversity: India is among most diverse societies with a plurality and diversity of cultures which marks it out as perhaps the largest multi-cultural society in the world.
- Caste Diversity is peculiar to Indian society. It may be called an extreme form of closed class system. The status of individuals in the social hierarchy is determined by birth.
- Racial Diversity: Historically Global Migration towards India is the primary reason behind absence of a uniform racial composition of its inhabitants. India has rightly been termed as 'melting pot' of races and tribes.

## PYQs Corner

*(Write the Answer and Get Free Evaluation)*

### 1 Family Structure

(i) Explore and evaluate the impact of 'Work From Home' on family relationships. **(2022)**

(ii) Customs and traditions suppress reason leading to obscurantism. Do you agree? **(2020)**

(iii) The life cycle of a joint family depends on economic factors rather than social values. Discuss. **(2014)**

### 2 Marriage Institution

(i) Do you think marriage as a sacrament is losing its value in Modern India? **(2023)**

### 3 Caste

(i) Why is caste identity in India both fluid and static? Discuss the impact of post-liberal economy on ethnic identity and communalism. **(2023)**

(ii) Has caste lost its relevance in understanding the multi-cultural Indian Society? Elaborate your answer with illustrations. **(2020)**

(iii) "Caste system is assuming new identities and associational forms. Hence, caste system cannot be eradicated in India." Comment. **(2018)**

(iv) Debate the issue of whether and how contemporary movements for assertion of Dalit identity work towards annihilation of caste. **(2015)**

### 4 Tribal Communities

(i) Given the diversities among tribal communities in India, in which specific context should they be considered as a single category? **(2022)**

(ii) Examine the uniqueness of tribal knowledge systems when compared with mainstream knowledge and cultural systems. **(2021)**

(iii) What are the two major legal initiatives by the State since Independence, addressing discrimination against Scheduled Tribes (STs)? **(2017)**

(iv) Why are the tribals in India referred to as the Scheduled Tribes? Indicate the major provisions enshrined in the Constitution of India for their upliftment. **(2016)**

CHAPTER 02

# Diversity of India

Diversity refers to the variety and range of human experiences, identities, backgrounds, and characteristics that exist within a population or group. It encompasses both visible and non-visible aspects.

Visible Diversity includes characteristics readily observable like race, ethnicity and gender identity.
Non Visible Diversity encompasses aspects that might not be immediately apparent like socio-economic spectrum, various religious belief (Hinduism, Islam, Christianity, Sikhism, Buddhism).

## LINGUISTIC DIVERSITY

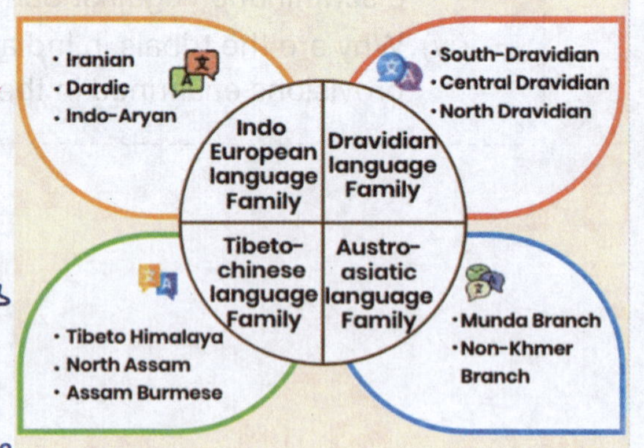


→ There is a famous saying about India's Linguistic diversity is "Kos Kos Par Badle Panni, char Kosh Par Bani".

→ Census 2011 reported → 19,569 raw mother tongue → 'rationalised' into 1369 mother tongues → regrouped into 270 mother tongues and 121 languages.

↱ More than 25% of the population speaks two languages, while about 7% speak three language.

- Language is the most powerful instrument of cultural identity. It is a source of both cohesion and conflict subjected to feelings of relative deprivation and domination of majority language speakers.

## Constitutional Provision Related India's Linguistic Diversity:

- Article 29 ensures the conservation of distinct languages, scripts, or cultures for any section of citizens.
- Article 343 designates Hindi in the Devanagri script as the Union's official language, allowing English usage for 15 years from the Constitution's commencement.
- Article 344 requires the formation of a Commission to recommend the progressive of Hindi far official purposes.
- Article 350, 350 A, 350 B, and 351 provide directives for addressing grievances, offering primary education in the mother tongue, appointing a Special officer for linguistic minorities, and promating and developing the Hindi language, respectively.

## Benefits of India's Multilingualism

- Territorial Unity: Co-existence of multiple languages promotes inter-state cultural exchanges, reinforcing a shared national identity despite regional differences.
  - Recognition of 22 official languages in Eight Schedule of Indian Constitution helps in promating unity.
- Equality Among Languages: Indian Constitution promotes equality among languages by recognizing multiple official languages.
  - Three-language formula aims to treat all languages equally → providing students with opportunity to learn their mother tongue, a regional language, and a national or international language.
- Prevention of Balkanization: Establishment of linguistic states through State Reorganisation Act of 1956 has proved a sense of autonomy to linguistic groups → addressed marginalisation of feeling → separatist movements.
- Facilitating Public Administration: Use of regional languages in state and local administration ensures that governance is accessible, inclusive and effective.
  - Supreme Court ordered translation of Judgements in regional languages like Hindi, Odia, Tamil, Marathi → to make justice more accessible for citizens.
- Enriched Literary Heritage: India's linguistic diversity → produced a rich

corpus of literature → ranging from ancient Sanskrit texts like Vedas to modern regional works in Bengali, Tamil, and Hindi.

- Being multilingual strengthens cognitive abilities like memory, attention span, and problem-solving → exhibit better cognitive flexibility → translates to a more skilled and adaptable workforce.
- Exposure to multiple languages and cultures fosters open-mindedness and empathy.
  - "Learning another languages is not only learning different words for the same things but learning another way to think about things" → Flora Lewis.

## OBJECTIVES OF INDIAN MULTILINGUALISM

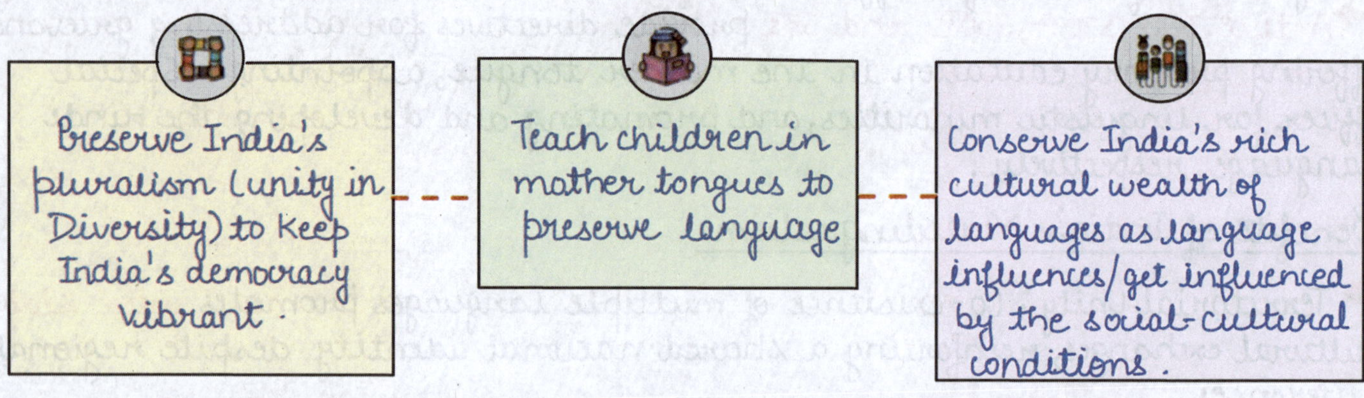


### Issues of Inquiry associated with Linguistic Diversity

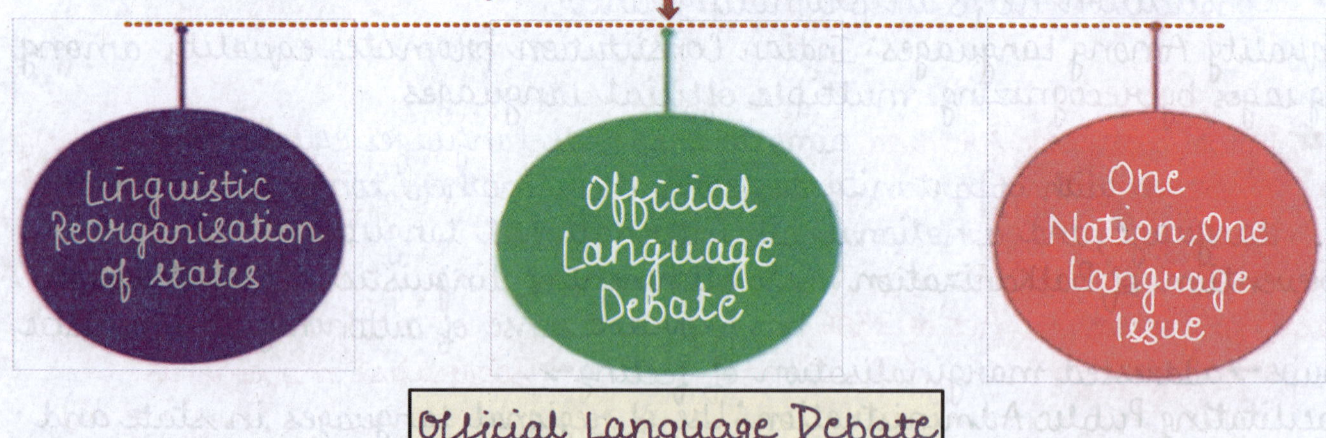


## Official Language Debate

### Pre-Independence Period

- English was the official language of administration. The Indian nationalist movement recognized the importance of language in unifying the diverse populace.

## Constituent Assembly Debates (1946-1949)

- Initial Proposals: As India move towards independence, Constituent Assembly debated which language(s) should be the official language of the new nation.
- English and Hindi were strong contenders.
- Munshi-Ayyangar Formula suggested → Hindi as the official language with continued use of English for a transitional period.

## Post-Independence Period

- Article 343 declared Hindi in the Devanagari script as the official language of the Union, with English to be used for official purposes for 15 years (until 1965).
- Official Languages Act, 1963: In response to significant protests, particularly in non-Hindi speaking states, against the imposition of Hindi.
  - Official Language Act was enacted in 1963, allowing for the continued use of English alongside Hindi for official purposes even after 1965.

## Language Protest (1965)

- Anti-Hindi Agitations: The announcement that Hindi would become the sole official language in 1965 sparked violent protests in Tamil Nadu and othern southern states.
  - Agitations were led by Dravidian parties, particularly DMK (Dravida Munnetra Kazhagam).

## Amendments and Resolutions

- Official Languages (Amendment) Act, 1967: Enacted in response to the protests. It ensures indefinite use of English for official purposes along with Hindi.
  - This amendment placated non-Hindi speaking states and ensured bilingualism in official communication.
- Three-Language Formula introduced by National Education Policy 1968 → which mandated the study of Hindi, English, and a regional language in schools to promote linguistic harmony.

## One Nation One Language: Continued legacy of official language debate

| Argument in Favour | Argument against |
|---|---|
| ▶ National Integration: A common language → bridge communication gaps → fosters a sense of national unity and belonging.<br>▶ Administrative Efficiency: Standardization of one language → streamlined administrative processes and communication.<br>→ Public service delivery became more streamlined + accessible<br>▶ Reduced Educational Disparity: Single language could standardize education → reducation in regional disparities in educational outcomes → through streamlined Textbooks, curriculum, and teacher training.<br>▶ Uniform legal proceedings and documentation → legal process more standardised, efficient and accesible.<br>→ It becomes easier for citizens to understand their legal rights and obligations.<br>▶ Check on Public Expenditure: It will put a halt on "National Translation Mission" whose focus was to make knowledge texts accessible, in all Indian languages listed in the VIII schedule of Constitution.<br>▶ Policy formulation and implementation will be more effective, participatory and inclusive.<br>▶ Example: Singapore has a multi-ethnic population (Chinese, Malay and Indian)<br>→ It opted for English as → made this state a global business hub. | ▶ Europeanization of India: Idea of singularity of language, is itself a European Idea → contrast to it India always believed in Unity in diversity.<br>▶ Threat to linguistic diversity and cultures could be threatened by imposing a single language.<br>→ It may lead to erosion of cultures identity through homogenization of culture.<br>▶ Social Agitation and Unrest: Feeling of relative deprivation by non-Hindi or minority language groups → led to Supra State regionalism.<br>▶ Vialation of Linguistic Rights can be seen in enforcement of Hindi as a national language.<br>→ It undermines the principle of linguistic equality + rights of individuals to use their mother tongue.<br>▶ Undermine democratic inclusivity of diverse linguistic groups and compromises the democratic fabric of the nation.<br>▶ Threat to National Unity: Rise of political apprehension → language based politics in State like Andhra Pradesh, Maharashtra, Tamilnadu → rise of regional parties like DMK.<br>→ Karnataka Governments mandated Kannada in school → reaping political mileage out of anti-national issues.<br>▶ Example: Imposition of Sinhala as official language of Sri Lanka marginalizing Tamil speakers → ethnic and linguistic conflict. |

**Way Forward:**

- Future of India's language policy lie in embracing diversity, not imposing uniformity. By strengthening 3-language formula and promoting a culture of multilingualism, India can ensure national unity while celebrating the rich culture of languages that define its unique identity.

## 3-Language Formula

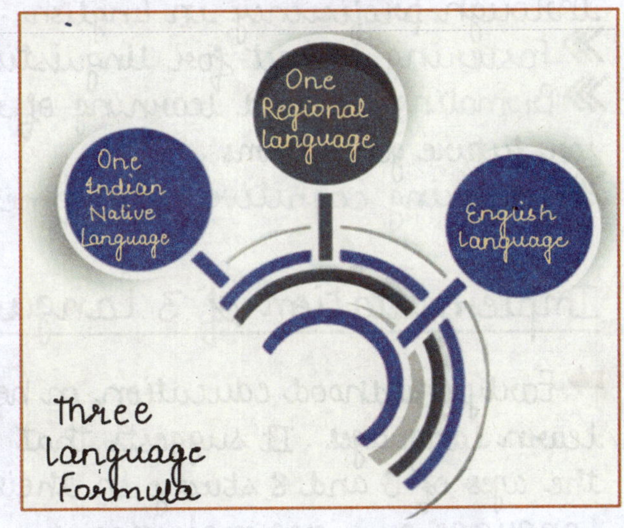


**About:** The National Education Policy of 1968 introduced the three-languages formula and NEP 2020 reinstated the same.

- It advocates every student in India should learn three-languages: two of which should be native Indian language, and the third should be English.

## Challenges with 3 language formula

- **Inconsistent Implementation:** TLF allows for mother tongue education, but inconsistent implementation weakens its effectiveness.
- **Endangered Languages and Inclusivity:** Focus on major languages might neglect and endanger smaller, indigenous languages.
- **Increased Student Burden:** Students face a heavier workload due to the additional language requirement.
- **Misconceptions About Hindi:** The policy's justification often cites a high Hindi-Speaking population, but census data reveals a lower percentage of native Hindi speakers.
  - Political apprehension to make Hindi national language creates resistance, particularly in South India.
- **Uneven Resourcing:** State like Tamil Nadu lack resources to teach Hindi effectively while Hindi-speaking state's don't prioritise incorporating South Indian languages.
- **Funding Constraints:** It requires significant investment in qualified language teachers, which can be challenging for resource-constrained state government.

## Need of 3 Language Formula

- Bridging the linguistic gap → to enable effective communication across the country.
- Providing career opportunities + competitive edge in job market through proficiency in English.
- Fostering respect for linguistic and cultural diversity.
- Promoting use and learning of regional languages can help preserve them for future generations.
- Enhancing cognitive development through learning multiple languages.

## Implementation of 3 Language Formula

- Early childhood education in helping children learn languages. It suggests that kids between the ages of 3 and 8 study in their native language or a regional tongue.

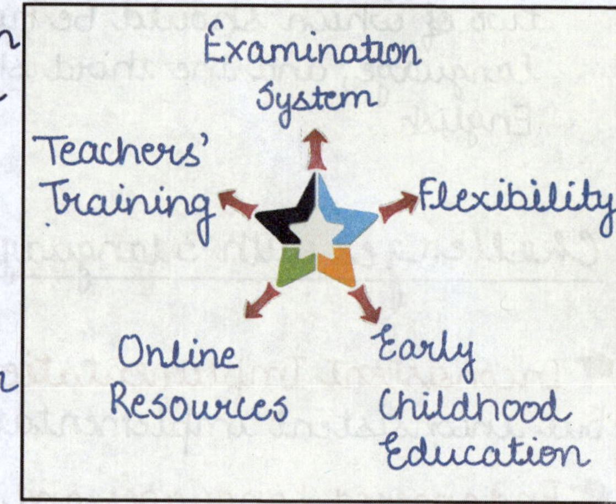


- Flexibility: It permits a wide range of language options.
  - Third language can be English or any other language of the student's choice.
- Teacher's Training: NEP 2020 acknowledges the necessity of trained educators in order to successfully apply the Three Language Formula.

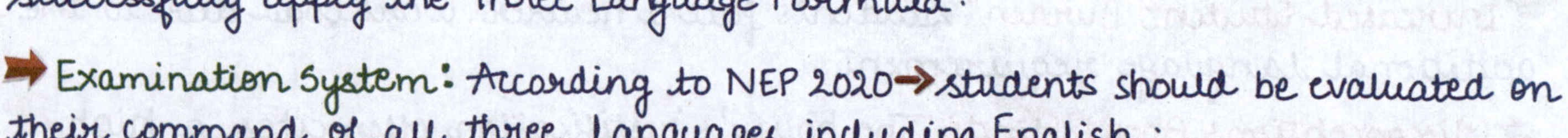

- Examination System: According to NEP 2020 → students should be evaluated on their command of all three languages, including English.
- Online Resources: To enables students to learn in their native tongues → encouragement of creation of online resources and instructional materials in native Indian languages.

# RELIGIOUS DIVERSITY

**Status:**

- Hinduism is dominant religion in India, with approximately 79.8% of population.
- India is a land of many faiths, with Islam (14.2%), Christianity (2.3%), Sikhism (1.7%), Buddhism (0.7%), and Jainism (0.4%).
- Four of world's major religions - Hinduism, Buddhism, Jainism, and Sikhism - originated in India.
- Presence of Constitutional Secularism → government does not endorse any partiular religion and guarantees freedom of religion to all its citizens.
- Religious Tolerance: Despite its diversity, India generally promotes religious tolerance and peaceful coexistence between different faiths.
  - ⋙ Philosophies like Sarva Dharma Sambhava, Sulh-i-Kul principle, compassion towards all religions promoted religious tolerance in India since Independence.

The Registrar and census commissioner released the data on population by religious communities of Census 2011.

Muslims (14.2%)
Christian (2.3%)
Sikh (1.7%)
Buddhist (0.7%)
Jain (0.4%)
Hindu (79.8%)

## Issues Associated with Religious Diversity

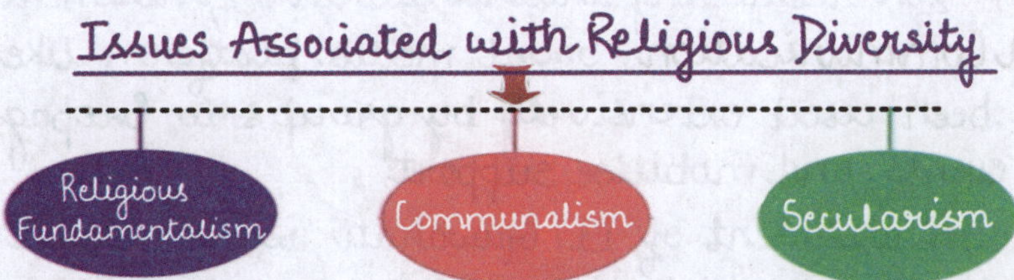


## Religious Fundamentalism

- Religious Fundamentalism is a tendency within a religion that emphasises a strict literal interpretation of its sacred texts or doctrines.
- Adherents believe these core principles are immutable truths and foundation for morality and social order.
- Characterised by Visible pattern of religious militancy through which self-styled true believers tries to arrest the erosion of religious identity and practice.

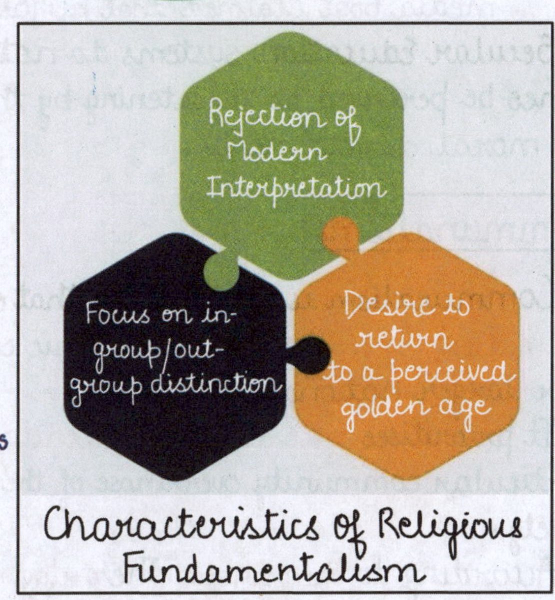

Characteristics of Religious Fundamentalism

## Causes of Religious Fundamentalism

- Modernization leads to rapid social changes, economic development, and adoption of new cultural norms → create a sense of threat to traditional religious values and identities.
- Secularization: Lead to decline in social significance of religion by → Privatisation of religious affairs, and Differentiation i.e. religion should be restricted to cultural domain only.
  - Ex: Rise of organisations like Popular Front of India (PFI) can be seen as a response to perceived secular policies that marginalise Muslims communities.
- Idealogical Cohesion generated unity among its followers → which can be appealing in times of social or political turmoil.
  - RSS has been effective in promoting a cohesive Hindu nationalist ideology → it helped them to mobilise support for various causes like anti-conversion laws.
- Charismatic Leadership can attract and inspire followers, often using their personal appeal to galvanise support for fundamentalists causes
  - Zakir Naik was banned in India in 2016 for allegedly inciting violence and promoting enmity between religious groups.
- Supply of potential Recruits: Since religion is opium of masses, a relatively deprived section is required to foment fundamentalist feelings.
  - Socioeconomic factors like unemployement, poverty and lack of education can provide a fertile ground for recruiting individuals into fundamentalist movements.
- Technological and Communication: Social media platform like whatsapp, Facebook, and Twitter have been used extensively by groups to propagate religious ideologies organise events, and mobilise support
  - Tauseef Ali Farooqui, a student of IIT Guwahati, was arrested after a social media post claimed that he joined terror organisation ISIS.
- Secular Education systems do not incorporate religious teachings → can sometimes be perceived as threatening by those who believe that religious values are essential for moral development.

## Communalism

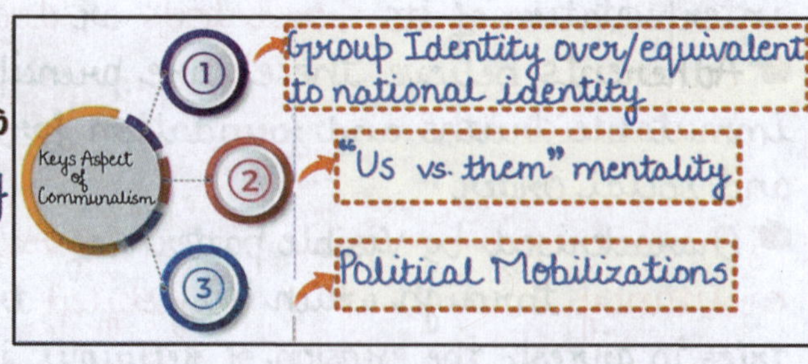


- Communalism is an ideology that emphasises primacy of one's religious or ethnic community over larger national identity.
- It prioritises interests and identity of a particular community over those of the whole society.
- According to Ram Ahuja "The antogonism practised by the members of one community against the people of other community and religion can be termed as communalism."

According to Bipin Chandra "Communalism is an ideology which shapes vision of members of a community formed on the basis of common religion about themselves, other religious communities, nationalism and state."

According to Gyanendra Pandey, communalism is a form of colonialist knowledge, which in its Indian usage, implies a condition of suspicion, fear, and hostility between the members of different religious communities.

As per NCRB data, 378 cases of communal or religious rioting were registered in 2021, 857 in, 2020, 438 in 2019, 512 in 2018 and 723 in 2017.

## Stage of Communalism

**Communal Consciousness:** It is initial stage where people develop a sense of belonging and affinity with their religious community. They identify with shared customs, traditions, and beliefs.

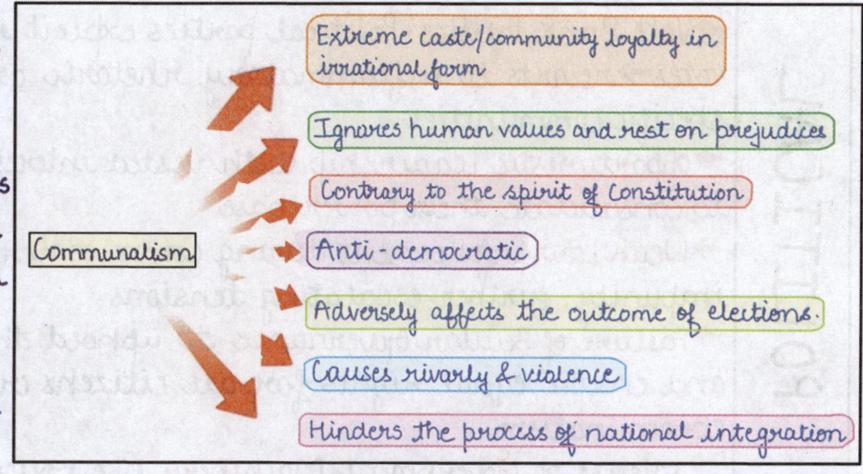


- Ex: Hindus celebrating Diwali or Muslims celebrating Eid al-Fitr are expressions of communal consciousness, highlighting their respective religious traditions.

**Liberal Communalism:** Focus shifts towards political representation and safeguarding interests of one's religious community.

- This stage denotes people belonging to different religious communities that do not have common secular interests (Socio, Economic and Political).
- Ex: Formation of the Muslim League in British India → aimed to represent the political interests of Muslims.

**Extreme Communalism** is most dangerous stage. Here, the "Us vs. them" mentality intensifies, leading to suspicion, hostility, and even violence towards other religious communties.

- This stage emphasises superiority of one's own religion and the incompatibility of different religious communities coexisting peacefully.

After Holistically understanding stages one can rightfully say that "A man of religion is not communal but the one who plays politics by Linking it with religion is communal.

## Factors Responsible for Communalism in India:

| Factors | Description |
|---|---|
| HISTORICAL LEGACY | → British Divide and Rule Policy to maintain control like separate electorates for Hindus and Muslims → sowed seeds of distrust between communities.<br>→ Violent Partition of India based on religion created deep wounds and memories of religious violence.<br>→ Historiography Debates about events of Mughal era and rise of Hindu nationalism → created a sense of grievance and animosity.<br>→ Unfinished Business of partition era like Kashmir issues, territorial disputes or status of religious minorities → led to ongoing tension. |
| POLITICAL | → Vote Bank Politics: Political parties exploit religious sentiments to garner votes → resorts to inflammatory rhetoric or divisive policies targeting specific communities.<br>→ Opportunistic Leadership with vested interest → stoke communal tensions to consolidate their power base.<br>→ Weak Law Enforcement during communal riots → create a climate of impunity, further escalating tensions.<br>→ Failure of Secular Governance to uphold the principles of secularism and ensure equal rights for all citizens creates a breeding ground for communalism.<br>→ Misuse of Government Machinery like police forces, to target specific communities → erode trust in the government. |
| ECONOMIC | → Competition for Scarce Resources like jobs, housing, or water can lead to competition and scapegoating of minority communities.<br>→ Unequal Development across religious communities → creates a sense of economic disparity and resentment.<br>→ Marginalization of Minorities can create frustration and a sense of injustice leads to social unrest.<br>→ Lack of Education and Upward Mobility make individuals more vulnerable to communalist utopian ideologies.<br>→ Growth of Communal Business Networks: The rise of business networks based on religious identity can create a sense of economic exclusion for those outside the network, potentially fueling communal tensions. |
| | → Religious Stereotypes and Prejudices perpetuated through socialization or misinformation → leads to distrust and hostility. |

| | |
|---|---|
| SOCIAL | → **Lack of Interfaith Dialogue** creates a sense of "otherness" and hinder social harmony.<br>→ **Social Segregation** based on religion limits opportunities for inter-community interaction → perpetuating misconception and biases.<br>→ **Social Media Echo Chambers** exposes user primarily to information that reinforces their existing biases. |
| ROLE OF MEDIA | → **Sensationalized Reporting** and inflammatory reporting on religious issues can exacerbate tensions and create a perception of widespread conflict.<br>↱ Ex: Tablighi Jamaat issue coverage during Covid 19 Pandemic.<br>→ **Communal Bias in Coverage** demonizes one community can contribute to a sense of victimhood and a desire for revenge.<br>↱ Ex: Communalisation of Sexual offences.<br>→ **Hate Speech Platforms**: Social media platforms like Facebook and Whatsapp have been accused of allowing spread of hate speech and communal propaganda.<br>→ **Lack of Fact-Checking** led to proliferation of fake news and misinformation. |

## Types of Communalism

▶ **Assimilationist**: When a large religious community tries to assimilate a smaller one in such a way that latter culture gets subdued.
- → Ex: Hindu codes applicable to Sikh, Buddhist, Jain as well as tribes.
- → GS Ghurey called tribal backward Hindus.

▶ **Welfarist**: Advocating for special programs or affirmative action to uplift a disadvantaged community → People work for the welfare of one's own community.
- → Ex: Community and religion specific scholarship like Jaina.

▶ **Retreatist Communalism** involves withdrawing from dominant society and creating separate space for community, as a response to perceived discrimination or hostility.
- → Ex: Bahaism members are prohibited from participating in political processes.

▶ **Retaliatory**: It is a reactive form characterised by hostility among communities → a community responds violently or through social unrest to perceived injustices or attacks by the dominant community.

▶ **Separatist**: It involves desire to form a separate state or homeland for the community, driven by a sense of religious and cultural distinctiveness.
- → Ex: Demand for Greater Nagalism, Bodoland.

Secessionist Communalism is the most extreme form → actively seeking to break away from existing nation-state and create an independent nation based on religious or ethnic identity.
  - Ex: Demand for Khalistan, Azad Kashmir.

## Evolution of Communalism in India

### Ancient India

- **Religious Tolerance:** Empires like Mauryas and Cholas promoted religious pluralism, with rulers patronising different faiths → put a check on birth of communalism.
- **Philosophical Undercurrents** like Hinduism's concept of Sarva Dharma Sambhava and Jainism's emphasis on ahimsa fostered and promoted religious tolerance.

### Medieval India

- **Rise of Religious Competition** with arrival of Islam and establishment of Muslim sultanates → introduced a new religious dynamic.
- **Theological Debates** and occasional conflicts between religious group emerged it was period of peaceful coexistence.
  - Abolition of Jizyah and promotion of Din-i-ilahi by Akbar highlight peaceful coexistence.
- **Impact of Invasions:** Destruction of Hindu temples during invasions by Mahmud Ghazni rulers fueled resentment and a sense of Hindu identity.

### Pre-Independence India

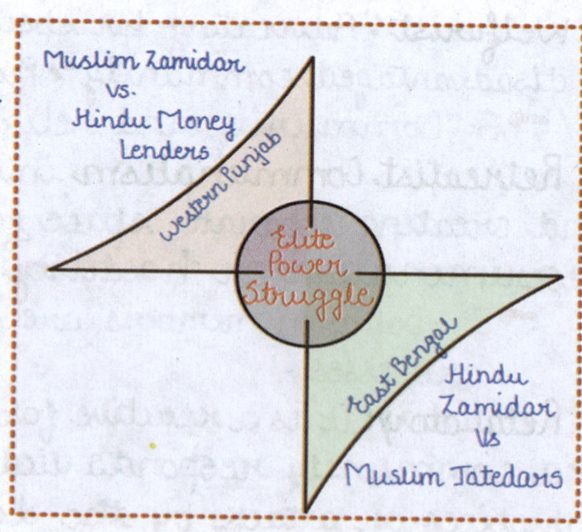


- Inadequate opportunities for aspiration and interest of middle class created the ground for communalism.
- Socio-Economic reality was such that religious distinction coincided with class distinction.
  - Power struggle between upper and lower strata manufactured the fabric of communalism.
- Colonial Divide and Rule Policy exploited existing religious fault lines to weaken nationalist movements.
- Formation of Religious organisations like Hindu Mahasabha and the Muslim League solidified religious identities and political demands.

➜ Increased Tensions fueled by competition for resources, political representation, and growing national consciousness contributed to communal violence.

## Independent India

➜ Overthrow of colonial state was only a necessary condition to fight communalism but not sufficient.

Reasons:

- Failure of National Leadership to unify different sections of society
  - ➜ restricted to policy of negotiations with leaders of different religious organisations.
- Hindu touch was dominant in nationalist agenda like ➜ Ganesh Festival, Shivaji Festival, taking dip in Ganga.
- Resentment among educated middle class muslim because of over emphasis on ancient Indian Culture and undermining Medieval Indian Culture

Lack of Cultural Integration ➜ Stereotyping ➜ Hostile attitude towards other ➜ Violent Manifestation ➜ 'Other' Communities surviving on technique of 'Invisibility' ➜ GHETTOIZATION ➜ Lack of Cultural Integration

➜ Post Independent government failed to come to terms with communalism.

## Major Communal Events in Post Independence

### 1960s:

- Revival of communalism and riots in Ranchi, Jamshedpur, Rourkela due to influx of Hindu refugees from East Pakistan created competition for resources and anxieties about demographic change.
  - Political parties like Jan Sangh exploited these anxieties for electoral gain, stoking communal tensions.
- 1969: Ahmedabad Riots (Jan Sangh vs. Muslim Organisations):
  - Jan Sangh's opposition to the secular policies of Indira Gandhi government led to tensions.
  - Cow slaughter, a sensitive issue of Hindus, became a flashpoint, triggering violence against Muslims.

### 1970s:

- 1974: Clashes between Dalit Panthers and Shiv Sainiks:
  - Dalit Panthers, a dalit rights group, challenged caste inequalities, leading to clashes with Shiv Sena.

**1980s:**

- **Clashes in Punjab:**
  - Sikh nationalist movement demanding an independent Khalistan state clashed with Indian government.
  - Religious tensions and political violence escalated, leading to a period of insurgency in Punjab
- **1983: Nellie Killings (Targeting Bengali-speaking Muslims) in Assam:**
  - Long-standing tensions between indigenous Assamese people and Bengali-speaking migrants, including Muslims, over language, identity,
  - Political manipulation and rumours fueled the violence against Bengali-speaking Muslims.
- **1984: Anti-Sikh Riots:**
  - Assassination of Prime Minister Indira Gandhi by Sikh bodyguards triggered widespread violence against Sikh across India.
  - Political failure to control the violence and a climate of impunity for perpetrators fueled the riots.

**1990s:**

- **1992: Riots Across India Following Babri Masjid Demolition:**
  - Demolition of the Babri Masjid by Hindu nationalists sparked nation-wide communal violence targeting Muslims.
  - Deep-seated historical grievances related to the mosque's location on a site believed to be the birthplace of Lord Rama fueled the violence
- **2002: Gujarat Riots:**
  - The Godhra train burning incident, where a coach carrying Hindu pilgrims was set on fire, triggered widespread violence against Muslims.
  - Allegations of government complicity and inaction by police forces exacerbated the violence.

**2000s Onwards:**

- **2012: Bodos vs. Bengali Muslims in Kokrajhar, Assam:**
  - Ethnic tension between Bodos, an indigenous tribe, and Bengali-speaking Muslims over land rights and competition for resources.
  - Political manipulation and rumours fueled the violence.
- **2013: Hindu-Muslim Riots in Muzaffarnagar:**
  - A dispute over the alleged harrassment of a Hindu girl by a Muslim boy trigged violence that spread across the western Uttar Pradesh.
  - Inflamatory rhetoric by politicians and sensationalized media coverage exacerbated the tensions.

👉 **2020: Delhi Riots:**

- Passage of the Citizenship Amendment Act (CAA) 2019, seen as discriminatory towards Muslims, sparked protests
- Clashes between pro and anti-CAA groups escalated into violence that primarily targeted Muslims.

## Measures to Tackle Communalism

| Short Term Measures | Long Term Measures |
|---|---|
| ➡ Politics should be delinked from communalism ➡ put a check on increased instances of communal violence during elections and the use of communal remarks for vote banks.<br>➡ Strengthening Law Enforcement to ensure prompt action against communal violence and hate crimes with strict penalties.<br>➡ Monitoring Hate Speech in public forums, including social media.<br>➡ Establish Local Peace Committees involving community leaders from diverse backgrounds to mediate and prevent conflicts.<br>➡ Media Regulation for responsible journalism by media ➡ to prevent sensationalism and biased coverage that can incite communal tensions.<br>➡ Community Policing initiatives to build trust between law enforcement and diverse community.<br>➡ Rapid Response Teams to quell communal riots and provide immediate relief and protection to victims.<br>➡ Public Awareness Campaigns to promote communal harmony and educate citizens on the dangers of communalism.<br>➡ Educational Workshops in schools and | ➡ Educational Reform to integrate comprehensive education on secularism, cultural diversity, and religious tolerance<br>➡ Inclusive Economic Development to reduce economic disparities that can fuel communal tensions.<br>➡ Judicial Reforms to ensure swift and fair trials for communal violence cases.<br>➡ Political Accountability: Enforce strict measures against politicians and parties that engage in or incite communalism.<br>➡ Civic Engagement Programs and participation from all communities to foster a sense of belonging and shared responsibility.<br>➡ Cultural Exchange Programs that allow people from different communities to interact and understand each other's traditions and values.<br>➡ Strengthening Secular Institutions in governance and public life to uphold constitutional values.<br>➡ Research and Data Collection to understand root cause of communalism and monitor trends to inform policy-making.<br>➡ Urban Planning and Integration to prevent segregation of communities and promote mixed neighbourhoods.<br>➡ Long-Term Media Strategy: Develop a long-term strategy to engage media in |

| | |
|---|---|
| colleges to teach students about religious tolerance and secularism.<br>➡ Promoting Interfaith Dialogue to foster understanding and cooperation among different religious groups.<br>➡ Victim Support Services and rehabilitation services for victims of communal violence, including counselling and financial aid. | promoting stories of communal harmony and success in diversity. |

## Committee Recommendation

- Ragnath Mishra Committee "Role of Police has been highly controversial with respect to incidents of communal violence hence needs to be addressed on urgent basis."
- Sachar Committee recommends:
  - A specific bill for preventing communal violence, control measures, and rehabilitation of victims.
  - It stressed on posting Muslim police personnel in police station located in Muslim-concentrated areas to improve trust and communication with communities.
  - Sensitization Training of government employees, including police, on handling communal situations and respecting diverse communities.

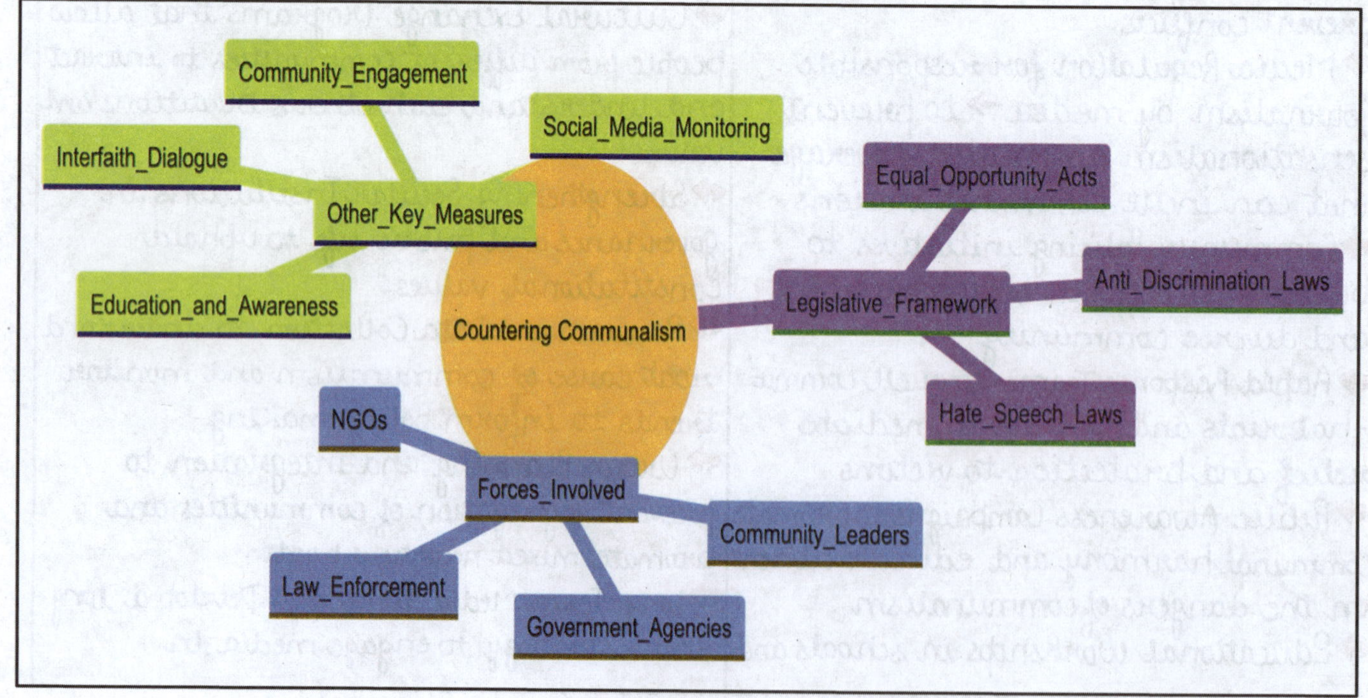

# SECULARISM

- **Meaning:** Refers to the principles of separation of religion and state, where the government is neutral towards all religions and does not promote or discriminate against any religions.
  - Secular term was added by 42nd Amendment (1976).
  - "India is Politically Secular not Socially."
- It has broadly two meanings:
  - Separation of religion from the state i.e. Dharm Nirpekshta.
  - Equal respect to all religions by state i.e. Sarva Dharma Sambhava.
- Indian constitution aims for a secular state where all religions are treated equally (Positive Secularism in India): State will have no religion of its own and all persons will be equally entitled to the freedom of consience and the right freely to profess, practice and propagate the religion of their choice.
  - **Support from State:** While on one hand, Government has given subsidies for Haj Yatra, it has also provided facilities for Amarnath Yatra.
  - **Equal Respect:** Every religion has liberty to celebrate functions like Eid, Diwali, Christmas, Guru Nanak Jayanti etc.
  - **Public Holidays** given on all major religious festivals.
- **Constitutional Basis:** Preamble Article 14, 15, 16, 25-28, 29-30, 44, 325 etc.
  - Secularism is part of 'Basic structure doctrine (SR Bommai and Others vs Union of India).

## Essential features of Indian Model

**State** is not completely identified with particular religion, yet state is not averse with the use of religious symbols.

No strict boundaries rather **porus boundaries between state and religion.**

No active hostility towards religion and no passive indifference.

Different religions are the foundations of the state.

Secularism is dependent on the ideas of Liberty, Equality, Fraternity and is considered as **integral component of democracy.**

A symmetrical intervention of state in different religions.

**Philosophy of Indian Secularism**

- Vedic concept of 'Dharma nirapekshata' i.e. the indifference of state to religion.
- **Sarva Dharma Sambhava:** It means equal respect to all religions.

## Objectives of Indian secularism:

- Brotection of Religious Freedom + Prevent Religious Persecution + Prevent Domination of One Religion + Bromotes interfaith harmony.
- Government stays neutral in matters of religion, and doesn't endorse any one religion over others.
- State offers legal protection to all religion and their followers.
- Breventing domination of one religion over another or discrimination within the same religion.
- Bromotes interfaith harmony and understanding.

## Concept of Secularization and its Manifestation

- Secularization is a sociological term that refers to the process by which religion loses its central role in society.
  - It comes into prominence in western society to curtail the authority of church and domesticate religious affairs.
- 3 Key Manifestation of Secularization:
  - Differentiation i.e. Religion will no longer be all encompassing and its presence will be restricted to only cultural domains.
  - Brivatization i.e since religion is a matter of faith it will be confined to the domestic sphere.
  - Decline in social significance of Religion because of its prohibition in the public sphere.

## Models of Secularism

| Western Secularism | Indian Secularism |
|---|---|
| It embodies a negative concept of secularism, i.e., the strict separation between religion and state.<br>No public policy can be solely based on religion, as religion is completely a private matter.<br>A single unified code of law is used to dispense justice regardless of | It embodies a positive concept of secularism, i.e equal respect for all religions or equal protection of all religions.<br>Public policies will be made on religious issues if there is a need to do so.<br>Certain personal laws of different |

| | |
|---|---|
| religious background<br>☛ It holds the principle of strict neutrality i.e. non-interference in affairs of each other. | religious boards are also considered while dispensing justice.<br>☛ It holds the principle of 'Principled distance', i.e interference of the State as and when required to uphold the Constitutional values. |

## Contemporary Aspects around Indian model of Secularism

| Aspect | Hindrances in Secularism | Promotion of Secularism |
|---|---|---|
| Anti-religious | ➤ In efforts to promote secularism, there may be pressure for religious minorities to assimilate into the dominant secular culture, leading to the erosion of distinct religious identities and practices. | ➤ Indian secularism doesn't favor one religion over another.<br>➤ The state treats all religions with equal respect and does not discriminate based on religious beliefs. |
| Western Import | ➤ Secularism is linked to Christianity that it is western and, therefore, unsuited to Indian conditions. | ➤ Indian secularism emphasizes the equal treatment and respect for all religions which aligns well with India's multicultural society |
| Minority Appeasement | ➤ India's secular policies amount to minority appeasement, where religious minorities are given preferential treatment at the expense of the majority community → Resentment & communal divides. | ➤ Protects Minority Rights: Through constitutional provisions and affirmative action policies, minorities are provided with safeguards against discrimination and marginalization. |
| Interventionist | ➤ Secularism is coercive and that it interferes excessively with the religious freedom of communities. | ➤ Indian secularism follows the concept of principled distance, which also allow for non-interference. |
| Vote Bank Politics | ➤ India's secularism is criticized for being undermined by communal politics, where politicians exploit religious identities for electoral gains → Religious tensions + communal violence | ➤ Secularism in India ensure that political decision are made based on principles of justice and inclusivity, rather than catering to electoral gain |

# Judicial Precedents on Secularism

**Shirur Mutt case, 1954**

- Supreme Court coined 'Doctrine of Essentiality'.
- The court opined that only the religious practices which were "essential and integral to religion" shall be protected under law.
- Ex: It was invoked during Ayodhya Case, 1994 → court opined that mosque is not integral to Islam and 'namaz' can be offered anywhere.
  - This doctrine was also invoked in recent Sabarimala case, 2018.

**Keshavananda Bharti vs State of Kerala 1973**

- The court reaffirmed the secular nature of the Constitution.

**Indira Nehru Gandhi vs. Raj Narain (1975)**

- Secularism means that state shall have no religion of its own and all person of the country shall be equally entitled to the freedom of their conscience and have the right to freely profess, practice and propagate any religion.

**S.P. Mittal vs. Union of India (1983)**

- Supreme Court held that government officials cannot participate in religious activities is unconstitutional.

**Indra Sawhney vs. Union of India (1992)**

- Supreme court upheld the validity of reservation with an upper cap of 50% → based on principle of social and educational backwardness, rather than religion.

**S.R. Bommai vs. Union of India (1994)**

- Secularism is part of the basic structure of Indian Constitution.

**M. Ismail Faruqui vs Union of India (1994)**

- Supreme Court ruled acquisition of a religious place of worship by government does not violate the right to freedom of religion, as long as adequate compensation is provided.

**Communalism Combat vs Union of India (2006)**

- Supreme Court issued guidelines to prevent hate speech and communal violence by politicians and religious leaders.

**Hijab Ban Case, 2022**

- Karnataka HC in 2022 ruled that hijab is not an essential religious practice under Islam and is not protected under Article 25.

# Shayra Bano Case

## Issues Challenged

- Triple Talaq (Talaq-e-Biddat) allows a Muslim husband to instantly divorce his wife by uttering the word "talaq" three times.
  - Challenged the constitutionality of this practice → as it violated a woman's right to equality and dignity.
- Nikah Halala occurs through triple talaq, for a woman to remarry her former husband, she needs to marry another person, consummate the marriage, and then get divorced again.
  - It was challenged as degrading and discriminatory towards women.
- Polygamy not directly practised by Ms. Bano's husband → but it raised concerns about legality and fairness of a practice allowing a Muslim man to have multiple wives at the same time.

## Status

- On 22nd August 2017, by a 3:2 majority, the 5 judge constitutional bench held that the instantaneous practice of triple talaq is unconstitutional.
- Parliament implemented Muslim Women (Protection of Rights & Marriage) Act 2019 to materialize the same.
- Key Provisions of the Act:
  - Talaq-e-Biddat is declared null and void.
  - The Act declared Triple Talaq a criminal offence → attracting up to three years imprisonment with a fine.
  - It declared it as Cognizable Offence → if formation is provided by married women or any person related to her by blood or marriage.
  - Offence may be compounded by Magistrate upon the request of the woman.
  - Provisions of subsistence/allowance will be decided by Magistrate + women can seek custody of minor children.

| Arguments in Favour Act | Criticism of Act |
|---|---|
| Protects Women's Rights from unilateral and harmful practice of triple talaq. | Criminalization of Divorce creates unnecessary legal complications litigation. |
| Promotes Gender Equality by addressing a discriminatory practice → that makes womens vulnerable. | Selective Targeting of a specific religious community. |
| Criminalizing triple talaq discourages the practice and associated social stigma | Fear of Potential Misuse of the law by women similar to dowry cases. |
| | Limited Scope: Only addresses triple talaq, doesn't address issues like polygamy |

| ➡ Deters Misuse of talaq by husbands who might have previously uttered it impulsively or without considering the consequences for their wives. | |
|---|---|

## Sabrimala Issue

### Issues Challenged

- It is centred around age-old practice of barring women of reproductive age (between 10 to 50 years) from entering Sabarimala Temple in Kerala.
- It was based on the belief that menstruating women rendered the temple impure.

| Arguments in Favour of Restriction | Arguments Against Restriction |
|---|---|
| Religious communities should decide what consitutes ERP, else it would be termed as an act of judiopapism<br>Diversity vs Discrimination: What is observed in Sabarimala is different tradition and custom not discrimination<br>Not an act of Misogyny: Women in menstruation age group were seen antithetical to celibate nature of deity.<br>It was difficult for women to observe 41 days penance for deity.<br>In Pluralistic society like India, entertaining PIL's against religious practices can cause serious damage to constitutional and social fabric of India. | Not an ERP → not protected under Article 25.<br>Individual dignity of women can not be at the mercy of masses.<br>Patriarchy in religion can not triumph over freedom to practise religion.<br>Violation of fundamental rights of women under Article 14 and article 15.<br>Prohibition was a form of practicing untouchability and it was questioned under "Doctrine of Living Tree."<br>Fundamental Rights were meant for individ-uals not dities.<br>Redefining Purity: Menstruation is a natural biological process and shouldn't be considered impure. |

Supreme Court Stance: In a landmark judgement Indian Young Lawyers Association vs. State of Kerala, 2018 Supreme court lifted the ban → declaring it unconstitutional and discriminatory.

→ It was lifted by a majority of 4:1 and the dissenting judge was Indu Malhatra.

# REGIONALISM

**Concept of Region:** It is a homogeneous area, physically and culturally distinct from neighbouring areas. People have awareness that they are similar, however distinct from others.

- Regionalism is rooted in India's diversity with respect to caste, religion, language class etc., when all these factors get geographically concentrated along with feeling of relative deprivation → translates into Regionalism.

Develop regional indentitites, loyalty tilted towards region rather than nation or state.

Based on Awareness — Regionalism

## Characteristics of Regionalism

- **Roots in Disparity:** Regionalism arises from economic, social, political, and cultural differences between regions
- **A Sense of Belonging:** At its core, regionalism is about feeling connected to and taking pride in a particular place.
- **Focus on Local:** Prioritizing development and interests of a specific region, sometimes at the expense of others.
- **Limited Perspective:** A regionalist view can unintentionally exclude or disadvantage people from outside the region.
- **Beyond Geography:** It is driven by a strong emotional attachment to a place, rather than just practical considerations.

## Forms of Regionalism

- **Separatism:** A strong desire for a region to become a completely independent state, separate from the existing country.
  - Ex: Demands for Bodoland in Assam, Gorkhaland for ethnic Gorkha (Nepali) people in West Bengal.
- **Demand for full & Independent Statehood:** A region demands to become a separate state within the existing federal structure of India, with a significant degree of autonomy.
  - Ex: Manipur, Tripura, Mizoram, Arunachal Pradesh got statehood and recently Delhi also put forward the demand of complete statehood
- **Demand for Regional Autonomy:** A region seeking greater control over its internal affairs within the existing Indian union. They want more power in decision-making regarding resources, culture, and development.
  - Ex: DMK in Tamil Nadu, Akali Dal in Punjab, Telugu Desam party in Andhra Pradesh, Assam Gana Parishad in Assam → demanding financial and governance autonomy.

▸ Secessionist: It involves militant and fundamentalist groups demanding a separation from India on the basis of ethnicity or any other factor.

- Ex: NSCN (IM), Islamic fundamentalist group in J&K, ULFA in Assam.

▸ Supra-State Regionalism: A form of cooperation between different regions within a country to achieve common goals that benefit all participating regions.

- Ex: Protest of Southern Indian States against Term of Reference of 15th Finance Commission.
- North Eastern Council (NEC) aims to promote economic and social development of the eight northeastern states.

▸ Inter-State Regionalism: It involve contrasting identities of one or more states with one another and associated with territorial regions.

- Ex: Dispute between Maharashtra and Karnataka on border issues.

▸ Intra-State Regionalism: It refers to regional aspirations within a single state in India. Different communities within a state may lobby for recognition of their distinct cultural or developmental needs.

- Ex: Tribal Issues in Manipur.

## Emergence of Regionalism in India

⋙ Nature of Independent Government: India adopted a democratic government with goal of nation-building. This process aimed to create a strong, unifed nation based on democratic values, secularism, national unity and social justice.

- Different regions/states aspired for a fair share of the development efforts → negligence from mainstream development or dissatisfaction led to dis-enchantment.

⋙ Integration of Princely States: Persistence of loyalty to former princely territories → reflected in electoral advantage of princes.

⋙ Linguistic Reorganisation of States: States like Andhra Pradesh, Kerala, Tamil Nadu, and Gujarat were formed primarily based on language → formally linguistic regionalism gained ground in Indian politics.

⋙ Selfish Politics: In Independent India to fulfil their selfish political aspirations → politicians explored narrow and sectarian sentiments of marginalised masses.

- Creation of more states meant more governors, chief ministers, members of legislative Assembly.

## Factors Responsible for Regionalism in India

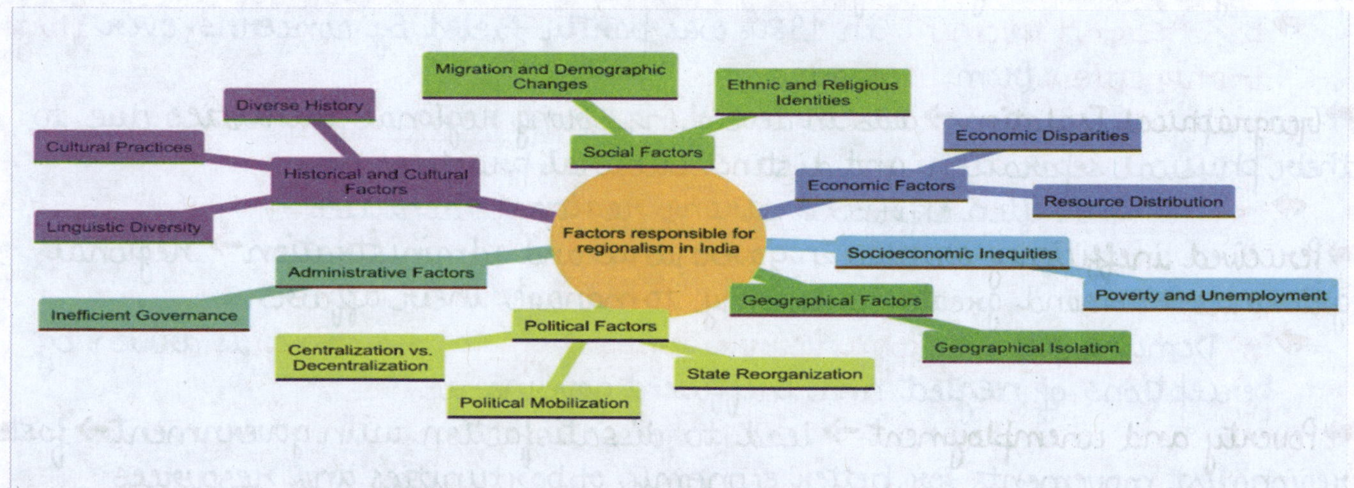


- **Diverse History:** Historical experiences of regions, such as distinct Kingdoms and colonial experiences, have shaped regional identities.
  - Ex: Dravidian movement in Tamil Nadu → tracing back to ancient Dravidian Civilisation.
- **Linguistic Diversity** contributes to regional pride and identity, leading to demands for recognition and autonomy.
  - Ex: Creation of Telangana as a separate state from Andhra Pradesh.
- **Varying Culture Practices,** festivals, and traditions reinforce regional identities and distinguish one region from another.
  - Ex: Onam, highlight distinct regional identity of Malayalis in Kerala.
- **Economic Disparities** among regions → feeling of relative deprivation → regionalism.
  - Ex: Bodaland movement in Assam arose from economic neglect and under development of Bodo-majority areas.
- **Resource Distribution Conflicts** → over natural resources → intensify regionalism as regions seek to control and benefit from their own resources.
  - Ex: Cauvery River water dispute between Karnataka and Tamil Nadu.
- **Political Mobilisation** by regional political parties on ground of regional identity and interests.
  - Ex: Shiv Sena in Maharashtra → appeals to Marathi pride and identity.
- **Centralisation vs. Decentralisation:** States government perceived a tilted balance of power towards central government as a threat → demand for regional autonomy.
- **Ethnic and Religious Identities:** When ethnic and religious differences → translates into marginalisation or underrepresentation.
  - Ex: Gorkhaland movement in West Bengal → driven by ethnic identity of Nepali-Speaking Gorkhas.

→ Migration and Demographic shifts can create tension between local populations and migrants, leading to regionalist sentiments.

→ Ex: Assam Movement in 1980s was partly fueled by concerns over illegal immigration from Bangladesh.

→ Geographical Isolation → aids in developing strong regional identities due to their physical separation and distinct cultural practices.

→ Ex: Manipur often expressed strong regional identities.

→ Perceived inefficiency or bias in governance and administration → regional grievances → demand greater autonomy to manage their affairs.

→ Ex: Demand for Vidarbha (currently part of Maharashtra) is driven by perceptions of neglect and inefficient governance.

→ Poverty and unemployment → lead to dissatisfaction with government → foster regionalist movements for better economic opportunities and resources.

→ Ex: Naxalite-Maoist insurgency in state like Chhatisgarh and Jharkhand.

## Impact of Regionalism

| Positive Impact | Negative Impact |
|---|---|
| → If it accommodates the federal sentiments → plays an important role in nation buildings → Inclusive democracy<br>→ Right to Self-Determination: By allowing cultural autonomy + preservation of distinct traditions.<br>→ Participatory Governance: When regional issues are addressed at regional level → allows for greater citizen participation + responsive government.<br>→ Realisation of Multiculturalism: By fostering a sense of pride in regional identities and cultures, regionalism can contribute to a richer and more vibrant national culture.<br>→ Check Political Extremism: Tripura Tribal Autonomous District Council, 1985 served and preserved endangered tribal identity by providing a democratic platform → reducing bases of political extremism in the state. | → Secessionist and Violent tone: Extreme regionalism → demands for complete separation → threaten national unity and territorial intergrity.<br>→ Basis of Vote Bank Politics: Politicians exploit regional sentiments to gain votes → through divisive appeals based on language, ethnicity, or religion.<br>→ Hindrance in International Diplomacy: Regional tensions → spill over into foreign policy → absence of united front on global stage.<br>→ Feeling of Relative Deprivation: Unequal distribution of resources due to presence of strong regional leaders → rise of feeling of relative deprivation → regional conflict.<br>→ Ex: Manipur Ongoing Conflict.<br>→ Cultural Insularity: Because of reduced intercultural exchange and understanding.<br>→ Policy Fragmentation: With inconsistent implementation of national programs |

↱ Economic Development through region specific tailored economic policies and development projects, benefiting local economies.

↱ Tourism boosts by highlighting regional uniqueness can attract tourists, boosting local economies and promoting cultural exchange.

across different regions.

↱ Ex: West Bengal refused to participate in Ayushman Bharat scheme.

↱ Migration Issues: Competition for jobs for locals in state like Gujarat and Maharashtra → led to hostility towards migrants from Bihar and Uttar Pradesh.

## Regionalism: As a Threat to National Unity

| | |
|---|---|
| POLITICAL FRAGMENTATION | • Emergence and dominance of regional parties → lead to political fragmentation → as they prioritize regional interests over national interests.<br>• Coalition Governments lead to policy compromises and instability → hinders implementation of national development plans + environment of political uncertainty.<br>• Parochial Politics: Where leaders focus on narrow regional issues to the detriment of broader national interests. |
| ECONOMIC DISPARITIES | • Uneven development + resource allocation conflicts can escalate and disrupt national harmony.<br>• Investment Disparities due to favourable local policies or political influence, leaving other regions underdeveloped.<br>↱ It may lead to rise in feelings of relative economic deprivation. |
| SOCIO-CULTURAL DIVISIONS | • Reinforcement of linguistic and cultural identity → comes in clash with promotion of a unified national identity.<br>• Ethnic Conflicts and tensions → lead to violence and social unrest, threatening national stability.<br>• Cultural Protectionism → leads to isolationism and cultural clashes between different regions. |
| SECESSIONIST MOVEMENT | • Demand for Autonomy → emergence of secessionist ideology → direct threat to national integrity.<br>↱ Ex: Movements in Kashmir, Punjab, and northeastern states.<br>• Violence and Insurgency: Regionalism manifests into Insurgency and armed rebellion against the state → undermines national security and unity. |
| ADMINISTRATIVE CHALLENGES | • Policy Implementation: States may resist or modify national policies to suit regional preferences, leading to inconsistencies and inefficiencies. |

# Measures to Counter Regionalism in India

## Government Measures Taken to Promote National Integrity

- **North-Eastern Council** was setup in 1971 to provide a forum for inter-state coordination, regional planning and integrated development of the region to avoid intra-regional disparities.
- **Schemes to promate Nationalism**: Schemes like "EK Bharat-Shreshtha Bharat" have been launched to promote the country's cultural diversity and increase inhabitant's feelings of national togetherness.
- **Backward Region Grant Fund** was implemented to address regional development imbalances.
- **Pradhan Mantri Khanij Kshetra Kalyan Yojana** was launched for welfare of tribals and tribal regions and other affected by mining.
- **State Reorganisation Act, 1956**: Zonal Councils to promote interest of different geographic zones.
- **Federal Institution**:
  - NITI Aayog has been established to ensure federal equilibrium.
  - Interstate Council was established to make Inter-State Council Secretariat a thriving institution that supports coordination and cooperation between Centre and States in India.
  - GST Council: Promote Financial federalism and take on board all stakeholders.
- **Article 370 Abrogation** to integrate Jammu and Kashmir more closely with the rest of India, ensuring uniformity in laws and governance.
- **Sixth Schedule** → provides for autonomous district councils in certain tribal areas of Assam, Meghalaya, Tripura and Mizoram to address regional aspirations while maintaining national integrity.
- **Unlawful Activities (Preventions) Act (UAPA)** → to curb secessionist activities and maintain internal security by penalizing act that threaten the unity and integrity of India.
- **Armed Forces (Special Powers) Act (AFSPA)**: Implemented in regions facing insurgency, like parts of Northeast and Jammu & Kashmir, to maintain law and order and counter separatist movements.
- **Periodic delimitation of constituencies** ensure fair representation of various regions in the Parliament and State legislatures, balancing regional and national interests.

| Short Term Measures | Long Term Measures |
|---|---|
| Promote National Integration Programs that celebrate national unity | Educational Reform to integrate lessons on national unity + importance of diverse |

| | |
|---|---|
| encouraging people from different regions to participate. | cultures in school curriculums. |
| ↱ Enhance Language Education that promotes multilingualism, ensuring students learn multiple Indian languages | ↱ Economic Development in backward regions, ensuring balanced economic growth across the country. |
| ↱ Strengthen Communication Channels to address regional grievances promptly and effectively. | ↱ Political Decentralisation → strengthen local self governance → to ensure regional aspirations. |
| ↱ Equitable resource allocation development projects to underdeveloped regions to address economic disparities. | ↱ Infrastructure Development that connects various regions, such as roads, railways, and communication networks, fostering inter-regional connectivity. |
| ↱ Fast Track Grievances Redressal mechanism to address and resolve regional grievances and disputes efficiently. | ↱ Legal Reforms to address regional biases and ensure that laws promote equality and fairness for all regions. |
| ↱ Media Regulation to highlight positive stories of national integration and discourage content that promotes regionalism. | ↱ National Service Programs that involve working in different regions, promoting cross-cultural understanding. |
| ↱ Employment Opportunities in under developed regions to reduce economic disparities that fuel regionalism. | ↱ Federal Structure Strengthening: by ensuring a balanced distribution of powers and responsibilities. |
| ↱ Promote National Symbols like national symbols (like flag, anthem, and emblem) in regional events to foster a sense of national pride. | ↱ Revitalize National Integration Council to regularly review and address issues through continuous dialogue and policy recommendations. |

## RACIAL INTOLERANCE/RACISM

About: A group of people with distinct physical characteristics such as skin, colour, feature, heights and texture of hair

- All four major morphological types - Caucasoid, Mongoloid, Australoid and Negrito are present in Indian population
- Racism is the systemic manifestation of uneven distribution of power and prejudices related to culturally defined ideas of race.

- As per Synergia Foundation report 86% of North-Easterners in metro cities experiencing racial bias.
- Article 15, Article 16 and Article 29 of the Constitution of India prohibit discrimination on ground of "race".
- India ratified the International Convention on the Elimination of All Forms of Racial Discrimination (ICERD) in 1968.
- Every year, 21st March, is observed as International Day for the Elimination of Racial Discrimination.

## Types of Racism

**Internalised Racism**
- Lies within individuals
- Private beliefs and biases about race and racism, influenced by our culture
- May be unconscious or psychologically rooted often reflects historic, inter-generational trauma.

**Interpersonal Racism**
- Occurs between individuals, anecdotal.
- Biases that occur when individuals interact with others and their private racial beliefs affected their public interactions.

**Institutional Racism**
- Occurs within institutions and systems of power.
- Unfair policies and discriminatory practices of institutions (schools, workplaces, etc) that routinely produce racially inequitable outcomes for people of color and advantages for white people

**Structural Racism**

Racial bias among institutions and across society

Cumulative and Compounding effects of an array of societal factors including the history, culture, ideology, and interactions of institutions and policies

## Causes of Racial Intolerance

- **Lack of Cultural Synthesis:** Lead to rise of "US vs THEM" mentality → Threat to Status Quo → manifestation of racial intolerance towards Newcomers.

Lack of Cultural Synthesis → Stereotyping → Ghettaization → Survival Technique of Invisibility

- **Racioncentrism:** Tendency to view one's own race superior to others.
- **Colonial Hangover:** Colonial rule institutionalized racial hierarchies, fostering a mindset of racial superiority and inferiority that persists in various forms.
- **Relative Deprivation:** Marginalised groups have less access to education, employment → reinforce discriminatory attitudes.

➜ Presence of Fringe or Anti-National Element: Spread rumours + stereotypes + misinformation that reinforce prejudice.

➤ Infringe elements might engage in acts of vandalism, harrassment, or even violence against individuals or businesses belonging to a different race.

➜ Western Beauty Standards → valorise lighter skin and certain physical features, can contribute to racial discrimination against those who do nat fit these standards.

➜ Perpetuation of stereotypes and prejudices about different cultures and race leading to racial discrimination.

## Implications of Racial Intolerance

- **Social Fragmentation:** Racial intolerance can lead to a divided society → segregated and isalated communities within society → weakens social cohesion and can lead to social unrest.
- **Discrimination and Alienation:** Radical intolerance → hinder access to education, employment, healthcare, and other essential services → perpetuate cycles of poverty and disadvantage.
- **Economic Inefficiency:** Exclusion from mainstream economy → drives out innovation and productivity.
- **Increased Social Costs:** Addressing the consequence of racial intolerance, such as social unrest and health disparities, can be costly for governments and society.
- **Erosion of Democracy:** Racial intolerance undermines democratic principles by marginalizing certain groups and denying them equal participation in the political arena.
- **Human Rights Violations** → which can attract national and international condemnation and affects a country's reputation and relationships with each other nations.

### Case Study: Death of Nido Taniam

M.P. Bezbaruah Committee was set up by the Ministry of Home Affairs. It looked into the concerns of the citizens from the North Eastern States following the death of Nido Taniam in Delhi.

#### Recommendations of Committee to Tackle Racial Intolerance:

➜ **Legislative Measures:** Enact a new law or armed existing laws to specifically address racial discrimination.

↗ It includes defining racial discrimination, complaints mechanism, and ensuring prompt action against offenders.

- Dedicated Helpline: Establish a 24x7 helpline for Northeastern people in distress.
- Set Up Special Police Unit in the police force to deal with issues related to racial discrimination and violence against Northeastern people.
- Launch awareness campaigns to educate the public about the culture and contributions of the Northeastern people to promote understanding and acceptance.
- Inclusion in School Curriculum to foster a sense of unity and respect.
- Legal Aid and Support: Provide legal aid and support to victim of racial discrimination to ensure they receive justice.
- Community Policing initiatives to build trust between the police and Northeastern communities.
- Appoint Special Liaison Officers in metropolitan cities with significant Northeastern populations to address their concerns and grievances.
- Appoint a nodal officer in the Ministry of Home Affairs to coordinate efforts to address issues faced by Northeastern people.
- Organise cultural events showcasing rich heritage of the Northeast to promote cultural exchange and understanding.
- Provide adequate hostel facilities for Northeastern students in major cities to ensure their safety and well-being.
- Sensitization Programs for police, government officials and other stake-holders to address biases and prejudices against Northeastern people.
- Robust Grievance Redressal Mechanism to address complaints of racial discrimination and ensure timely resolution.
- Monitoring and Evaluation: Set up a monitoring and evaluation system to track implementation of these recommendations and assess their impact.

## Way Forward:

- There should be sensitizing programmes that focus on addressing issues of Indian obsession with particular races.
- Charismatic Personalities should lend their voice to the cause of racism.
- Police need to be trained, sensitized with respect to racial attacks.
- Confidence building measures → to assure security and well being of racial minorities in India.
- Educational Institution need to be more accomodative and inclusive.
- Sports needs to be promoted → Athletes of different race showcasing their talent and athleticism can help dismantle stereotypes often associated with race.

# ETHNO-NATIONALISM

**About:** Ethno-nationalism is the belief that a nation is defined by a shared ethnicity, prioritizing the culture, language, and heritage of a specific ethnic group and advocating for its political dominance within a territory.

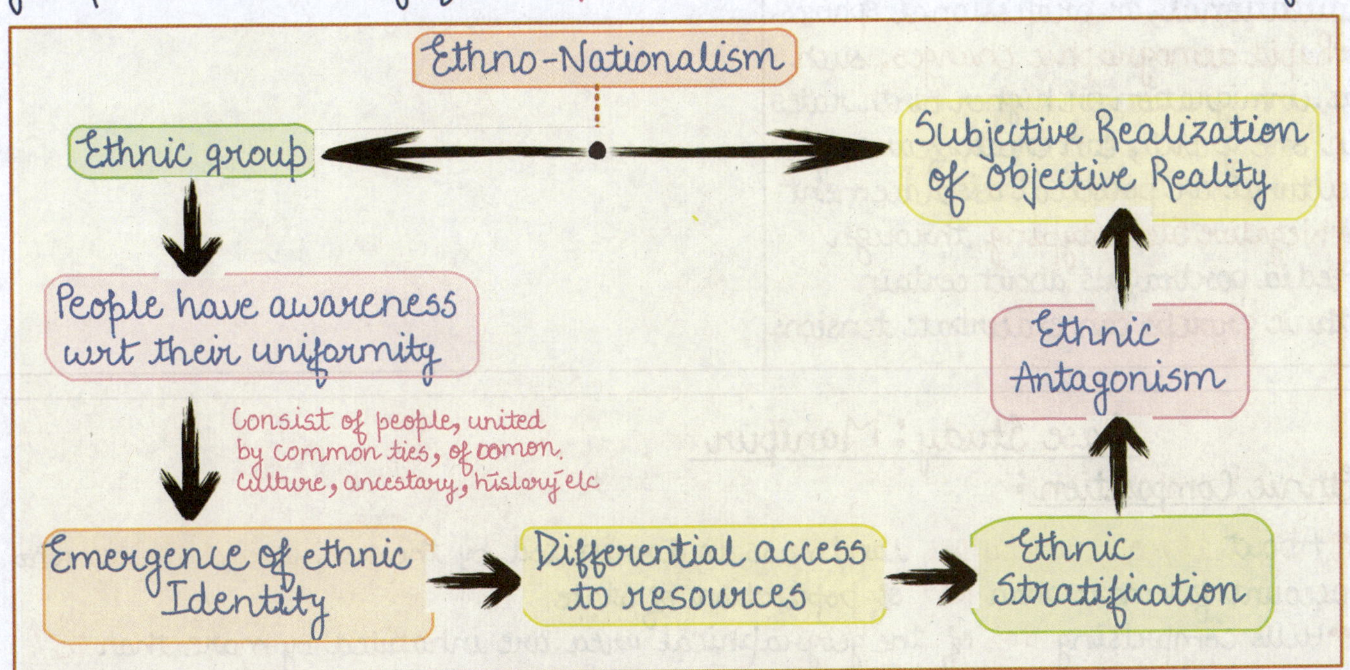


## Ethnic Antagonism

Ethnic antagonism is hostility or tension between different ethnic groups. It's a deep-seated dislike or distrust that can lead to conflict.

| Factors Responsible | Measures to Counter Ethnic Antagonism |
|---|---|
| ☛ Identity Threats: Perceived threats to ethnic identity or status can provoke defensive and hostile reactions.<br>☛ Historical Conflicts and wars between ethnic groups → leave end-uring legacies of mistrust and animosity.<br>☛ Exclusionary Policies that favour one ethnic group over others → lead to feelings of disenfranchisement + resentment. | ☛ Fair Representation in political institutions and decision-making processes.<br>☛ Implementation of Anti-Discrimination laws.<br>☛ Targeted Development Programs aimed at reducing economic disparities between ethnic groups.<br>☛ Inclusive School Curriculum that foster interaction and understanding among different ethnic groups.<br>☛ Rule of Laws → that fairly adjudicates disputes and protects rights of all ethnic groups. |

| | |
|---|---|
| Resource Competition such as land, jobs, and economic opportunities → heightens tension between ethnic groups.<br>Social Exclusion ethnic groups in educational, or professional spheres.<br>Rapid demographic changes, such as immigration or higher birth rates in one group, can create fears of cultural or political displacement.<br>Negative Stereotyping through Media portrayals about certain ethnic groups can exacerbate tensions. | Integrated Housing Policies to reduce Segregation and encourage diverse communities<br>Encourage and Support leaders who advocate for ethnic inclusion and harmony. |

## Case Study: Manipur

**Ethnic Composition:**

- About 10% of Manipur's landmass is dominated by the non-tribal Meitei who account for more than 64% of population of State.
- Hills comprising 90% of the geographical area are inhabited by more than 35% recognised tribes.
- Majority of Meiteis are Hindus followed by Muslims, the 33 recognised tribes, broadly classified into 'Any Naga tribes' and 'Any Kuki tribes' are largely Christians.

**Basis of Conflict:** Manipur High Court directed state to pursue a 10-year-old recommendation to grant Scheduled Tribe status to non-tribal Meitei Community.

| | |
|---|---|
| Meitei argument to support the demand of ST status?<br>Background: Schedule Tribe Demand Committee of Manipur (STDCM) initiated their campaign for ST status for the Meiteis in 2012.<br>Historical Context: The Meiteis were recognised as a tribe before Manipur's merger with India in 1949.<br>ST Status is seen as essential for preserving their community, ancestral land, culture, and language. | Advantaged Community argue that Meiteis hold demographic and political advantages + socioeconomically advanced compared to them.<br>Tribal groups perceived fear of job loss if ST status had been granted to Meiteis.<br>Loss of Land: ST status will enable the Meiteis to acquire land in the hills, potentially displacing tribal communities.<br>Political Motivations:<br>• Some views the demand for ST status as a tactic to undermine the political |

| | |
|---|---|
| ➩ Statehood Impact: Manipur's transition to statehood in 1972, Meiteis have expressed concerns about being marginalised in their own land.<br>➩ Infrastructure development and government employment dynamics favouring STs have further heightened insecurities among the Meitei community in Manipur. | aspirations of Kuki and Naga groups.<br>• It's also seen as a strategy by the dominant valley communities to expand their influence into the hill areas of Manipur. |

## Way Forward

- Evaluation of Criteria for ST status:
  - ➜ Should be Based on recommendations from committees like Lokur Committee (1965) → emphasising primitive traits, distinct culture, geographical isolation, shyness of contact, and backwardness.
  - ➜ Incorporate insights from the Bhuria Commission (2002-2004) and the Virginius Xaxa committee 2013, addressing critical issues such as livelihoods, education, health, displacement, migration, and legal matters.
- Repeal the Armed Force Special Powers Act (AFSPA, 1958) to improve human rights standards in the region.
- Ensuring a fair and transparent legal system → to prevent misuse of power by security forces.
- Enhance border surveilliance to prevent Myanmar migrant incursions, to strengthen national stability and security.

## PYQs Corner

*(Write the Answer and Get Free Evaluation)*

### 1 Religious Diversity

(i) Are tolerance, assimilation and pluralism the key elements in the making of an Indian form of secularism? Justify your answer. **(2022)**

(ii) What are the challenges to our cultural practices in the name of secularism? **(2019)**

(iii) Communalism arises either due to power struggle or relative deprivation.' Argue by giving suitable illustrations. **(2018)**

(iv) How the Indian concept of secularism is different from the western model of secularism? Discuss. **(2018)**

(v) Distinguish between religiousness/religiosity and communalism giving one example of how the former has got transformed into the latter in independent India. **(2017)**

(vi) How do the Indian debates on secularism differ from the debates in the West? **(2014)**

### 2 Regional Diversity

(i) Do you agree that regionalism in India appears to be a consequence of rising cultural assertiveness? Argue. **(2020)**

(ii) In the context of diversity of India, can it be said that the regions form cultural units rather than the States? Give reasons with examples for your viewpoint. **(2017)**

(iii) What is the basis of regionalism? Is it that unequal distribution of benefits of development on a regional basis eventually promotes regionalism? Substantiate your answer. **(2016)**

(iv) Growing feeling of regionalism is an important factor in the generation of demand for a separate state. Discuss. **(2013)**

### 3 Linguistic Diversity

(i) Has the formation of linguistic States strengthened the cause of Indian unity? **(2016)**

### 4 Diversity and Associated Issues

(i) Analyse the salience of 'sect' in Indian society vis-a-vis caste, region and religion. **(2022)**

(ii) How does Indian society maintain continuity in traditional social values? Enumerate the changes taking place in it. **(2021)**

(iii) What makes Indian society unique in sustaining its culture? Discuss. **(2019)**

(iv) Do we have cultural pockets of small India all over the nation? Elaborate with examples. **(2019)**

(v) The spirit of tolerance and love is not only an interesting feature of Indian society from very early times, but it is also playing an important part at the present. Elaborate. **(2017)**

(vi) Describe any four cultural elements of diversity in India and rate their relative significance in building a national identity. **(2015)**

CHAPTER 03

# Population and Associated Issues

According to Census 2011

**INDIAN POPULATION**

- Most Populated States → Uttar Pradesh (20 crore) > Maharashtra (11 crore) > Bihar (10 crore)
- Most Populated Union Territory → Delhi (1·67 crore)
- Least Populated States → Sikkim (6 lakh) < Mizoram (10 lakh)
- Least Populated Union Territory → Lakshadweep (64,000)

**DENSITY OF POPULATION**

- States with Highest Density of Population → Bihar (1106) > West Bengal (1028)
- Union Territory with Highest Density of Population → Delhi (11320)
- States with Lowest Density of Population → Arunachal Pradesh (17) < Mizoram (52)
- Union Territory with Lowest Density of Population → Andaman & Nicobar (46)

- States with Highest Sex Ratio Kerala (1084) > Tamil Nadu (996)
- UT with Highest Sex Ratio Haryana (879) > Jammu & Kashmir (889)
- States with lowest Sex Ratio Puducherry (1037)
- UT with lowest Sex Ratio Daman & Diu (618)

- Literacy Rate in India stands at 73%
- Male Literacy Rate stands at 80·9%
- Female Literacy Rate stands at 64·6%
- Crude Death Rate (CDR) → World Bank → India's CDR in 2023 was 6·6.
- Infant Mortality Rate (IMR) → NFHS-5 → IMR in India is 35·2 per 1000 live births.
- Maternal Mortality Rate (MMR) → NFHS 5 → MMR in India is 97 per 100,000 live births.

Kautilya had written in his Arthashastra that "a large population is a source of political, economic and military strength of a nation."

## DEBATE : ASSET vs LIABILITY

| Parameter | Asset | Liability |
|---|---|---|
| Workforce | Large pool of labour for industry and innovation. Ex: According to PLFS 2024, Labour Force Participation Rate (Age >= 15 years and above) increased from 45.2% to 46.9% | High unemployment rate → wastage of potential. Ex: As per PLFS 2024 Survey Male Unemployment Rate (Age >= 15 yrs and above) stands at 6.7% whereas female is 8.5%. |
| Market | Increased demand for goods and services, stimulating its economic growth. Ex: Indian economy is a Consumption driven economy (consumption > 50% share in GDP). | Unequal distribution of wealth limits consumption power for a large segment of the population. Ex: World Inequality Report 2022 → In India top 10% and top 1% of population holding 57% and 22% of total national income respectively. |
| Human Capital | Increased productivity and innovation can transform Human Resource into Human Capital. | Uneducated population limits economic potential. |
| Demographic Variation | Boost economic growth and tax revenue if managed effectively. | Large dependent population (young and old) → put strains on resources. |

## MODELS AND THEORIES

### Malthusian Theory of Population Growth

- Core Premise: Thomas Robert Malthus posited that human population inherently possesses the capacity for exponential growth → following a geometric progression.
  - Whereas food production increases at a slower → following an arith-metic rate.

**Malthusian Checks:** Malthus argued that unchecked population growth would trigger negative feedback mechanism (like famine, war, and disease), known as Malthusian checks → to bring population back into equilibrium with resource limitations.

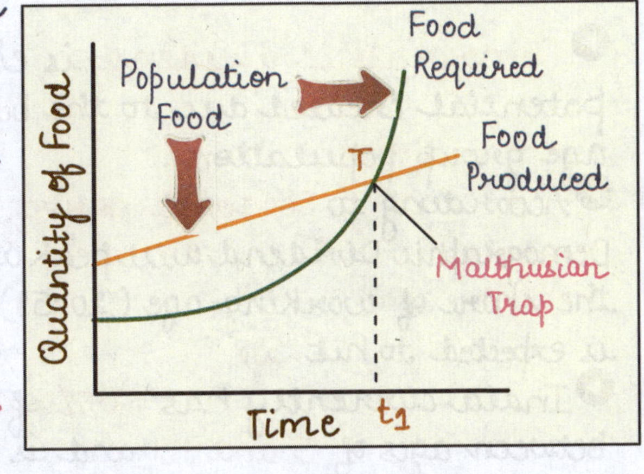


## Demographic Transition Theory

- **Demography** refers to characteristics of population which studies trends and processes associated with population.
  - Ex: Birth Rate, Death Rate, Migration Structure, Human Capital.
- **Demographic Transition Theory** suggests that population of any region changes from high birth and high deaths to low births and low deaths as society progresses from rural agrarian and illiterate to urban industrial and literate society.

### Stages of Demographic Transition

**Stage 1:**

- **High Birth Rate:** High Reproductive Rate → People Compensating for High Mortality.
- **High Death Rate:** Life expectancy is low due to limited healthcare, sanitation, and technology.
- **Slow Population Growth:** Despite high BR, high DR kept population growth stagnant.

**Stage 2:**

- **Declining Fertility:** Birth rates remain high in the beginning of the second stage but it declines with time.
- **Rapid Declining Mortality:** Improvements in sanitation, healthcare, and food security leads to a significant drop in death rates.
- **High Population Growth:** The gap between declining fertility and rapidly declining mortality creates a period of population explosion.

**Stage 3:**

- **Low Fertility and Mortality:** Both birth rates and death rates become low and relatively stable.
- **Factor Responsible:** Access to contraceptives, increase in education level and standards, improved sanitation and healthcare level.

# INDIA'S DEMOGRAPIC DIVIDEND

- Demographic dividend is economic growth potential created due to the bulge in working age group population.
- According to Economic Survey 2018-19, India's Demographic Dividend will peak around 2041, when the share of working-age (20-59) years population is expected to hit 59%.
- India currently has 62.5% of its population between ages of 15 and 59 and is steadily rising and will reach its peak around 2036 (65%).
- Demographic dividend availability began in 2005-2006.
- India has one of the youngest populations with a median age of just 28 yrs, compared to China (37 years), Western Europe (45 years), and Japan (49 years).
- Bulge in working-age population: India's working-age population started in 2005-06 and will last till 2055.

## Factors Shaping India's Demographic Transition

India's demographic transition, characterized by a decline in both birth and death rates, is a complex phenomenon driven by a confluence of socio-economic and programmatic advancements.

Women participation in Workforce → Reduction in TFR
Increase in Savings and Investments
Independent population > Dependent population
Increase in Domestic Consumption
Swelling of Labour Force

- Economic Growth: India's GDP per capital has increased from $2590 in 2000 to $2,411 in 2022 (World Bank).
  - It allows families to invest more in fewer children's education and heathcare
- Urbanisation: Exposure to social change and modern lifestyle preferences contributes to a reduction in fertility rates.
  - According to World Bank, urban population has grown from 27.8% in 2020 to 35% in 2020.
- Reduced infant and child morality: With improvement in healthcare facilities → families feel more confident in having fewer children.
  - India's under-five mortality rate has declined from 77 (as per NFHS 3) to 41.9 per 1,000 live births (NFHS 5).
- Women Empowerment: According to NFHS-5 and National Statistical Office (2021 and 2022) literacy rate is 71.50%, with literate males at 84.40% and literate females at 70.30%.

- **Government Interventions** like Mission Parivar Kalyan launched in 2016 focuses on increasing access to contraception and promoting smaller families.
  - Bring down the Total Fertility Rate at 2.0 i.e. population replacement level.
- **Evolving Family Structure**: Shift towards nuclear families and feminisation of households altered the preference towards less children.
  - According to Kantar data, at all-Indian level, 50% were nuclear in 2022, up from 37% of households in 2008.
  - In the Southern region, nearly 69% of households are nuclear from 50 percent in 2008.

## Challenges Associated with India's Demographic Dividend:

- **Jobless Growth**: In last 3 decades India's economy grew at over 5.8% per annum with job growth being close to 1% per annum.
  - Employment elasticity has fallen from close to unity in the 70s to 0.4 in the 90s to less than 0.1 today.
- **Automation** will lead to displacement of labour causing emotional stress to them and their families.
  - Nearly 12 million Indian women could lose their jobs by 2030 owing to automation, according to a McKinsey Global Institute report.
- **Dependence on informal sector**: Around 90% of labour force (mostly unskilled and semi-skilled) is employed in the less productive and low paying informal sector.
- **Low human development parameters** have negatively affected efficiency of work-force to engage in high productivity employment opportunities.
  - At rank 134 on Human Development Index, 2023-24 and 111th in Global Hunger Index, 2023
- **Low female labour force participation**: Periodic Labour Force Survey 2022-23 estimates that LFPR for female is 37% only.
- **Lack of equality education required skill sets**: Report of Aspiring minds, at least 47% of graduates in India are not employable for any industry role.
- **Poor Skill Development**: According to National Policy on Skill Development and Entrepreneurship report, in India just 4.7% of the workforce had formal training, compared to much higher rates in the US (52%), Japan (80%) and South Korea (96%).
  - According to Indian Skill Report, 2019, only 45.6% of youth graduating from educational institution are employable.
- **Stagnant manufacturing sector**: Though the sector has a multiplier effect over employment generation, it contributes just 16% of GDP.

## Policy measures in addressing the challenges

➤ Rapid and Inclusive growth with high employment elasticity has to be central to any employment strategy → will generate more jobs.

→ Ex: Growth of stronger industrial clusters and MSMEs will create more employment per unit of capital, and support inclusive growth.

➤ Promoting Labour Intensive Industries such as food processing, leather and footwear, wood manufacturers and furniture, textiles and apparel and garments.

→ Ex: Economic Survey 2019-20 suggests integrating 'Assemble in India' under 'Make in India' particularly in network products → Boost to India's Export.

➤ Decentralisation of Industrial activities is necessary for balanced regional development.

➤ Development of rural areas puts a check on the migration towards cities.

→ Ex: Implementing more schemes like Providing Urban Amenities to Rural Areas, Shyama Prasad Mukherji Rurban Mission.

➤ Investment in human capital: There is an urgent need to increase investment in sector such as education, health and nutrition.

→ Ex: Interim Union Budget 2024-25 emphasised the need for 6% of GDP in Indian education sector.

➤ Development of skills through a combination of apprenticeships and training institutes run by the private sector → essential to address academic-industry mismatch.

➤ Technological interventions can enhance productivity through increased market access, real-time information, quick dispute resolution, and development of transparent mechanisms.

→ Ex: India's edtech sector is beneficiary of the same.

India's workforce is only a potential not a guarantee. Its dividend depends upon two factors → quality of workforce and employment opportunity and if not harnessed it may lead to demographic disaster, unrest and chaos in the society.

## Paradox in India's Demographic Dividend

| Parameters | Northern States | Southern States |
|---|---|---|
| Fertility Rates (FR)<br>National Replacement Level = 2.0 | High FR: States like Bihar (3.0) and Uttar Pradesh (2.35) >> National average (TFR = 2.0) | Low FR states like Kerala (1.8) and Tamil Nadu (1.76) have achieved fertility rate below replacement-level. |

| Population Growth | Faster Population growth due to higher fertility rates → put a strong strain on educational and healthcare infrastructure | Slower population growth due to lower fertility rates → lead to ageing population in the South → impact the workforce and social security systems. |
|---|---|---|
| Literacy Rates (Particularly among females) | Low Literacy rate: In states like Bihar (51.50%) and Uttar Pradesh (57.18%) (as per 2011 Census) → low participation in the workforce. | Higher Literacy Rate: states like Kerala (92.07%) and Tamil Nadu (72.14%) (as per 2011 Census) → high participation in the work-force. |
| Urbanisation (National average rate = 31.1%) | Low Urbanization Rate: state like Jharkhand (24.05%) and Uttar Pradesh (22.27%) (2011 census) → limits access to better education, healthcare, and job opportunities. | High Urbanization Rate: states like Tamil Nadu (48.4%) and Kerala (47.72%) → greater access to education, healthcare, and job opportunities. |
| Social Structure | Patriarchal social structures are prevalent → influencing family planning decision and female education. | Strong presence of matriarchal and matrilineal systems + higher female literacy → lower fertility rates. |

**Political Apprehension:** Southern states have successfully implemented family planning programs → leads to a decline in population growth But with changing nature of politics it developed apprehension like:

- **Potential loss of seats:** Southern states fear they might lose parliamentary seats in future delimitation exercises.
- Weakening of Regional Autonomy because of decreasing influence in the national policy and government.
- **Reward vs Penalty:** Southern states argue that their success in population control shouldn't be penalised by reducing their representations and reduction in budgetary allocation.

## FACTORS AFFECTING THE GROWTH AND DISTRIBUTION OF POPULATION

**SOCIO-CULTURAL FACTORS**

- Cultural factors like religious pilgrimage sites (Varanasi) or historical centres can attract large tourists
- Government policies such as family planning initiatives or special economic zones can influence population growth rate
  - Ex: Male and Female sterilization, contraceptive and awareness programmes can influence the population growth rate.

| GEOGRAPHICAL FACTORS | |
|---|---|
| | ▶ Availability of Water tends to attract larger populations.<br>➤ Fertile Indo-Gangetic plains, with their perennial rivers like Ganga and Brahmaputra supported dense populations historically.<br>▶ Landforms: Flat plains and fertile valleys are more favourable for agriculture and infrastructure development.<br>➤ The Deccan Plateau, with its less fertile black soil, has a lower population density compared to the Indo-Gangetic Plain.<br>▶ Climate: Coastal areas with a pleasant climate, like Kerala and Goa → attracted people for settlement and tourism compared to arid regions of Rajasthan.<br>▶ Soil: Fertile soil is essential for agriculture to ensure food security.<br>➤ Black soil of Deccan Plateau supports argiculture, but not as intensively as the alluvial soil of the Indo-Gangetic plains. |

| ECONOMIC FACTORS | |
|---|---|
| | ▶ Minerals: Presence of valuable minerals like gold, oil, or diamonds can attract industries and workers, leading to population growth.<br>➤ Ex: Discovery of coal deposits in Jharkhand attracted industries → led to growth of urban centres like Dhanbad.<br>▶ Urbanisation: Cities offer a concentration of jobs, education, healthcare, and cultural amenities.<br>➤ Mumbai and Delhi have witnessed rapid population growth because of it.<br>▶ Industrialisation: Industries create jobs and economic opportunities, attracting people to settle near factories and production centres.<br>➤ Development of textile industry in cities like Ahmedabad and Surat. |

## Determinants of Population Change

- **Fertility Rate:** It is the number of live births during a reference period per 1000 women of reproductive age.
- **Total Fertility Rate:** It refers to the total number of live births that a women would have if she lived through the reproductive age group (15-64 years).
- **Crude Birth Rate (CBR):** Crude birth rate specifies the number of live births estimated at midyear and is reported per 1,000 living people.
- **Crude Death Rate** is the ratio of total registered deaths occurring in a specified calendar year to the total mid-year population of that year, multiplied by 1000.
  - ➤ According to World Bank, India's CDR in 2023 was 6.6.
- **Infant Mortality Rate (IMR)** is number of deaths of children under one year of age per 1000 live births.

➤ According to the NFHS-5, the infant mortality rate (IMR) in India is 35.2 per 1,000 live births.

- **Maternal Mortality Rate (MMR):** Death of a woman (per lakh live births) while pregnant or within 42 days of termination of pregnancy.
  ➤ According to NFHS-5 (Conducted in 2018-19) → maternal mortality ratio (MMR) in India is 97 per 100,000 live births.
- **Migration:** The movement of people with the intention of establishing a new residence, either permanently or temporarily, in a different geographical location.

## TOTAL FERTILITY RATE

**Current Status:** As per National Family Health Survey NFHS-5 conducted by MoHFW during year 2019-21, Total Fertility Rate (TFR) has declined to 2.0 children per woman from 2.2 children per woman as per NFHS-4 resulting in achievement of replacement level of fertility, which is 2.1 children per woman.

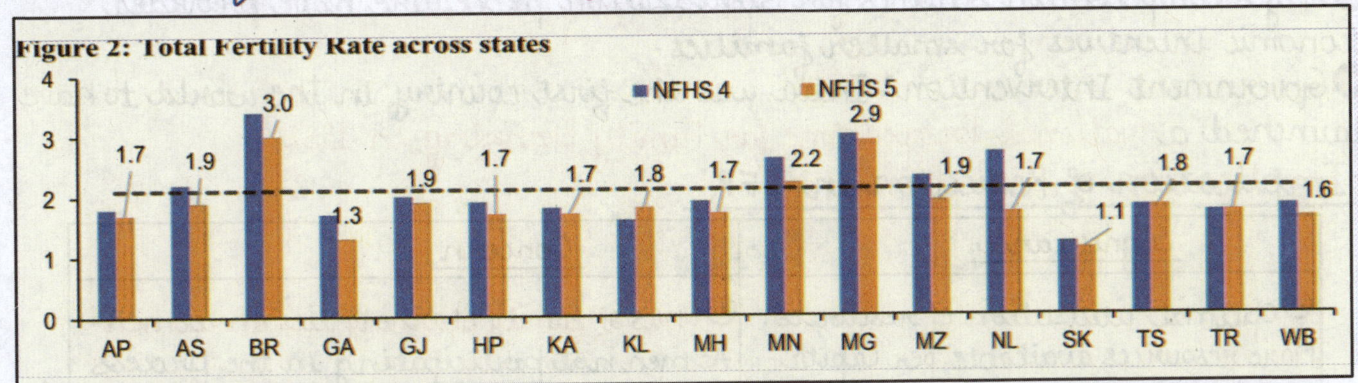


### Cause of High Fertility Rate in Some States:

- **Poverty:** Children are seen as an economic assets (More hand to work) → contribute to family income through labour in agriculture or small businesses
  ➤ NITI Aayog's own calculation of multidimensional poverty for 2022-23 estimates 11% of the population to be still in poverty.
- **High Infant and Child Mortality Rate:** Preference of male child + low status of women → lack of awareness of reproductive rights among women.
- **Poor Accessibility to Family Planning:** Limited access to family planning services and contraceptives restricts couple's ability to control family size.
- **Universalization of Institution of Marriage:** Societal pressure to marry and have children → influence couples to have children.
  ➤ They might have gone for adoption.
- **Joint family Norms:** Financial burden of raising children can be shared by extended family members → reduce the precceived economic pressure to limit family size

## Causes of Low Fertility Rate in some states:

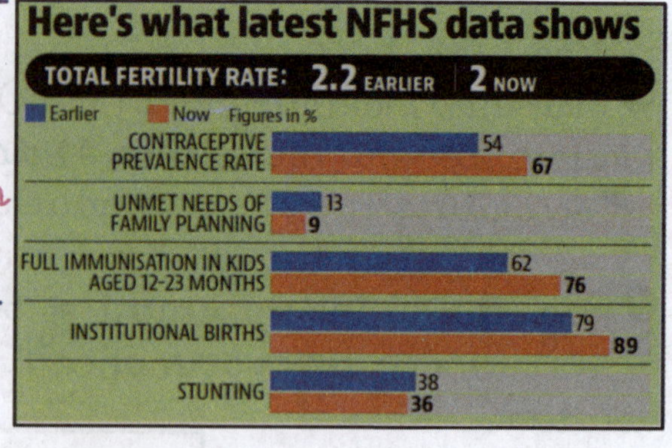


- **Urbanisation**: urban living characterised by confined living spaces and higher costs of child rearing → leads to low TFR.
  - → According to NHFS 5 → TFR is at 1.6 in urban areas and 2.1 in rural India.
- Increased Women Education empowers women to pursue careers and delay child bearing.
  - → Ex: Female Literacy rate in Kerala stands at 92.07% and TFR stand at 1.8.
- Improved healthcare and Family Planning reduced infant mortality rates → removes the pressure to have many children to ensure survival.
  - → Effective use of contraceptives and drug delivery protected maternal health also
- Reversible Spacing Methods like increasing the gap between children has empowered couples to plan their families.
- Wages compensation schemes for sterilization procedure have provided economic incentives for smaller families.
- Government Intervention: India was the first country in the world to have launched a National Programme for Family Planning in 1952.

## Implication of Reduction in TFR:

| Significance | Concern |
|---|---|
| Optimal utilisation of resources: More resources available per capita for education, healthcare, infrastructure<br>Status of Women: Empowers women with opportunities for education, career advancement, and reproductive control.<br>Women In Workforce: Increases female labour force participation, leading to economic growth and women's empowerment.<br>Political Landscape: Changing population structure may influence voting patterns. | Onus of family planning lies on women: As men not participating in the process and "shrugging responsibility"<br>➤ NFHS 5 reveals uptake of female sterilization up to 38% against 36% in 2015-16.<br>TFR lower than 2.1 → Generation is not producing enough children to replace itself, eventually leading to an outright reduction in population.<br>Labour Shortage: Shrinking workforce can lead to labour shortages in certain sectors → hinders economic growth. |

Declining TFR: A Paradox -: As many young people enter the workforce, the burden of supporting a growing elderly population increases. It strains the social security systems and healthcare infrastructure → hindering sustained economic growth if not addressed proactively.

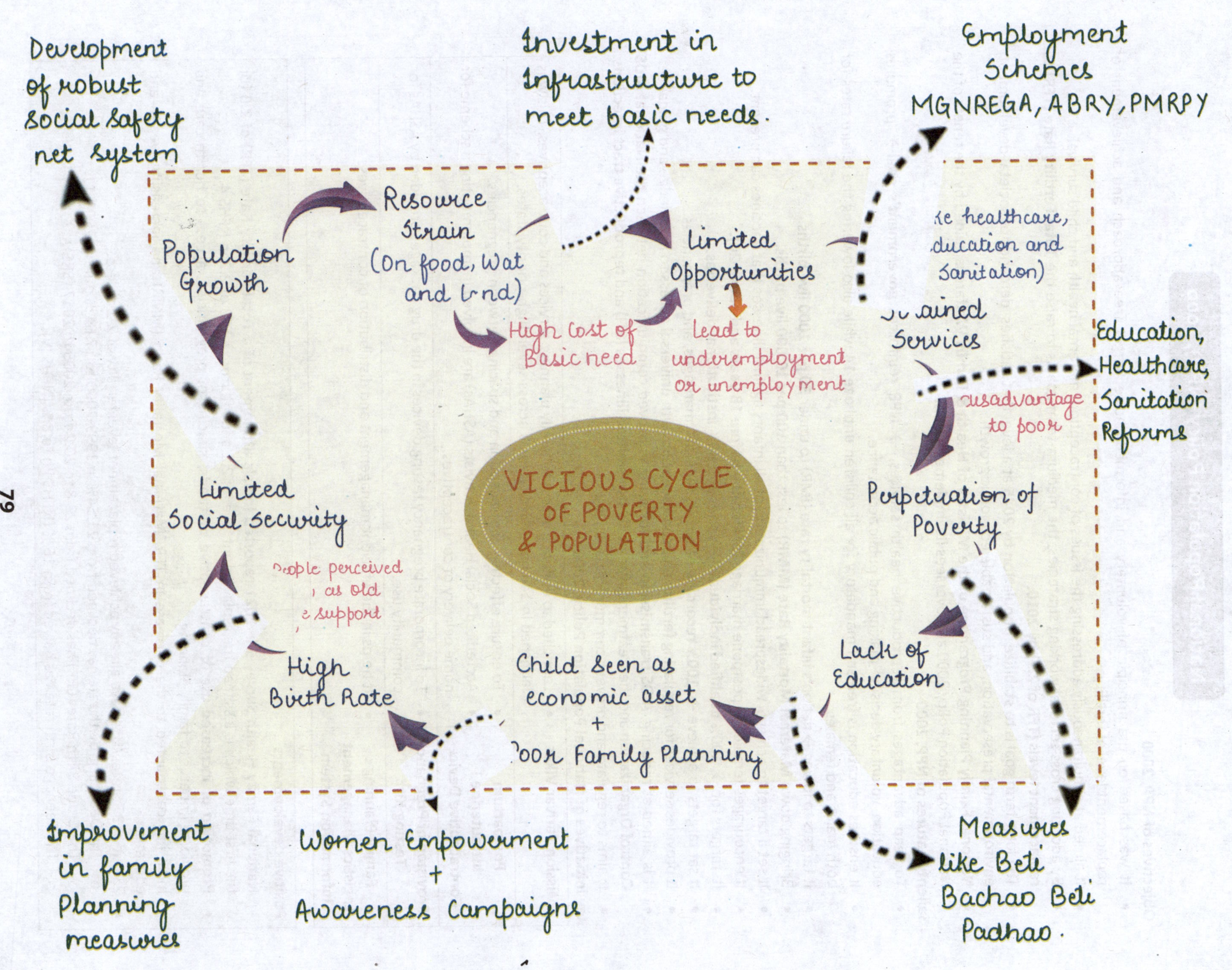
VICIOUS CYCLE OF POVERTY & POPULATION
Population Growth
Resource Strain (On food, Wat and l nd)
High cost of Basic need
Limited Opportunities
Lead to underemployment or unemployment
ke healthcare, ducation and Sanitation)
. ained Services
usadvantage to poor
Perpetuation of Poverty
Lack of Education
Child seen as economic asset + oor Family Planning
High Birth Rate
eople perceived as old e support
Limited Social Security
Development of robust social safety net system
Investment in Infrastructure to meet basic needs.
Employment Schemes MGNREGA, ABRY, PMRPY
Education, Healthcare, Sanitation Reforms
Measures like Beti Bachao Beti Padhao.
Women Empowerment + Awareness Campaigns
Improvement in family Planning measures

## National Population Policy (NPP), 2000

**Objectives of NPP, 2000**

- It was based on the principle of voluntary and informed choice, target free approach and achievement of replacement level of fertility.
- It aimed at simultaneously addressing the issues of contraception, maternal health and child survival.
- By adopting cross-sectoral working strategies, the medium-term goal is to raise the **Total Fertility Rate (TFR) to replacement levels (TFR of 2.1) by 2010.**
- The long-term goal is to **stabilize population by 2045** at a level that satisfies demands of societal development, environmental preservation, and sustainable economic growth.
- **National Family Planning Programme of the Ministry of Health & Family Welfare** is guided by the tenets of the National Population Policy 2000 and oversees its implementation.

**Salient Features of NPP, 2000**

- To reap advantages from reproductive health services, → **NPP** reinforces **government's goal**→ promotes education, voluntary decision-making and public acceptance.
- It ensures **education is free** and mandatory for all children until **age 14** while also lowering the failure rates for both males and females.
- It targets to lower → nation's **infant mortality rate** (IMR) to under **30 per 1000 live births.**
- Bringing down **Maternal Mortality Rate (MMR)** to less than **100 per 10,000 live births.**
- It set a target to achieve widespread immunization of all infants against illnesses that vaccines can prevent.
- It encourages females to postpone marriage **(preferably before 18 years and above 20).**
- It targets for → **100% qualified individual** deliveries and **80% institutional deliveries.**
- It set targets to achieve → **100% recording of births**, funerals, marriages, and pregnancies.
- It provides services for **regulating fertility** and **contraception** with **universal access** to knowledge and guidance.
- It is aimed at reducing **AIDS transmission** and fostering improved communication between the **National AIDS Control Organization** and the treatment of **sexually transmitted illnesses (STI)** and **reproductive tract infections.**
- It aims to regulate and prevent communicable illnesses.

**Key initiatives of National Population Policy, 2000**

| | |
|---|---|
| **Mission Parivar Vikas** | • Launched to enhance access to family planning services and contraceptives. This was launched in 146 high-fertility areas across seven high-priority states. |
| **Postpartum Intrauterine Contraceptive Device** | • To ensure effective contraception and spacing between pregnancies.<br>• Accredited Social Health Activists (ASHAs) are involved in implementing a scheme for home delivery of contraceptives. |
| **Provision of Pregnancy Testing Kit** | • To incorporate pregnancy testing devices in the drug packages provided by ASHAs for community use. |
| **Family Planning Logistics Management Information System** | • It helps in the efficient management and distribution of contraceptives. |

**Positive developments**

- **National Family Health Survey 5 in 2021 reported India's attainment of a Total Fertility Rate (TFR) of 2.0** for the first time which is less than the replacement level of 2.1 and fell from a TFR of 2.2 in NFHS 4.
- **Promotion of increased use of contraceptive methods**, spacing of pregnancies, access to health care and providing impetus to family planning.
- India has contributed to the decrease in TFR, Maternal Mortality Ratio (MMR) and increasing wealth and education.
- 25 out of 37 States/UTs have already achieved replacement level fertility of 2.1 or less.
  - The Decadal growth rate has declined from 21.54% in 1999-2000 to 17.64 % during 2001-11.
  - The Crude Birth Rate (CBR) has declined from 23.8 to 20.2 from 2005 to 2017 (SRS).
  - The Teenage birth rate has halved from 16 % (NFHS III) to 8 % (NFHS IV).

# MIGRATION

## Concept and Statistics

- Migration refers to geographical mobility between one region and another involving the change in residence for a considerable period of time.
- According to Migration in India Report 2020-21, India's migration rate is 28.9%, with migration rates of 34.9% and 26.5% in Urban and rural areas respectively.
- SDG 10.7: To facilitate orderly, safe, regular and responsible migration and mobility of people through the implementation of planned and well-managed migration policy.
- International Migrant Stock Report, 2019: India is top source of international migrants.

## TYPES OF MIGRATION

### Based on Geographical Scale

- **Internal:** Migration within a country (Varanasi → Coimbatore)
- **External:** Migration across international borders (India → USA)

### Based on Duration

- **Permanent:** Migration with intention of settling in a new location.
- **Temporary:** Migration for a limited period (migrant worker for seasonal work, students for education)

### By Cause or Motivation

- **Forced:** Migration due to external pressures, such as war, persecution, natural disasters, or environmental degradation (Rohingyas displacement)
- **Voluntary:** Migration by choice → driven by economic opportunities + education, or a better quality of life. (Ex: Rural to Urban Migration).

## Factors affecting Migration and Reverse Migration

| Migration | | Reverse or Counter Migration | |
|---|---|---|---|
| **Push Factor** | **Pull Factor** | **Push Factor** | **Pull Factor** |
| **Economic Factors** | | | |
| • **Agricultural Distress + Fragmentation of Cultivable land** → Led to volatile **agricultural prices** and high **input costs** → Agriculture became a non-profitable sector → Forcing farmers outmigration.<br>• **Lack of alternative employment opportunities:** As per **International Labour Organization, 2019** report "rural areas have fewer and lower-quality job opportunities".<br>• **Decline in Village industries:** E-Commerce platforms + Globalization + Competition from cheaper manufactured goods → Decline of traditional village industries<br>• **Low standard of living:** Inadequate access to healthcare, education. | • **Industrialization:** Creates a demand for labour, employment opportunities with higher wages.<br>• **Globalization:** Brings **international companies** in domestic market → Offers **diverse job opportunities** → Attracting **skilled** and **unskilled** workers.<br>• **Commercialization of Agriculture:** individuals seek jobs related to processing, packaging, and distribution of agricultural products.<br>• **Better infrastructure like** healthcare facilities, sanitation systems, education facilities → translates into **High Standard of Living.** | • **Negative Flux in Destination areas:** Congestion in Urban cities, Overcrowding and increasing pollution made life of migrants hell.<br>• **Limited Income opportunity:** Job opportunities in urban areas demands high-skilled or specialized knowledge → which will act as a pull-back factor<br>• **Urban Burden:** High living costs in cities → can be a significant burden.<br>• **Aggregation of slums:** They will act as strong urban deterrent → slums were characterised by poor living conditions, overcrowding, lack of sanitation and limited access to basic services. | • **Skill development programs** like **Pradhan Mantri Kaushal Vikas Yojana** provide rural youth with training in job-oriented skills relevant to rural industries or agri-preneurship<br>• **Improvement in Rural Infrastructure** through Rural development initiatives like **Deen Dayal Upadhyaya Grameen Kaushalya Yojana** and **Sansad Adarsh Gram Yojana.**<br>• **Developments of Counter Magnets:** Initiatives like **Atmanirbhar Bharat** promote creation and growth of SMEs whereas Programs like **Rural Haat** provide platforms for local artisans and entrepreneurs. |
| **Socio-Cultural Factors** | | | |
| • **Differential Access to resources:** Due to ethnic religious and linguistic identities.<br>• **Occupational Division of Labour** on the basis of Caste and Gender.<br>• **Lower status** of women due to Patriarchy.<br>• **Perceived Modernism:** Media portrayals of urban lifestyles → create a sense of aspiration among individuals from rural areas. | • **Urbanism:** Promotes anonymity + heterogeneity → minimisation of inequalities.<br>• **Institution of Marriage:** Either Bride or Groom or both**(neolocal family)** have to migrate to a new destination.<br>• **Urban social movements:** Cities are advocating for **women's rights** and **gender equality.** | • **Lack of Cultural Integration:** Denial from **existing social fabric** → feelings of **isolation & alienation** → desire to return to the source area.<br>• **Ghettoization:** limits exposure to diverse **perspectives** and **opportunities** for social mobility.<br>• Replication of **Cultural Inequalities** existing in source regions like caste and | • **Feeling of Nativism:** yearning to reconnect with their roots, culture, and familiar surroundings → Generates emotional pull towards place of origin.<br>• **Family Reunification:** desire to be closer to ageing parents, siblings, or extended family → act as a strong pull factor for returning to one's source region. |

| | | religious discrimination. | |
|---|---|---|---|
| **Socio-Political Factors** | | | |
| • **Violence** creates a dangerous environment, forcing people to flee for safety like **ongoing insurgency** in northeastern states like **Nagaland** has driven people to migrate .<br>• **Corruption** can lead to lack of trust in authorities → limited opportunities for economic upliftment.<br>• **Lack of Government will:** Inadequate government services like healthcare, education and employment.<br>• **Development led to Displacement:** Constr uction of the **Sardar Sarovar Dam** on the **Narmada River** displaced thousands of tribal families. | • **Political Freedom:** Cities are seen as hubs for activism and social movements.<br>• **Safety and Security Better:** Cities with a stronger police presence are considered as more safe especially for women and marginalised groups.<br>• **Implementation of Scheme:** Cities with concentration of government offices → minimises **bureaucratic hurdles.**<br>• **Increased opportunities for political participation:** Urban centers have a more politically active population with **higher voter turnout rates.** | • **Son of Soil Policy:** With reservation to local native people it may alienate the others. Like **Assam Accord (1985)** aimed to address illegal immigration from Bangladesh. However, it has also been criticised → for creating a climate of fear and discrimination against **Bengali-speaking Muslims.**<br>• **Politicization of Region:** Politicization of regions like **Maharashtra for Marathis** with potential for violence → will act as a strong push back factor. | • **Change in Political Leadership:** Rise of regiona political parties **Shiv Sena** in Maharashtra politics might incentivize some Marathi-speaking migrants who left state to return and contribute to the party's growing influence.<br>• **Region acts as a Political Magnet for** Increased hate crimes, targeted violence, or political rhetoric that excludes or marginalises certain groups → people will prefer to counter migrate to the source region . |

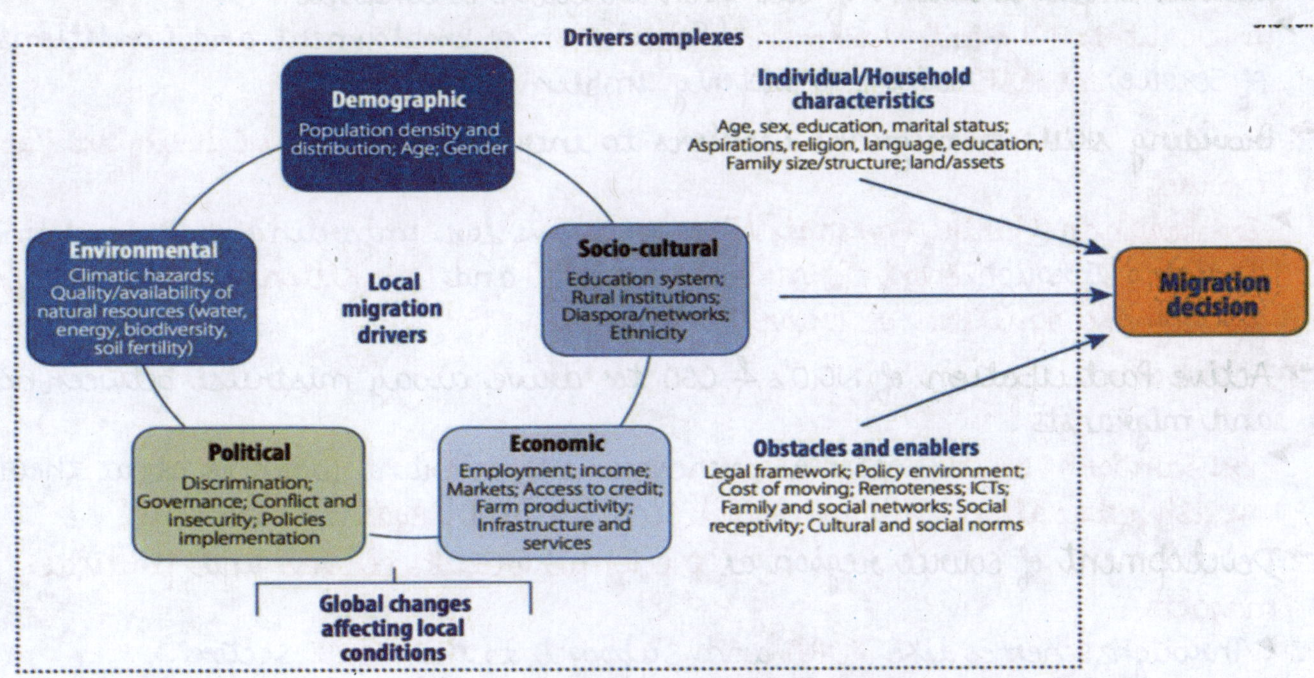

## Consequences of Migration:

### At Source Region:

- **Economic Impact:** Employable people migrate led to loss of human resources, however if migration draws upon surplus labour, then it is a win-win situation.
- **Demographic Impact:** Male specific migration will lead to an increase in dependent population → an increase in feminisation of work and agriculture.
- **Socio-Cultural Impact:** Migration will act as an agent of Social Change i.e. new ideas related to technology, family planning gets diffused to source region.
  - Absence of adult male → dislocation of family, violence against women, increased incidence of Juvenile delinquency.

### At Destination Region:

- **Arena of Conflict:** Migrants are perceived to take away jobs of locals, increase competition for basic amenities and services.
  - Feeling of relative deprivation → lead to crime and violence.
- Mismanaged migration leads to slum proliferation.
- Political Mobilisation of natives and migrants as resources are limited and scarce.
- **Information of Labour:** As most migrants were devoid of skill, information, bargaining power → stuck to exploitative labour arrangement.

## Way Forward

- Judicial implementation of act both in letter and spirit.
  - Inter-State Migrant Workmen (Regulation of Employment and Conditions of Service) Act, 1979 still not properly implemented.
- Providing skills to migrant workers to increase their desirability in labour market.
  - Ex: Pradhan Mantri Kaushal Vikas Yojana is for imparting skill development training through Short-Term Training (STT) and Up-skilling and Re-skilling through Recognition of Prior Learning.
- Active Participation of NGO's & CSO to drive away mistrust between native and migransts.
  - Ex: Sampark (NGO) creates awareness among migrant workers about their health, education, finance, social security and legal entitlements.
- Development of source region as economic growth centres and political magnets.
  - Through schemes like PURA and support to the MSME sector.

- Politicization of migration needs to be checked.
- Policies should be designed so as to include migrants.
- Collection of Credible data for target specific intervention instead of one-size fit approach.

## PYQs Corner

*(Write the Answer and Get Free Evaluation)*

1. Discuss the main objectives of Population Education and point out the measures to achieve them in India in detail. **(2021)**

2. "Empowering women is the key to control population growth." Discuss. **(2019)**

3. "Demographic Dividend in India will remain only theoretical unless our manpower becomes more educated, aware, skilled and creative." What measures have been taken by the government to enhance the capacity of our population to be more productive and employable? **(2016)**

4. Discuss the changes in the trends of labour migration within and outside India in the last four decades. **(2015)**

5. Critically examine whether growing population is the cause of poverty OR poverty is the main cause of population increase in India. **(2015)**

CHAPTER 04

# Urbanisation

## URBANISATION

**About:** According to European Environment Agency "Urbanisation is the increase in the proportion of people living in towns and cities. It occurs because people move from rural areas to urban areas. This usually occurs when a country is still developing".

- SDG 11 is about making cities and human settlements inclusive, safe, resilient and sustainable.
  - Cities represent the future of global living. The world's population reached 8 billion by 2022, over half living in urban areas.

### Concepts and Statistics

- **Urban Agglomeration:** This term was introduced in 1971 census. It is a large, continuously built-up area comprising a central city or multiple towns, often with surrounding outgrowths, that exhibits high population density and strong economic and social connections.
  - Ex: Railway colonies, university campuses, port areas, military camps.
- **Overurbanization:** It is a situation where the rate of urbanisation outpaces the ability of cities to provide essential infrastructure, jobs and services for growing population.
  - Ex: An example of this can be seen in the expansion of Gurugram on the outskirts of Delhi.

➩ Counter-Urbanisation: It is the migration of people from urban areas towards rural areas or smaller towns, marking a reversal of the traditional trends of urbanisation.

➩ Census Town: It is a settlement classified as urban by the census because it meets specific conditions.
- ⋙ At least 5,000 inhabitants
- ⋙ A density of 400 people per sq. km.
- ⋙ At least three quarters of its male working population must be "engaged in non-agriculture pursuits."

➡ Urbanisation Rate: As per World Bank, urbanisation rate in India increased from 17.4% in 1950 to 35% in 2015.

➡ Urban Population: As of 2021, India accounts for the second largest urban population in the world after China.

➡ According to 2011 Census, 31.16% of India's population lived in urban areas.

➡ Urban Migration: Urban-to-urban migration itself contributes 20% to total migration + rural-to-urban migration → this internal movement accounts for 40% of all migration in India.

➡ Urban Financing: As per 12th Five Year Plan → India spends only $17 per capita per year on urban infrastructure, whereas the requirement is $100

➡ Tamil Nadu is the most urbanised state (48.4%) of population living in urban areas, followed by Kerala (47.7%) upstaging Maharashtra (45.2%).

# Urbanisation in India

## Pre-Independence Period

- Municipal Corporations: East India Company established first municipal corporation in India at Madras in 1688, followed by Bombay and Calcutta in 1726.
- Self-Governance: Lord Ripon's Resolution of 1882, gave Indians the right to local self-government.
  - ➤ It would develop the municipal institution which had been under the direct control of the British Crown.
- Urban Settlements: Britishers developed three principal port cities (Mumbai, Kolkata, and Chennai) for trade.
  - ➤ Britishers also started the wave of Urban Agglomeration by establishment of civil lines and cantonments.

## Post Independence Phase (1947-1990)

- Industrialisation and Planned Development through Five Year Plans led to the establishment of public sector enterprises.
  - Cities like Bangalore and Pune started emerging as industrial and educational centers.
- Rural-Urban migration increased as people moved to cities in search of better employment opportunities.
- Urban Planning and Development Authorities: Cities like Delhi saw establishment of urban planning bodies like Delhi Development Authority in 1957 to manage urban growth.

## Liberalisation Phase (1990-2000)

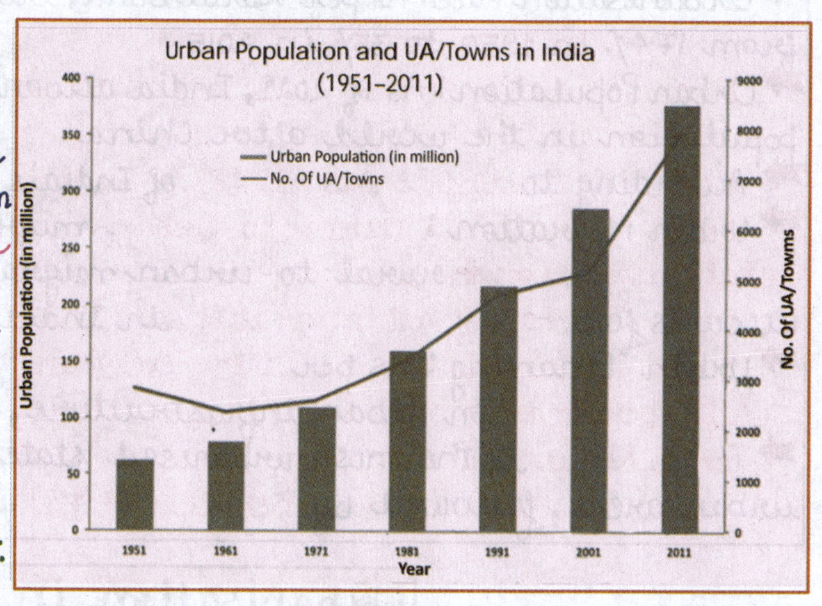


- Driving Force: Urbanisation in this phase was mainly driven by natural increase in population (around 60%), followed by rural urban migration.
- Economic Reforms: The liberalization of the Indian economy in 1991 led to rapid economic growth, which spurred urbanization.
- Increased Foreign Investment: The inflow of Foreign Direct Investment (FDI) contributed to the development of urban infrastructure and real estate.
- Emergence of IT Hubs: Cities like Bangalore, Hyderabad and Gurgaon became prominent IT hubs, attracting a skilled workforce from across the country.

## Post-Liberalisation Phase (2000-Present)

- Driving Force: Share of natural increase in urban population declined to 44%, whereas share of reclassification of rural areas into urban areas strengthened and the share of rural-urban migration increased to 24%.
- Rapid Urbanisation: As per Census 2011, Urbanisation in the country as a whole increased from 27.7 percent in 2001 to 3.1 percent in 2011.
- Smart Cities Mission: The Government of India launched the Smart Cities in 2015 promote sustainable and inclusive urban development.

- **Urban Infrastructure Development**: Projects like the Atal Mission for Rejuvenation (AMRUT) and the Pradhan Mantri Awas Yojana (PMAY) aimed at improving urban infrastructure and providing affordable housing.
- **Rise of Tier-II and Tier-III Cities**: Smaller cities began to develop rapidly due to better connectivity, improved infrastructure, and government incentives, reducing pressure on larger metros.
- According to the World Bank, India's urban population in 2022 was 35.87% of the total population.

## Perspective in Process of Urbanisation

- **Socio-cultural phenomenon**: It is "melting pot" of people with diverse ethnic, linguistic, and religious backgrounds. Eg. Kolkata city development.
- **An economic process**: The city is a focal point of productive activities. It exists and grows on the strength of economic activities existing within itself. Ex: Mumbai.
- **A geographical process**: It deals with migration or change of location of residence of people and involves the movement of people from one place to another.

Economic Activities → drives → Migration → Brings Cultural Diversity → Alter the geographic landscape & socio' fabric → further influences → Economic Activities

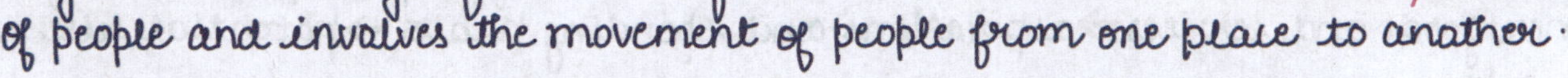

## Salient Features of Urbanisation and Indian Urban Cities

- **Rapid Population Increase**: As per Census 2011 India's urban population has registered an annual exponential growth rates of 2.76% registered during 2001-11.
  - India is home to nine metropolitan cities → Mumbai, Pune, Delhi, Ahmedabad, Surat, Chennai, Kolkata, Bangalore, and Hyderabad.
- **Migration Driven** because of Push factor like agrarian distress, lack of employment opportunities and Pull factors include better jobs prospects, education, healthcare, and improved living standards in urban areas.
  - As per Observer Research Foundation migration accounted for about one fifth of urban addition.
- **Economic Transformation**: Urbanisation in India is characterised by economic transition from an agrarian economy to industrial and servic sectors.
  - India's Urban Population contributes 63% to Gross Domestic Product, and is expected to rise to 75% by 2030.
- **Regional Disparities**: Urbanisation is non-uniform across India.
  - Tamil Nadu accomodates 48.4% of urban population in contrast to 22.27% of Uttar Pradesh.

➡ Informal Economy: Large section of urban population is in informal sector like street vending, small scale manufacturing, and service jobs because of absence of adequate skill and knowledge.

➡ Strained Infrastructure: Urban areas struggle with inadequate infrastructure, traffic congestion, pollution, and insufficient public services.

➡ Slum Proliferation: Rapid Urbanisation → demand for housing + considerable shortage of affordable housing → growth of informal settlements and slums.

↪ According to Census, 2011 → 17.4% of urban Indian households lived in slums.

➡ Urban Poverty: A significant portion of the urban population live in poverty, with limited access to basic services like clean water, sanitation, and healthcare.

➡ Satellite Towns: Urbanisation in India is not limited to large metropolitan cities but also includes the development of satellite town and peri-urban areas around major cities.

➡ Cultural Melting Pots: Indian cities with people from various regions, languages, and religions coexisting and contributing to a rich cultural mosaic.

➡ Social Stratification: Urban areas also reflect social stratification and inequalities → Ghettoization on basis religion, caste, class is manifestation of the same.

➡ Growth in Consumerism and Materialism: Urban life exposes people to different consumer goods and services → aspirations and spending habits → potential rise in materialism.

## Drivers of Urbanisation

**ECONOMIC**

- Job opportunities: Availability of diverse employment options attracts people. Example: IT jobs in Bengaluru.
- Industrialisation: Growth of industries creates new jobs market. Example: Textile industry in Surat.
- Higher wages: Urban areas often offer higher salaries. Example: Higher wages in Mumbai's financial sector.

**SOCIAL**

- Better Education: Access to quality education institutions. Example: Universities in Delhi.
- Healthcare Services: Availability of advanced medical facilities. Example: AIIMS in New Delhi.
- Lifestyle and Amenities: Improved living standards and facilities. Example: Malls and entertainment centers in Pune.

POLITICAL

- Government Policies: Policies encouraging urban development. Example: Smart Cities Mission
- Infrastructure Development: Development of urban infrastructure. Example Metro systems in various cities.
- Safety and Security: Better law enforcement and security measures. Example: Improved policing in Hyderabad.

ENVIRONMENTAL

- Climate Change: Environmental changes pushing rural migration Example Migration due to drought in Maharashtra.
- Natural Disasters: Displacement due to natural calamities. Example: Floods in Kerala leading to urban migration.
- Land Availability: Availability of land for housing and business. Example: Expansion in outskirts of Bengaluru.

TECHNOLOGICAL

- Advance in Transportation: Improved connectivity through transportation Example: Bullet train project between Mumbai and Ahmedabad.
- Communication Networks: Enhanced communication infrastructure. Example: Widespread internet access in urban areas.
- Innovation Hubs: Concentration of tech startups and innovation. Example: Startup ecosystem in Hyderabad's HITEC City.

## Problems and Issues Associated with Urbanisation/Urban Cities

### Socio-Economic Issues

- Skyrocketing Housing Cost because of mismatch between population and available housing infrastructure + Corruption → lead to shift towards slums
- Slums and Overcrowding: Large and small slums lack basic amenities and healthcare, education facilities.
- Social Disconnect: The fast-paced urban lifestyle, coupled with higher access to power for some, can foster individualism and weaken community ties.
- Unplanned Urban Expansion like prioritisation of building construction over essential municipal services like sanitation and waste management.

**Why Land Potential is Locked in Urban Cities?**

01 Urban Land Ceilings and Regulation Act, 1976: Put ceilings to prevent hoarding or excessive holding of land in urban agglomerations by few people.

02 Underutilised Land held by Public Sector Enterprises like Bharat Sanchar Nigam Limited.

03 Unutilized Land held by Government Agencies like DRDO and Railway hold a significant portion of unutilised land, which can be repurposed.

04 Land Acquisition Act, 2013 sets compensation for aquired land at market value, leading to high cost of Acquisition.

- Ghettoization reflects social stratification and inequalities → on the basis of religion, caste, class.
- Informalisation of Workforce: According to Women in Informal Employment: Globalizing and Organizing report 79.2% workforce in urban areas are under informal sector.
- Increasing Crimes: As per NCRB 2022-23 report, even being the National Capital, Delhi is reported as the most unsafe metropolitan city for women.

## Infrastructure and Environmental Issue

- Mobility-driven transmission like local train services, metro services operating at exceeding passenger capacities → became a conduit based viral transmission of disease.
- Slum Vulnerability: Uneven urban population distribution coupled with high cost of living and inadequate affordable housing → proliferation of slums.
  - In Mumbai and Kolkata, 54% and 32% of the city population respectively, reside in slum areas.
- Traffic Congestion in cities like Mumbai lack of proper traffic management → leads to congestion → causing air and noise pollution.
- Water Scarcity and Sanitation Deficits: Intermittent water supply, coupled with inadequate drainage and sewage system → create water scarcity and sanitation problems.
  - Ongoing Water Crisis in Summer Season of Delhi.
- Urban Floods became a frequent disruptive phenomenon because of unsustainable design and planning.
  - Ex: Bengaluru floods 2022 → cost a loss of over Rs 225 crores.

## Water Disposal Issues

- Industrial Pollution and Untreated Waste: Untreated industrial effluents and sewage discharged into rivers contaminate water bodies, posing environmental and health hazards.
  - Ex: Yamuna river became ecologically dead in Delhi.
- Improper Waste Handling pollutes the environment and threatens public health.
  - Ex: Vector-borne diseases like Dengue and Chikungunia are common in metro-cities nowadays.

# IMPACT OF URBANISATION

1 Marriage Institution
2 Family
3 Caste System
4 Tribes
5 Elderly
6 Childrens
7 Transgenders

## Marriage Institution

- **Shift in Marital Patterns:** Survey by Bharat Matrimony in 2022 revealed that 60% of urban marriages in cities like Mumbai, Delhi, and Bangalore are love marriages → reflecting shift from traditional arranged marriages.
- **Delayed Marriages:** According to NFHS-5, median age at first marriage for women in urban areas increased to 22.1 years, up from 20.4 years in the last decade.
- **Increased Legal Awareness** and use of legal avenues for marital disputes and domestic issues in urban settings → lead to greater independence, rising divorce rates in cities.

## Family

- **Nuclear Families:** Census 2011 indicates that 52.1% of households in urban areas were nuclear, up from 46% in 2001 → highlighting the deviation from joint to nuclear family structures.
- **Changing Roles:** International Labour Organisation noted that 43% of urban families has led to a 30% increase in daycare centres and a 20% rise in old age home facilities in last decade.

## Caste System

- **Urban Anonymity:** The anonymity of urban life reduces caste-based discriminations and prejudice in daily life.
- **Diminishing Caste Barriers:** A report by National Council of Applied Economics Research in 2018 found that 78% of urban youth felt that caste is less significant in urban areas compared to rural settings.
- **New Forms of Discrimination:** As per Indian Institute of Dalit Studies 2019 study, Dalits in urban areas still face discrimination in housing and employment, with 38% reporting bias in job searches.
- **Caste Panchayats** experienced a significant decline in authority and influence as their perceived power diminished.
- **Caste Identity:** Urbanisation + Education + individual achievement → erode caste identity, with reduced adherence to rules of commensality and untouchability in urban areas.

## Tribes

- **Displacement:** Ministry of Tribal Affairs reported in 2020 that over 1.5

million tribal people have been displaced due to urban development projects in the last two decades.

Cultural Assimilation: Indian Anthropological Society in 2019 highlighted that urbanisation has led to a decline in traditional tribal practices → assimilated in dominant Hindu Fold.

## Women

Employment Opportunities: Urbanisation has opened up numerous employment opportunities for women, leading to greater financial independence and empowerment.

- According to PLFS (2022-23), female labour force participation rate in India was 37%.

Women Issues Presistent in Urban Societies

Education: Increased access to education in urban areas has led to higher literacy rates and professional qualifications among women.

- According to the 2011 Census, literacy rate for urban women stands at 76.9%.

Safety Concerns: Despite increased educational opportunities, safety issues at workplaces remain a concern for urban women.

- Sexual harassment at workplace is very common in urban life.
- Delhi registered itself a most unsafe metropolitan city for women.

Freedom of Choice: Exposure to quality education and liberal environment in urban areas → empowers women with greater freedom of choice in making personal decisions compared to their rural counterparts.

Dual Role and Workload: Urban women face the task of balancing professional and personal responsibilities, leading to a potential increase in their overall workload.

## Elderly

Isolation: A Study of Agewell Foundation in 2020 found that 45% of elderly individuals in urban areas experience loneliness and isolation, compared to 30% in rural areas.

Dependence on Service: There is growing dependence on old age homes and healthcare services for elderly care reflects growing reliance on institutional care for the elderly.

## Children

- **Education and Opportunities**: Urbanization provides better educational facilities and extracurricular opportunities, leading to overall development.
- **Lifestyle Changes**: Rise of Cardiovascular Diseases in young generation linked to progressive urbanization and coinciding - tobacco use, unhealthy diets, physical inactivity and harmful use of alcohol.
- **Security and Stress**: According to NCRB survey, urban children report higher levels of stress and insecurity, with a 15% increase in juvenile crime rates in metropolitan areas over the past decade.
  - Where Maharashtra reported highest numbers of crimes committed by juveniles, Delhi reported crime increased by 42% by Juveniles in NCRB report 2023.

## Transgenders

- **Visibility and Activism**: Centre for Law and Policy Research noted that urban areas have become hubs for transgender activism, with cities like Mumbai and Delhi hosting numerous support groups and events for trans-gender rights.
- **Discrimination and Employment**: National Human Rights Commission, 2020 report found that 92% of transgender individuals in urban India face discrimination in employment → resorting to begging or sex worker for survival.

## Factors that hinders the realisation of true potential of Government Initiatives

### Implementation Issues

- Lack of coordination between central, state, and local governments → leads to delays, stalled projects, and unclear roles.
- Bureaucratic hurdles, Red Tapism and corruption impedes efficient allocation and utilization of funds.
- Inadequate capacity at the local level, with limited manpower and expertise for effective project execution.

### Planning and Resource Constraints:

- Rapid urbanisation outpaces the ability to plan and develop infrastructure effectively.
- Limited budgetary resources can restrict the scope and scale of initiatives, making it difficult to meet the growing demands of urban populations.

- Difficulty in land acquisition, a crucial aspect of infrastructure development causes delays and project cost escalations.

**Social and Equity Concerns:**

- Non-inclusive nature of initiatives might not adequatly address the needs of marginalised communties, leading to uneven benefits and potential displacement
- Lack of Community participation in planning can result in projects that don't address local priorities effectively.
- Resettlement and rehabilitation plans for those impacted by development projects were inadequate.

**Sustainability Concerns:**

- Short-term focus on project completion might overlook long-term sustain-ability considerations like environmental impact and resource management.
- Limited focus on creating walkable and public transport-oriented urban spaces can lead to increased reliance on private vehicles and contribute to pollution.

## Some Institutional Recommendations

### 6th Report on Local Governance: Administrative Reforms Commission

- Decentralised and Empowerment: It advocated for greater decentralization of power and decision-making to local bodies like municipalities.
  - It would empower them to better address the needs of their communities
- Unified Metropolitan Transport Authority (UMTA): It suggested the creation of UMTAs in metropolitan areas → responsible for integrating and managing public transportation services → aim to improve traffic management and overall mobility.
- Imported Service Delivery: It called for a focus on improving delivery of essential services in urban areas, such as water supply, sanitation, and waste management.
- Role of State Legislature: It recommended establishing separate Standing Committees on Local Bodies within state legislature → for better oversight and support to local governance initiatives.
- Adequate infrastructure in all towns, advance action for lying down adequate infrastruture should be taken to avoid insufficiency of services.
- Collection and disposal of garbage in all towns and cities with a population above one lakh, the possibility of taking up PPP projects for collection and disposal of garbage may be expired.

## "Reforms in Urban Plannings Capacity in India": NITI AAYOG

- **Rapid Growth:** India is experiencing a significant urban population boom, with projection suggesting over 600 million people living in cities by 2030.
- **Uneven Distribution:** Urbanisation is not uniform across India, with major metro cities growing much faster than smaller towns, leading to regional disparities.
- **Rural-to-Urban Migration:** A major drive of urban growth is people seeking better job opportunities, education, and healthcare in cities.
- **Informal Settlement:** Rapid urbanisation often outpaces the development of affordable housing, leading to a rise in slums and informal settlements lacking basic amenities.
- **Infrastructure Deficits:** The rapid pace of urbanisation often strain infrastructure like transportation, water supply, and sanitation.
- **Socio-Economic Diversity:** Cities are becoming more diverse, bringing together people from various backgrounds and creating new social dynamics.
- **National metro rail policy:** To ensure that metro projects are not considered in isolation, but as part of a comprehensive plan of overall public transportation
- **Waste to Energy authority:** NITI Aayog suggested creation of an authority may be called Waste to Energy Corporation of India (WECI) → to speed up the process of cleaning up municipal solid waste.
- **Sustainable Urban Planning:** The report call for strategic urban planning that prioritizes planned infrastructure development, environmental protection, and the creation of green spaces.

## FUTURISTIC MEASURES

- **Investment in Public Transport:** NITI Aayog emphasises need to expand public transportation capacity and improve service quality to reduce reliance on private vehicles and congestion.
  Eg: Model of DMRC and BRTS shall be replicated throughout India.
- **Slum Upgradation and Relocation:** There is a need for comprehensive plans for upgrading existing slums or relocating residents to areas with better infrastructure and Sanitation facilities.
- **Strengthening Public Health Infrastructure:** NITI Aayog suggests increasing public health spending to address the doctar shortage and improve healthcare access in urban areas.
- **Community Engagement:** Fostering community engagement is crucial for encouraging a sense of ownership and participation in public health initiatives and overall urban development.

➡ Financial management: Introduction of Standardised, time-bound, audited balance sheets across ULBs would help improve financial management as well as spur further reforms in this area.

Urban Governance and Urban Financing have been discussed with sufficient detail in "Pulse Indian Polity & Governance".

➡ Power Utilities: Municipal bodies and DISCOMs should be empowered and responsible for power distribution and incorporate power conservation measures in building bye-laws.

➡ Increases job opportunities in focus on rural areas through programs like IRDP, NREP, and TRY to → put a check on rural to urban migration.

## Key Takeaways from Successful Case Studies on Urbanisation

### Singapore:

- Land use Zoning policies → Maximises efficient use of land area → for balancing residential, commercial, and industry needs.
- Green Spaces: Despite high urban density, Singapore maintains numerous green spaces, parks, and vertical gardens.

### Barcelona, Spain:

- Urban Regeneration: City underwent urban regeneration for 1992 olympics, transforming former industrial areas into vibrant public spaces and residential areas.
- Extensive Public Transport network including buses, trams and an efficient metro system, promoting sustainable urban mobility.

## PYQs Corner

*(Write the Answer and Get Free Evaluation)*

1. Does urbanization lead to more segregation and/or marginalization of the poor in Indian metropolises? **(2022)**
2. How is the growth of Tier 2 cities related to the rise of a new middle class with an emphasis on the culture of consumption? **(2022)**

CHAPTER 05

# Globalisation and Indian Society

## GLOBALISATION

**About:** The IMF (International Monetary Fund) defines globalisation as: "the increasing integration of economies around the world, particularly through the movement of goods, services, and capital across borders.

- Transnational corporations (TNCs)
- Global money markets

economic

- Growth of online social networks
- Migrant families and diaspora

social

political

- Global governance
- Global action on climate change

cultural

- The growth of global culture
- The glocalisation of products*

### Prominent Views on Globalisation

Rabindranath Tagore- Book "Nationalism"
- Promotes a global village, cosmopolitan society.
  Quotes- "At every land there are my kith and kin, to reckon whom, Keen I have been."

▶▶ Thomas Friedman sees globalization as a force for good, promoting economic growth, innovation, and the spread of democracy.

Bill Gates believes globalisation lifts people out of poverty and creates a more interconnected world for tackling global challenges.

Kofi Annan- "It has been said that arguing against globalisation is like arguing against the laws of gravity."

» Tony Blair - "Globalization is a fact, not a choice, and it's heretostay."

» Noam Chomsky - "Globalization Begets Inequalities."

Amartya Sen - Globalization has enriched the world scientifically and culturally and benefited many people economically as well.

## WAVES OF GLOBALISATION

### Globalisation 1.0 (Pre 1914)

- This era was marked by a surge in international trade, driven by advance-ments in transportation and communication technologies like steamships, rail roads and telegraph.
- European powers colonised vast territories, creating global empires.
- Global Governance is almost absent here.

### Globalisation 2.0 (1950 - 1980's)

- Rise of multinational corporations and the Bretton Wood system, which pegged major world currencies to the US dollar.
- Rule-based international governance → through establishment of institutions like UN, IMF, World Bank, GATT/WTO.

### Globalisation 3.0 (1980's - 2000)

- Philosophy of Neoliberalism emphasised deregulation, privatisation, and free markets.
- Rise of information and communication technologies, internet, and Containerization → which revolutionised global trade and communication.
- Global Supply Chains were established as factories crossed international borders.

### Globalisation 4.0 (2000 - Present)

- It is characterized by advancement of cutting-edge technologies like artificial intelligence and rapid growth of information technology.
  - These technologies shorten travel times, dissolve barriers, expand brains, and unite people worldwide.
- Service Sector become highly disruptive because of changing human-technology relations and also replacing human jobs with AI.
- Integrated with Industry: New technologies such as AI, machine learning, cloud computing big data and integrating it with industrial processes enables service delivery and competition.

➡ **Evolving work Culture:** Changing nature of work such as work from home, gig work can perform their tasks remately without physical presence.
➡ **Fourth Industrial Revolution:** Industry 4.0 combines humans and technology incorporating cyber-physical systems, IoT, big data analytics, AI, 3D printing, and autonomous vehicles, shaping the future of the service sector.

## FACTORS LEADING TO GLOBALISATION

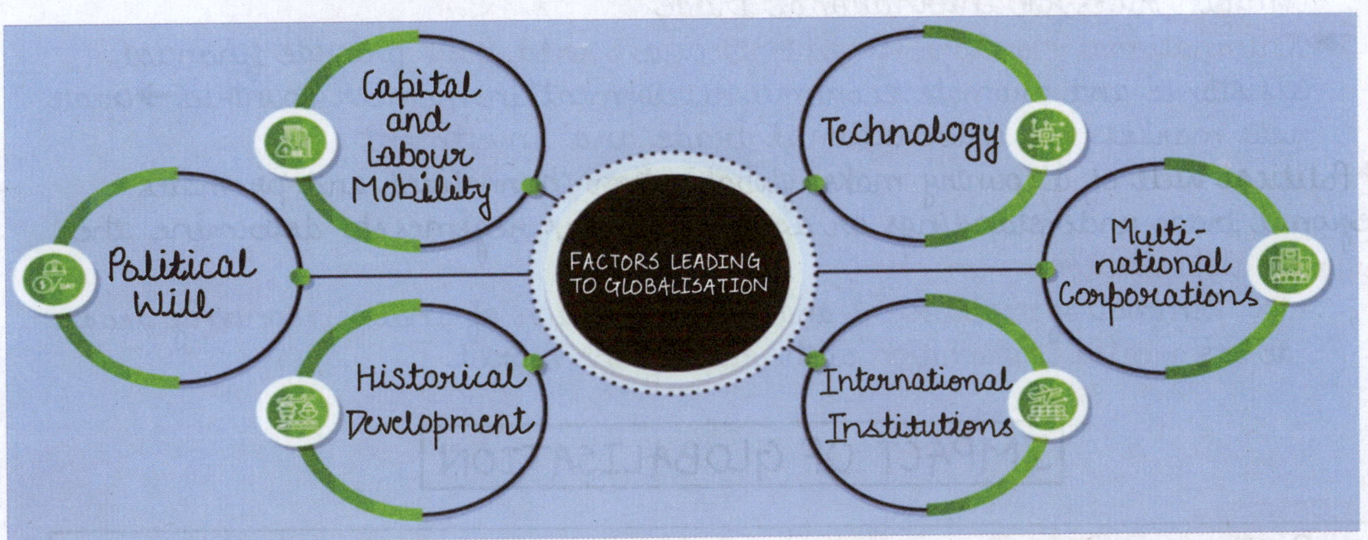


➡ **Historical Development** of trade routes facilitating the movements of goods between Kingdoms and Countries.
➡ **Technology** made international trade efficient, accessible and profitable.
- Advancement in transportation and communication → slashed the cost and time of moving goods, people, and information across borders.
- Rise of personal computers, the internet, and digital communication tools has further accelerated globalization.

➡ **Capital and Labour Mobility** encourage international trade and allows companies to take advantage of lower production costs in some countries.
- Financial liberalisation allow capital to flow more freely across borders → increased investment in form of FDI/FPI.
  - Service Sector in India recieved highest FDI inflow in the fiscal year 2023-2024 and this sector also contributes the highest in GDP.
- Labour mobility across the borders fills labour shortages and allows companies to access a wider talent pool.
  - As per World Migration Report 2024, India has been the top recepient of remittances globally for many years.

➡ Multinational Corporations (MNCs):

⋙ Global Production Chains: MNCs establish production facilities in different countries → taking advantage of cheap labour → to minimise cost of production.

- Ex: Apple design its iPhones in California but manufactures them in China.

⋙ Foreign Direct Investment brings capital, technology, and jobs to developing countries and fosters economic growth.

➡ International Institutions create a more predictable and stable environment for global commerce.

⋙ World Trade Organisation works to promote free trade and establish common rules for international trade.

⋙ International Monetary Fund (IMF) and World Bank provide financial assistance and promote economic development in member countries → create new markets for international trade and investment.

➡ Political Will of a country makes globalisation channelized and promotes regional trade understandings or agreements, tax regimes etc determine the scope of globalization.

- Ex: Removal of tax barriers and liberalisation of Indian economy leads to its greater integration with rest of the world.

## IMPACT OF GLOBALISATION

| Positive Impacts | Negative Impacts |
|---|---|
| ➡ Unleashing Local Growth: Multi-national corporation (MNCs) have invested heavily → created a surge in job opportunities for the local population.<br>➡ Nurturing Homegrown Giants: Globalisation has empowered large Indian companies to transform into multinationals. Ex: Tata Motors and Infosys.<br>➡ Voice on Global Stage: With Indian MNCs significantly contributing to global trade, India gains a stronger voice at multilateral forums like WTO → advocating for fairer trade practices. | ➡ Trade deficits where a country imports more than it export. It can strain the economy.<br>• India has an ongoing trade deficit with China.<br>➡ Dark side of connectivity like illegal movement of drugs, arms, and people across borders.<br>➡ Rise of Transnational Threats: Free flow of goods and ideas can also allow spread of terrorism and other criminal activities<br>• Ex: Left Wing Extremism in India.<br>➡ Global Health concern have been increased → travel and trade can accelerate the spread of infectious diseases like COVID-19.<br>➡ Financial Domino Effect: Interlinked economies means a financial crisis in one country can |

| | |
|---|---|
| ➡ Choice for Consumer: Consumers have an option to choose from a wide range of products and services available across globe.<br>➡ Foreign Direct Investment along with cutting-edge technologies, propelling advancements in domestic production methods.<br>➡ Educational Callaboration between foreign and Indian universities provides access to superior educational and medical service, → fostered skilled and knowledgeable workforce.<br>➡ Robust Financial Sector: Globalization enhances efficiency of banking, insurance, and financial sectors → fostering competition and innovation.<br>➡ Inclusive Growth: Expansion of the internet to remote rural areas, coupled with infrastructural development, leads to inclusive growth.<br>➡ Pluralistic Society: Globalization fosters integration of people from traditionally marginalised backgrounds into mainstream.<br>➡ Evolutionary Governance: Free flow of ideas and best practices in governance → influence new policy initiatives in health, education and technology.<br>➡ Status of Women: Access to global thoughts, ideas and opportunities for women helping in improving their status. | trigger slowdowns in others.<br>• Ex: Global Financial Crisis 2007.<br>➡ Differential Benefits: Agriculture often lags behind manufacturing and service industries.<br>➡ Neocolonialism is a new form of coloniza-tion, where powerful countries exert economic influence instead of military force → Threatening Sovereignty.<br>• Ex: China's Belt Road Initiative.<br>➡ Unsustainable Growth: Tilted focus on economic growth → leads to environmental neglect, threatening biodiversity and future generations.<br>➡ Materialism on Rise: Increased wealth can exacerbate problems like corruption.<br>➡ Cultural Homogenization: Concerns exist that dominant cultures are seen as superior, leading to a loss of cultural diversity.<br>• Ex: English is perceived as language of success in some countries.<br>➡ Debt trap: A rise in consumer credit can lead to a "buy now, pay later" culture that fuels excessive consumerism. |

## IMPACT OF GLOBALISATION ON FAMILY

➡ On Structure of Family:

➡ Disintegration of Joint Family and rise in Nuclear families due to increasing mobility of younger generation for work and education.

- According to Census 2011, share of nuclear families grew up to 52.1% from 51.7% in 2001 in the fourth wave of globalisation.

➜ Emergence of new forms of family like single parenting, neolocal families live-in relationship, living with friends under one roof etc.

➠ On Functions of Family:

➜ Shifts in Economic Role: Initially families were both units of production and units of consumption.

- Globalisation + Industrialization → Factory System of Production → Family became a unit of consumption only.

➜ Educational Role: It allows families to supplement their children's education beyond the traditional classroom → increased use of educational apps, online courses, and even virtual tutors and mentors.

➜ Decline in case of spouse selection as love marriages and internet marriage sites like Shaadi.com, Bharat Matrimonial are playing a crucial role in match making.

➜ Note: Despite changes in functions of family, even today there are cert functions performed by family:

- Primary socialization of children and agency of social control.

➠ On Interpersonal Relationship:

➜ Democratic Relationship and parenting instead of authoritative because of influence of western progressive ideas.

➜ Better Status of Women: With access to quality education and global workforce → more women joining the workforce → their financial dependence is reduced.

- As per PLFS Report 2022-23 Female Labour Force participation Rate in country has improved significantly by 4.2% to 37.0% in 2023.

➜ Ties with extended kin have been strengthened due to penetration of digital technology led social media, whatsapp group, video call → improved quality of relationship.

➠ On Interaction Pattern:

➜ New Occasions for Celebrations like Valentine's day, Mother's day, Father's day.

➜ Shifting dining patterns from "Sit and Eat together" to watching TV or chatting on computers during meals.

➜ Online Friendship: Cultural globalisation has fostered online friendship networks → lead to rise of vlogging culture and social media interaction → shaping social connections.

➠ On Family Value System: Globalization leads to the erosion of traditional family values and customs in India

➜ It gives boosts to individualism over collectivism.

# IMPACT OF GLOBALISATION ON MARRIAGE

| Positive Impacts | Negative Impacts |
|---|---|
| Increased Choice and Independence leading to a shift from arranged marriages based on compatibility.<br>Women's Empowerment led to a decline in dowry practices and greater decision-making power within marriage.<br>Financial Security and Delayed Marriage: Globalization → better job opportunities → allowing couples to achieve financial stability before marriage.<br>As per NFHS 5, the median age of marriage of women improved from 16.2 years in 1992-93 to 19.2 years in the year 2019-21.<br>Openness to Intercultural Marriages: Globalisation → fosters cultural exchange → rise in intercultural marriages → broadens perspectives and enriches family life.<br>Focus on Shared Values: Globalization → couples to prioritize shared values and interests over traditional considerations like caste or religion.<br>Search Across Geographical Barriers: In influence of global and western lifestyle many Punjabi families are prioritising NRI grooms. | Secularisation of Marriages: Exposure to diverse marriage → fosters individual choice, → leads to secular ceremonies over religious aspects.<br>Erosion of Traditional Values: Emphasis on individualism + career aspirations → lead to delayed marriages → weaken the extended family support system traditionally seen in India.<br>Increased Divorce Rates: Exposure to Western ideas + changing gender roles + Secularization of Marriage → a rise in divorce rates.<br>Consumerist Influences: Media portrayals of extravagant weddings or Big Fat weddings → create financial strain and dissatisfaction.<br>As per Indialends survey 20% of all loans taken by young Indians in 2018-19 were to fund their own wedding.<br>Clash of Cultures: Intercultural marriages, while positive in some ways, but also leads to challenges in adjusting to different customs, traditions, and expectations, causing conflict within the marriage. |

# IMPACT OF GLOBALISATION ON INDIAN CULTURE

India is a patchwork of many religious, dialects, cultures, music genres, architectural styles, and so forth, all bundled together into a single, cohesive nation. From the perspective of globalisation, we can examine this rich culture and identify several instances of westernization as well as the blending of various characteristic and civilizations into our exquisitely weaved blanket.

## Four Key Aspect of Inquiry

## Homogenization

- Cultural Homogenization describes the phenomenon where distint cultural practices, beliefs, and identities are replaced or overshadowed by a dominant, often Westernised or global culture.
- Increased Exposure: Globalisation fosters spread of ideas, information, and cultural products through media, travel, and trade.
- Homogenization of taste and preferences: Dominant influence of Western culture → through American media and consumer goods.
  - Ex: Entry of Avocados, Peanuts Butter, Corn flakes in Indian food pattern.
- Global Brands: Rise of MNCs selling standardized products creates a sense of cultural similarity across different countries.
- Homogenization of language: Use of English has increased manifold in urban areas and is perceived as the language of elits.
  - According to UNESCO's Atlas of the World's Languages in Danger of Disappearing 2009 → 196 Indian languages are in danger of extinction.
- Homogenisation of dressing: Convenience and comfort of western dresses → pulled away the young generation from traditional outfits to modern dresses like T-shirt, jeans and shorts.
- Homogenisation of Art and Music: Indians are getting attracted to foreign dance forms like Salsa, Hip hop.
  - In the field of Music, there is a rise of Pop music, and rap culture.
- Homogenisation in values and rights like democracy, scientific temper, rationality, human rights, child rights, and banking culture.

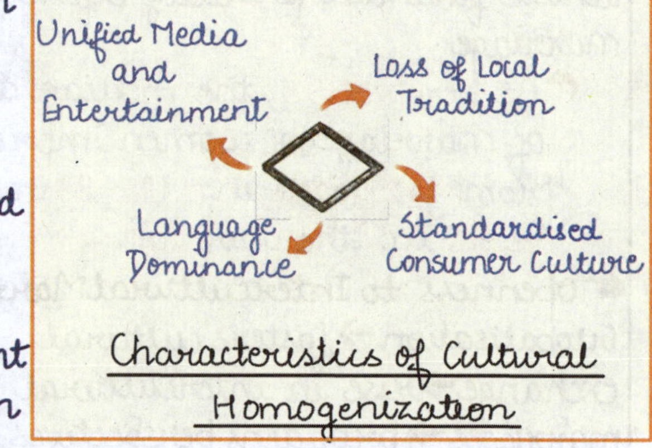


Characteristics of Cultural Homogenization

## Glocalization of culture = Globalization + Localisation

➡ Glocalisation refers to the process where global cultural products, ideas, and practices are adapted to fit specific characteristics of local cultures. It's a two-way street:

» Global Goes Local: Elements of global culture are adapted to resonate with local preferences and traditions.

- Ex: McDonald's offers vegetarian options in India to cater to religious dietary restrictions.

» Local Goes Global: Local cultural elements are incorporated into global practice or disseminated internationally.

- Ex: Yoga has become a global phenomenon.

Characteristics
- Celebration of Diversity
- A dynamic Process
- Local Control while engaging in global outlook
- Two-Way Flow for Cultural diffusion

Characteristics of Glocalization

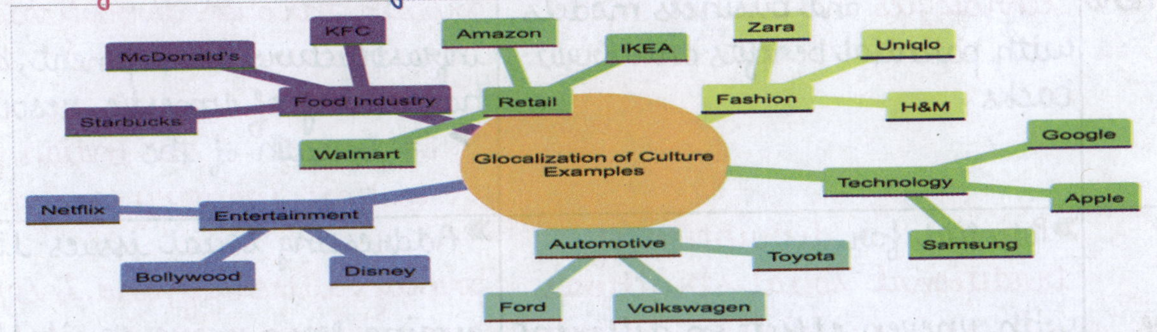


➡ Glocalisation of Flavars: Global fast food chains like McDonald's offer Indian-inspired options (Paneer Tikka Burger) catering to local tastes.

➡ Multilingual Education: French, German, and Spanish are taught alongside regional languages, equipping students with a wider range of communication skills.

➡ Dubbing of Hallywood, Chinese, and Korean movies gain popularity, often dubbed in local languages for wider reach.

➡ Glocalization of Traditions: New celebrations like Valentine's Day and Friendship Day alongside festivals like Diwali and Holi remain strong.

## Debate: Westernisation VS Modernisation

| Feature | Westernization | Modernisation |
|---|---|---|
| Core Objective | » Emulation of Western cultural norms, practises, and institutions. | » Overall advancement of Indian Society through social, economic, and political development. |

| | | |
|---|---|---|
| Process | Superficial adoption of Western elements, often rapid and externally driven.<br>Ex: Colonisation forces | Indigenous transformation, emphasising internal needs and a gradual, context-specific approach.<br>Ex: Development of Panchayat Raj System. |
| Scope | Restricted to speech, clothing, food habits, music etc. | Fundamental change in value, attitude, behaviour, and infrastructure.<br>Ex: Gender Inequality |
| Cultural Impact | Potential homogenization and erosion of traditional Indian values and customs. | Possibility of adaption and innovation within Indian Culture, leading to a more dynamic and inclusive identity. |
| Economic Development | Introduction of specific Western technologies and business models, with potential benefits and drawbacks. | Focus on broad-based economic growth through diversification, infrastructure development, and harnessing of domestic resources.<br>Ex: Growth of the Indian pharmaceutical industry. |
| Social Change | Potential for disruption of traditional social structures, with uneven effects on different groups. | Addressing social issues like poverty, illiteracy, and inequality, aiming for a more equitable and just society.<br>Ex: Affirmative action like Reservation. |

## Revival of Culture

- **Yoga's Global rise**: Yoga is experiencing a surge in popularity, both in India and around the world.
  - It is evident in success of programs like Ravi Shankar's "Art of Living" and the worldwide celebration of International Yoga Day on 21st June.
- **Ayurveda's Renewed Interest**: Ayurvedic medicine is enjoying a resurgence in popularity, not just in India but also internationally.
- **Religion's Resurgence in Uncertain Times**: As globalisation increases interconnectedness → led to feeling of uncertainty → led to a resurgence of religious faith → evident in the use of religion in politics and social movements.

→ Going Local, Going Global: There's a growing appreciation for locally-made handicrafts in the global market.
- Traditional Indian art forms like Chikankari and Bandhani are prime examples of this trend.

→ Tourism's Positive Impact: The rise of global tourism is encouraging local communities to preserve their unique cultural traditions and heritage.
- Increased tourism in Kerala has led to a revival of traditional houseboat building and the revival of local cuisine to cater to tourists.

→ Philanthropy and foundations: Aga Khan Trust for Culture has restored historical sites across India, such as Humayun's Tomb in Delhi → Showcasing India' rich architectural heritage for future generations.

## IMPACT OF GLOBALISATION ON WOMEN

**Positive Impacts:**

→ Increased Job opportunities because of establishment of MNCs + growth of export-oriented industries in sectors like IT, textiles, and service industries
- Tata Consultancy Services has the highest number of female employees in India, about 35% of its workforce.

→ Entrepreneurship: Better access to global markets, technology, and invest-ment → lead rise of entrepreneurship culture among women.
- Ex: Kiran Mazumdar-Shaw, founded Biocon, a biopharmaceutical company.

→ Access to Education contributed to the spread of educational opportunities, allowing more women to pursue higher education and acquire professional skills.
- As per MSM Unify survey more than half of students who desire to study abroad are women especially interested in STEM courses.

→ Skill Enhancement Initiatives like the National Skill Development Corporation and Digital India Program → facilitated skill training for women → enhances their employability in various sectors.

→ Empowerment: Employment led to Economic independence → improved their status within their families and communities.

→ Changing Societal Norms: Global cultural exchanges → promoting gender equality and encouraging women to participate in various sphere of life.
- Ritu Karidhal, a senior scientist at ISRO → played a key role in the Mars Orbiter Mission.
- Increased Acceptance towards women wearing western clothes, dating culture in urban areas, use of contraceptives.

→ Digital Inclusion: Proliferation of the internet + initiatives like "Internet Saathi" program by Google and Tata Trust → empowered rural women with digital literacy → enabled accessibility of information, education, and employment opportunities.

→ Networking and Advocacy: Social media campaign like #MeToo + online platforms like Twitter → allow women to connect, share experiences, and advocate for their rights.

→ Healthcare Access: Introduction of telemedicine platforms like Practo and mHealth initiatives have improved healthcare access for women, especially in rural areas.

→ Participation in Socio-Political Domain: Globalisation has gradually increased participation of women in leadership and decision-making positions.

↳ Ex: As per RBI report, elected women representatives constitute 45.6% of the total PRI representatives in India.

→ Advocacy for Rights: Global human rights frameworks and conventions influenced domestic legal reforms aimed at protecting and promoting women's rights.

↳ Implementation of Domestic Violence Act, 2005 and Sexual Harassment of Women at Workplace (Prevention, Prohibition and Redressal) Act 2013.

→ Implementation of Policies: International pressure and standards have encouraged implementation of initiatives like Beti Bachao Beti Padhao → to address gender discrimination and promote education and protection for girls.

## Negative Impacts:

➤ Persistence of patriarchal attitudes in society contributes to the commodification of women, increased harassment on social media, and higher rates of violence against women.

» Ex: As per NCRB report 2023, "Cruelty by Husband or His Relatives (31.4%) Kidnapping and Abduction of women, Assault on Women, and Rape are prominent crimes against women.

➤ Low Wages and Poor Working Conditions in the garment and textile industries many women work long hours for low pay under poor conditions.

» Ex: In Tamil Nadu's textile mills, female workers face exploitative labour practices.

➤ Informalisation of Female Labour Force: Due to skill mismatch from global standard most of the women in workforce are ended up as domestic help or confined to informal sector.

» Only 14-15% of workers in the formal sector are women.

- **Work-life balance challenges:** As women are subjected to a dual burden → long working hours and household responsibilities → impacting their performance and hindering success.
  - Example: Juggling work commitments with cooking and childcare responsibilities.
- **Gender inequalities** have been amplified by globalisation in terms of resources, time allocation, access to opportunities, and decision-making power.
  - Ex: Glass Ceiling in corporate posts and limited agency for women.
  - Skewed access to technology and Gender pay gap is still persistent.
- **Objectification and Commodification of Women** through advertising and media that portrays women primarily as object of desire.
  - It is evident in beauty product commercials → that sets unrealistic standards of beauty.
  - Advertisements for alcohol that use women's bodies to sell the product.
- **Trafficking and Violence:** Increased mobility of people across borders made women more vulnerable to trafficking for forced labour or sexual exploitation.
  - According to the 2022 Trafficking in Persons Report by the U.S Department of State, nearly 59% of identified trafficking victims in India were female, and almost half were children.

## IMPACT OF GLOBALISATION ON YOUTH

| Positive Impacts | Negative Impacts |
|---|---|
| → Hybridisation of value + Cultural exchange among youth → demand for a composition society.<br>» Indian youth celebrate Holi by incorporating western music and fashion.<br>→ Globalized World: Young Indians are actively acquiring digital skills to connect and callabarate with peers worldwide through social media platforms.<br>→ Ambition and Entrepreneurship: Aspiring young entrepreneurs are launching tech startups to tap into the global market. | → Cultural Erosion among youth: Weakening of cultural identity raises the concern for potential loss of local culture.<br>» Popularity of Western music and fashion trends → decline in appreciation for traditional Indian art forms and regional textile.<br>→ Generational Gap: Shift towards nuclear families + distant from elders → loss of intergenerational knowledge, values and wisdom.<br>→ Adoption of sedentary lifestyles characterized by a lack of physical activity + |

➡ Synergy Between Religion and Modernity: Indian youth advocating for gender equality within religious institutions, ➡ reflecting a desire to modernise practices while upholding core values.

➡ Youth empowerment and participation Increased awareness has made youth more vocal about their rights and demands, leading to greater participation in policymaking.

» Ex: Youth outrage leads to implementation of Public Examination (Prevention of Unfair Means) Act, 2024.

excessive screen time ➡ led to an increase in health disorders.

➡ Vicious Cycle of Urban Poverty: Economic Globalisation fueled migration towards urban centres ➡ rise in urban poverty and unemployment

➡ Cyberbullying and Online Predators because of increased internet access ➡ highlights the need for digital literacy and parental guidance.

➡ Marginalisation of Rural youth as they lack access to quality education, job training, and technological resources necessary for competing in the global job market.

# IMPACT OF GLOBALISATION ON CASTE SYSTEM

➡ Weakening of caste hierarchy: Globalization has led to expansion of economic opportunities, education, and exposure to liberal ideas.

- Increased access to education + professional skill ➡ allows individuals from lower castes to compete for jobs dominated by upper castes.

➡ Acceptance of inter-caste marriages: Globalization fosters interaction between people from different backgrounds, leading to a social environment for inter-caste marriages.

➡ Shift From Caste Based division of labour to skill based division of labour because of rise of globalised industries, MNCs and Urbanisation and service based economies.

➡ International pressure and scrutiny because of increased awareness of caste discrimination and rise of social media platforms to gather support from the global community.

➡ Advocacy of Rights: Influence of global human rights discourse can be seen in the framing of the Scheduled Caste and the Scheduled Tribes (Prevention of Atrocities) Act 1989.

➡ Global Activism: Organisations like National Campaign on Dalit Human Rights have used global platforms to highlight caste issues.

- They participated in international forums like United Nations, bringing global attention to caste-based discrimination in India.

➡ **Economic Inequality:** Globalization → brought economic growth → increased income inequality because high-paying jobs have been largely concentrated among educated and relatively privileged sections.

- As per Oxfam India report 2023, the top 5% of Indians own over 60% of country's wealth, while bottom 50% only have 3%. The richest 1% of Indians own 40.1% of the country's wealth.

➡ **Caste Capitalism:** Globalisation gave impetus to capitalism whose benefits were reaped by a limited section of lower caste → created class with caste.

Globalization's impact on the caste system is multifaceted. While it present opportunities for change and social mobility, it's crucial to address inequalities and discrimination to ensure everyone benefits from globalization.

## PYQs Corner

*(Write the Answer and Get Free Evaluation)*

1. What is cryptocurrency? How does it affect global society? Has it been affecting Indian society also? **(2021)**
2. Is diversity and pluralism in India under threat due to globalisation? **(2020)**
3. Are we losing our local identity for the global identity? Discuss. **(2019)**
4. To what extent globalization has influenced the core of cultural diversity in India? Explain. **(2016)**
   Discuss the positive and negative effects of globalization on women in India. **(2015)**

CHAPTER 06

# Role of Women and Women Organisations

Gender refers to socially constructed aspects of differences between men and women. It is manifested at every level of society.

Gender Stereatyping is oversimplified beliefs about trait, behaviours, and roles that belong to men or women. It's like putting people in boxes based on their gender.

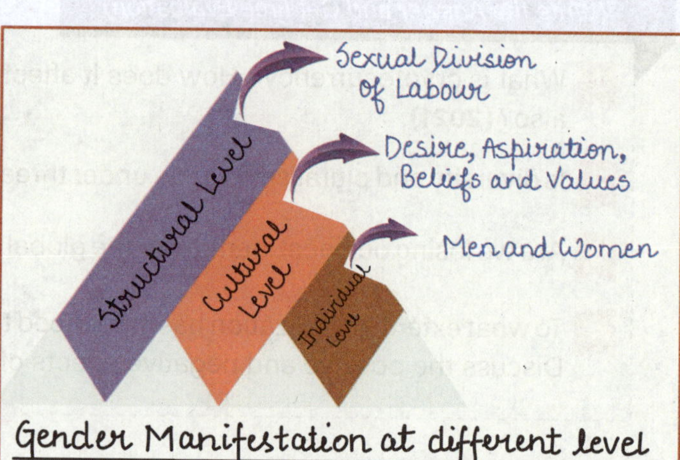

Gender Manifestation at different level

| Women Stereatyping | Social Position |
|---|---|
| 01 Caring and Nurturing | → Domestic Division of Labour i.e women is confined to domestic sphere |
| 02 Soft Skill | → Pink Collar Jobs |
| 03 Emotional and Non-Rational | → Glass Ceiling in Institution and Organisation |
| 04 Weak, passive and dependent | → Subject to domestic violence and sexual harassment. |

## Constitutional Safeguard Available to Women

- Article 14 → Men and women to have equal rights and opportunities in the political, economic and social spheres.
- Article 15(1) → Prohibits discrimination against any citizen on the grounds of religion, race, caste, sex etc.
- Article 15(3) → Special provision enabling the state to make affirmative discriminations in favour of women.
- Art 16 → Equality of opportunities in matters of public appointments for all citizens.
- Article 23 → Ban trafficking in human and forced labour.
- Article 39(a) → State shall direct its policy towards securing all citizens, men and women, equally, the right to means of livelihood.
- Article 39(d) → Equal pay for equal work for both men and women.
- Article 42 → State to make provision for ensuring just and humane conditions of work and maternity relief.
- Article 51(A)(e) → To renounce the practices derogatory to the dignity of women.
- Article 300(A) → Right to property to women.
- 73rd & 74th Amendment Act 1992 → Reservation of 1/3rd of seats in local bodies of panchayats and municipalities for women.

## Legislative Framework to Protect Women

- Sati (Prevention) Act 1987 → Practice of Sati which was first abolished in 1829, was revised and made illegal in 1987. It aim for prevention of practice of sati and its glorification in India, except for Jammu and Kashmir.
- Amendment to Criminal Act 1983 → This act talks about domestic violence as an offence, rape is also made a punishable offence.
- Special Marriage Act 1954 → It has been amended to fix the minimum age of marriage at 21 years for males & 18 years for female.
- Hindu Succession Act 1956 → Equal share to daughter from property of father, while a widow has the right to inherit husband's property.
  - Amendment Act in 2005 → enabled daughters to have equal share in ancestral properties.
- Immoral Traffic Prevention Act (ITPA), 1986 → replaced SITA, 1956 was amended in 1986 & renamed ITPA → enacted to prohibit or abolished traffic in women and girls for purposes of prostitution.
  - It was amended to cover both sexes + provided enhanced penalties for offences involving minors.
- Dowry Prohibition Act 1961 → Now Courts are empowered to act in his own Knowledge or on a complaint by any recognised welfare organisation on dowry murder.

→ Indian Evidence Act, 1872 → replaced by Bharatiya Sakshya Act, 2023 → burden of proof lies with husband and his family where bride dies within 7 years of marriage.

→ Domestic Violence Act 2005 → It seeks to determine domestic violence in all forms against women & make it a punishable offence.

→ Indecent Representation of Women (Prohibition) Act, 1986 → It prohibits indecent representation of women through advertisements or in publications, writings, paintings, and figures or in any other manner and for matters connected there with.

→ Sexual Harassment of Women at Workplace (Prevention, Prohibition and Redressal) Act, 2013 → Protect women from sexual harassment at their work place.

## Prominent Remarks on Women

→ "Women is the companion of man gifted with equal mental capacities" → Mahatma Gandhi

→ "You can tell condition of a nation by looking at the status of its women." → Jawaharlal Nehru

→ "Feminism is not just about women; its about letting all people live fuller live." → Jane Fonda.

→ "Women belong in all places where decision are made .... It shouldn't be that women are the exception". → Ruth Bader Ginsburg

→ "In politics, if you want anything said, ask a man; if you want any thing done, ask a woman" → Margaret Thatcher

→ "A woman with a voice, is by definition, a strong woman." → Melinda French Gates.

→ "The education and empowerment of women throughout the world cannot fail to result in a more caring, tolerant, just and peaceful life for all." → Aung San Suu Kyi

→ "Feminism isn't about making women stronger Women are already strong it's about changing the way the world perceives that strength." → G D Anderson.

## WOMEN AND PATRIARCHY

Patriarchy refers to the system of social structure and policies in which men dominate, oppress and exploit women.

» Concept of gender draws its legitimacy from patriarchy itself.

» Nature of control subjugation of women with respect to

class, caste, region or religion, ethnicity. Ex: (Brahmanical Patriarchy is not same as Tribal Patriarchy).

## Arena of Patriarchy

>>> **Family:** It act as an agent of cultural reproduction instead of social change through primary socialization. First lesson of patriarchy is learnt in the family itself.

| Manifestation of Patriarchy | Causes of Persistence |
|---|---|
| 01 Patrilineal Inheritance: Cultures, inheritance and family names are passed down through male line → sidelining women's rights to property and family legacy.<br>02 Gender Roles: Domestic duties are assigned to women and decision-making power to men → perpetuating male dominance in family affairs.<br>03 Preference for Sons → leading to practice like sex-selective abortion and unequal resources allocation between sons and daughters. | 01 Socialization from a young age to accept and perpetuate gender roles → boys encouraged to be assertive and girls to be nurturing<br>02 Inadequate legal and policy enforcement regarding inheritance and domestic violence → customary law take precedence over formal legal frameworks.<br>03 Women Economic Dependence on male family members reinforces their subordinate position within the family. |

>>> **Religion:** Patriarchal construction of social practices are legitimised by religious institutions as most of the religious practices accord superior position to male.

| Manifestation of Patriarchy | Causes of Persistence |
|---|---|
| 01 Religious Texts and Interpretations promote male superiority + prescribe subservient role for women.<br>02 Religious leadership positions are predominantly occupied by men → women resorting to subordinate roles.<br>03 Rituals and Practices reinforce gender inequality → restricting women's participation in religious affairs.<br>Ex: Sabarimala Issue. | 01 Institutional Endorsement upholds patriarchal norms and resist reforms that would promote gender equality.<br>02 Religious and Cultural Beliefs → deeply integrated into practice and norms → making them difficult to challenge or change.<br>03 Community Pressure discourages individuals from questioning or opposing patriarchal practices. |

>>> Caste: Sexuality of women is directly linked to caste purity, caste system and caste endogamy.

| Manifestation of Patriarchy | Causes of Persistence |
|---|---|
| 01 Double discrimination → faced by lower caste women based on both caste and gender → greater marginali--zation and exploitation.<br>02 Cased-based endogamy reinforces patriarchal control over women's sexuality and reproductive choices<br>03 Labour Division: Lower caste women relegated to menial and labour-intensive tasks, reflecting both caste and gender hierarchies. | 01 Social Stratification of caste system → perpetuates hierarchical relations, including gender hierarchies.<br>02 Weak Enforcement of Anti-caste discrimi--nation laws → allowing traditional caste and gender norms to persist.<br>03 Economic Dependence: Lower caste women → limited access to education + economic opportunities → reinforcing male depende-nce and upper caste authority. |

>>> Agriculture Sector: Around 84% women depend on agriculture for livelihood, mostly confined in low skilled jobs and Labour-Intensive jobs.

- According to Census 2011 → only 32.8% women are registered as primary workers.

| Manifestation of Patriarchy | Causes of Persistence |
|---|---|
| 01 Land Ownership: As per SECC 2011 → only 6.5% of women over the age of 18 in India own agricultural land.<br>02 Access to Resources: Women farmers often have less access to credit, tech--nology, and training compared to their male counterparts. | 01 Agricultural policies and programs → failed to address specific needs and rights of women farmers → perpetuating their marginalization.<br>02 Economic Inequalities in terms of resources lower their status and limited bargaining power. |

>>> Knowledge System: Patriarchal construction of Knowledge perpetuates patriarchal ideas → clearly reflected in educational institutions and media which reinforce male dominance.

| Manifestation of Patriarchy | Causes of Persistence |
|---|---|
| Educational Bias: Curricula + educat--ional materials → lacks representation of women's contributions to various fields. | Institutional policies and practices favor men, from recruitment and promotion criteria to networking opportunities. |

| | |
|---|---|
| ➜ Academic Hierarchies: According to UGC report ➜ women constitute only about 26% of professors and equivalent positions in India universities.<br>➜ Objectification and Commodification of women through media. | ➜ Cultural Attitudes, gender roles and capabilities influence the opportunities and support available to women in education and academia.<br>➜ Lack of mentorship support networks for women in academia and research fields perpetuates gender disparities. |

"The movement of women from private to public space could not challenge the nation of patriarchy since patriarchy also transformed from private to public."

Sylvia Walby.

## Female Labour Force Participation Rate (FLFPR)

### Statistics:

- As per Periodic Labour Force Survey Report 2022-23 ➜
  - Female Labour Force Participation Rate stands at 35.4% in 2003.
  - Rural Female Labour Force Participation Rate stands at 39.6%.
  - Urban Female Labour Force Participation Rate stands at 25.5%.
- Gender Gap Report 2024: India has slipped two places in global ranking to 129th in 2024 from 127th in 2023 out of 146 countries.
  - Economic Policy: India is among countries with lowest levels of economic parity, similar to Bangladesh, Sudan, Iran, Pakistan, and Morocco, with less than 30% gender parity in estimated earned income.

### Causes of Low Female Labour Force Participation Rate

➜ Lack of Suitable Job Opportunities especially for women in rural areas after the fall of farm jobs & lack of economic opportunities in non-farm employment.

➜ Increased Mechanization: Nearly 12 million Indian women could lose their jobs by 2030 owing to automation (McKinsey Global Institute Report)

➜ Increased women literacy by getting enrolled for higher studies in colleges reduced the workforce participation.

➜ Effect of household income: With increasing household incomes, especially over the last 3 decades, the need of a "Second income" reduced.

- This reduced women's participation especially in Subsidiary activities (Secondary income) due to change in preferences. This effect is especially seen in urban women workforce.

➜ Gender Discrimination: For every woman, 90% of the inequality she faces would be caused by discrimination because of gender.

- Higher Education: As of 2018-19, only 2% of working age women received formal vocational training, of which 47% did not join labour force (NSSO, 2018-19)
- Skill training: Women form only 17% of cloud computing, 20% of engineering and 24% of data/artificial intelligence Jobs. (WEF 2020)
- Wages: WEF's gender gap report 2022, where India was ranked at 135th position out of 146 countries.

→ Familial Responsibilities. Unpaid care work continues to be women's responsibility, with women spending on average five hours per day on domestic work.

- Women regularly sacrifice wages, career progression and education opportunities to meet family responsibilities, safety considerations etc.

→ COVID-Effect: Massive job losses for women, especially informal workers, and slower recovery of women-led micro businesses.

- Deepened gender digital divides, disrupted girls' schooling and placed millions of female health workers at risk

→ Under-reporting of women's work (Economic Survey 2022-23)

→ Other factors: lack of Sanitation, Sexual harassment at workplace, unsafe travelling, poor-child care facilities and care homes for elderly etc has prevented women from working in industries.

## Implication of Low Female Labour Participation Rate

### On Individual Level:

- Lack of Financial Autonomy: Low FLFPR → women lack their own income → increased financial dependency → limit women ability to make independent decisions and investment for personal development.
- Denial of Opportunity for social mobility → women stuck in existing social strata → unable to improve their socioeconomic status.
- Lack of Ability to Change or influence societal norms and policies. Women's absence in professional setting + decision making processes → perpetuating gender biases and hindering progress towards gender equality.
- Self Alienation of Women can lead to decreased self-esteem, mental health issues, and a sense of unfulfillment as they are not fully utilizing their skills and talents.

### On Family Level:

- Economic Strain: Due to an increased dependent population → limits family's ability to afford better education, healthcare, and overall quality of life → perpetuating a cycle of poverty.

- Increased Pressure on Male Earners can lead to stress, health problems, and strained family relationship due to the burden of economic responsibility.
- Limited Educational Opportunities due to limited financial resources, families might prioritize education of male children → perpetuating gender inequality.

**On National Level:**

- Reduced Economic Growth → significant portion of population being economically inactive leads to a loss in potential GDP growth.
  - Christine Lagarde (Ex-IMF Chief) remarks that → India's GDP can grow by 27% if women are brought to same level of men in terms of economic and workforce participation.
  - Amitabh Kant highlights that India cannot be a $5 or $10 trillion economy without women being a very major player in the Indian economy.
- Gender Inequality: Low Female LFPR reinforce gender inequalities → hindrance in achieving social equality → Obstructs national progress on multiple fronts, including education, health, and political stability.

| Government Measures taken to improve Low FLFPR | Way Forward |
|---|---|
| Code on Social Security, 2020: Contains provisions for enhancement in paid maternity leave from 12 weeks to 26 weeks, permitting women workers in night shifts with adequate safety measures. | Improve Access to Quality Education for all women, irrespective of caste or economic background. |
| Code on wages 2019 prohibits gender discrimination among employees in matters relating to wages. | Implement affirmative action policies to address caste-based discrimination + promote inclusivity in formal sector leading to women empowerment. |
| Beti Bachao Beti Padhao Scheme was launched with objective to guarantee survival, women safety, and education of female children. | Role of SHG in Women Empowerment such as Mahila Arthik Vikas Mahila Mandal, UMED Abhiyan have proven beneficial in development of women entrepreneurship. |
| Sexual Harassment of Women at Workplace (Prevention, Prohibition and Redressal) Act 2013 was enacted to ensure safe working spaces for women. | Addressing Structural Rigidities to create a more inclusive and flexible work environment. |
| | Encourage formulation of informal sector jobs, providing better job security and benefits. |

| | |
|---|---|
| ⋙ Grant in-aid for Working Women Hostel in cities, smaller towns and also in rural areas.<br>⋙ One Stop Centre (OSC) and Universalization of Women Helpline intended to provide 24 hours immediate and emergency response to women affected by violence.<br>⋙ Mahatma Gandhi National Rural Employment Guarantee Act, 2005 (MGNREGA mandates that at least one third of jobs generated under scheme should be given to women. | ⋙ Vocational Training is closely related with economic growth with capability to create employment for their income generation.<br>⋙ Promoting Gender-Neutral Social Norms through positive portrayals of women in diverse roles through media and educational programs.<br>➜ Ex: Nirmala Sitaraman (India's Finance Minister), Sudha Murty (Chairperson of the Infosys Foundation), Kiran Bedi (First Indian IPS officer can act as idols. |

# VIOLENCE AGAINST WOMEN

## Statistics

➜ According to NCRB there has been 4% increase in crime against women in an year with 12% increase in Rape Cases.

➜ According to NCRB 2022 report:

- ➜ Composition of Crimes: Cruelty by Husband or His Relatives" held highest share in crimes against women (31.4%), followed by "Kidnapping & Abduction of Women" (19.2%) and "Assault on Women with Intent to Outrage her Modesty" (18.7%).

## Causes of Violence Against Women

➜ Institutionalization of Patriarchy → created a framework where a male dominance is normalised + women's subordination is institutionalized → perpetuation of systemic inequality → justifies violence against women.

- ➜ Ex: Prevalence of dowry practices.

➜ Differential Process of Socialization asserts and reinforces traditional gender roles. As per Annual Status of Education Report (ASER) 2020 → dropout rate for girls increases significantly after primary school → to fulfill traditional roles.

➜ Women's economic dependency on men limits their autonomy and increase their vulnerability to violence.

- ➜ It restricts women's ability to leave abusive relationships and seek independence, perpetuating cycles of violence.

➜ Objectification and commodification of Women in media, advertising and popular culture → reduce women to mere objects of male desire → legitimising and perpetuating violence against them.

➜ Cultural Lag refers to the time it takes for societal norms and values to catch up with technological and social changes.

- Study by WeSpeakOut in 2018 estimated that 75% of Bohra women of Dawoodi Bohra sect had undergone female genital mutilation (FGM) despite being illegal and internationally condemned.

- Impact of Globalisation:
  - Corruption of Value System and the rise of materialism and individualism have contributed to a moral decay in society → undermined respect for women's rights and dignity → leads to increase violence.
    - Nirbhaya gang-rape case in 2012 highlighted serve moral decay and brutality present in society.
  - Increase in Cross Border Crime → Ministry of Home Affairs 2019 → thousands of women and children are trafficked across borders annually, primarily for forced labour and prostitution.
- Institutional Weaknesses
  - Lack of Stringent Laws: Many countries lack comprehensive and stringent laws to protect women for violence.
    - Weak legal framework fail to deter perpetrators and provide inadequate protection and justice for victims.
  - Poor Law Enforcement due to corruption, lack of resources and inadequate training of law enforcement personnel.
    - Human Right Watch Report, 2017 documented cases where police refused to file FIRs for sexual assault complaints → discouraged victims from seeking justice.
  - Poor Conviction Rate: Low conviction rates for crimes against women discourage victims from seeking justice and embolden perpetrators.
    - According to NCRB data of 2019 conviction rate for rape is as low as 27.8%.

## Manifestation of Violence against Women in Different Arenas

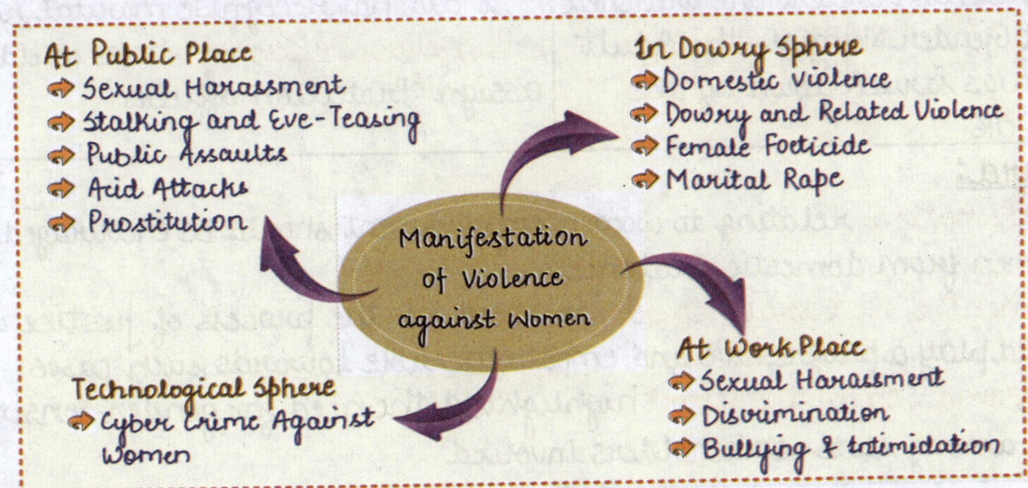

## In Domestic Sphere:

# Domestic Violence

**Status:** According to NCRB domestic violence constitutes the highest share of crime against women.

- The Supreme Court critically remarks that "alongwith IPC 498A Domestic Violence Act, 2005 is the most misused act.

**Key Reasons of Domestic Violence:**

- Cultural acceptance of domestic violence.
- Nuclear Families are more prone to domestic violence.
- Illiterate women, economically dependent women often bear the brunt of domestic violence.
- Patriarchal notions of ownership over women's bodies, labour, reproductive rights and level of autonomy.

| Domestic Violence Act, 2005 | Criticism of Act |
|---|---|
| It defines domestic violence as actual abuse or threat of abuse i.e. financial, physical, sexual, verbal and emotional. | Gender biased → There are increasing number of false cases. |
| Scope of term women has been widened → it includes 'live in partners', wives, sister, widows, mothers, single women, divorced wives. | Verbal abuse and mental harassment are open to subjective interpretation - this is being misused. |
| It is a civil act → which deals with right to secure housing, custody of children and compensation. | Lack of awareness → especially in rural areas. |
| It becomes cognizable and non-bailable only when protection orders are breached | Insensitivity of male police officers, judicial magistrates during hearing. |
| To make it Gender Neutral, the Adult male term was struck down by the court in 2016 | Absence of economic, legal, psychological support system for victim women |
| | It did not recognise marital rape. |
| | Budgetary Deficiency: States could not assign 'Protection officers.' |

**Way Forward:**

- NGOs participation relating to women empowerment should be encouraged to protect women from domestic violence.
- Establishment of Fast track courts to speed up the process of justice delivery.
- PRIs should play a progressive and empathetic role towards such cases.
- "Justice Verma Committee Report" highlighted the need for gender-sensitization training among state stakeholders involved.

## Dowry and Related Violence

### Dowry and Related Violence

**Key Reason for Persistence of Dowry:**

➡ Martial Arrangements Dowries from the basis of marriage and it has become a matter of social prestige and stigma.

➡ Acceptance of Dowry Culture by both Men and Women.

➡ Globalization led consumerist culture gave a push to dowry culture.

| Impact of Dowry | Way Forward |
|---|---|
| ➡ Gender Discrimination: Due to dowry system ➡ women are seen as a liability + subjected to subjugation.<br>➡ Affecting Career of Women: Poor presence of women in the workforce is directly proportional to dowry.<br>➡ Unmarried Women: Educated and professio-nally competent girls remain unmarried because of inability of parents to fulfill demand of dowry.<br>➡ Objectification of Women: Dowry is perceived as investment by the bride's family for plugging into powerful connections and money making opportunities.<br>➡ Crime Against Women: Unfufilled dowry promise leads to crime against women, ranging from emotional abuse and injury to even deaths. | ➡ Strengthen and strict implementation of anti-dowry laws, like Dwary Prohibition Act, 1961 ➡ with severe penalties against those demanding, giving, or accepting dowry.<br>➡ Stigmatization of Dowry through educational institutions, media and awareness campaigns.<br>➡ Incentivizing New Forms Martial Arrangement ➡ dowry free or where expenses were mutually shared.<br>➡ Women Empowerment enables the women to purse the career of her choice and strike dawn the patriarchal arrangement. |

**Available Framework to deal with Dowry:**

➡ Section 498 A of IPC deals with cruelty committed by husband and relatives ➡ it was a cognizable, non-bailable and non-compoundable offence.

➡ According to Supreme Court Section 498A of IPC has been used as a weapon rather than shield.

➡ Dowry Prohibition Act, 1961 ➡ prohibits the giving or taking of dowry.

## FEMALE INFANCIDE

Female Foeticide refers to 'aborting the female in the mother's womb'; whereas female infanticide is 'killing the girl child after her birth'.

- NFHS-4 data revealed a bias in favour of males having firstborn children 2.5% of first-born girls are lost during pregnancy, according to the 927 first-born children who had SRBs.
- Economic Survey 2017-2018 to identify 63 million 'Missing girls' in India until 2014.
- PCPNDT (Pre-Conception and Pre-Natal Diagnostic Technique) Act, 1994 → outlaw the use of sex selection method both before and after conception and to forbid the use of prenatal diagnostic method for selective abortion.
- Beti Bachao Beti Padhao, 2015 → To combat sex-selective abortion and the dropping child sex ratio, which was 918 girls for every 1,000 boys in 2011.

## Marital Rape

→ Section 375 of IPC → activities that constitute a man committing rape are defined under it.

→ Supreme Court, September 2022 ruled that women had right to safe abortions regardless of their martial status and that martial rape should be included in the definition of rape for the purpose of the Medical Termination of Pregnancy Act.

### Criminalising Martial Rape

| Arguments For. | Agrument Against |
|---|---|
| Consent and Autonomy: Martial rape law emphasize that marriage does not imply perpetual consent to sexual activity. | Cultural and Religious Considerations: Criminalizing martial rape interferes with cultural and religious practices → it will disrupt the sacred marriage institution. |
| Addressing Gender Inequality: Martial rape laws acknowledge and address the historical gender imbalances within the institution of marriage. | Instrument of Exploitation: Proving non-consensual sex within a martial relation-ship might be complex → eventually it will become an instrument of male exploitation. |
| Legal Protection from Abuse as it is an extreme from of domestic violence. | Privacy and Intrusion: Laws against martial rape could lead to unwarranted intrusion by state into intimate and private aspects of married life. |
| Closing Legal Loopholes by criminalizing marital rape. | Presumption of False Accusations → Driven by motives such as revenge, divorce proceedings, or gaining an advantage in child custody battles. |

| Promoting Healthy Martial Relationships based on mutual respect, trust and communication. | Potential for Legal Abuse → Criminalizing martial rape might be misused as a weapon in contentious divorce or separation cases. |
|---|---|

## At Public Place

### Sexual Harassment

About: It is unwanted and unwelcome behaviour of a sexual nature that violates a person's dignity and creates an intimidating, hostile, degrading or offensive environment in public space.

- It include → Unwanted physical contact or advances + Displaying sexually explicit material + Demanding sexual favours + Sending inappropriate texts or emails.

### Stalking and Eve-Teasing

→ Stalking involves repeatedly following or harassing a person in a way that causes them to feel afraid or unsafe.

- It include → Following someone + Sending unwanted letters + emails + messages + monitoring someone's online activity.

→ Eve-teasing is a euphemism used in South Asia for public sexual harassment or molestation of women by men.

- It includes → Catcalling or making lewd comments, Whistling or making suggestive sounds, Gesturing obscenely.

Measures to Counter:

- Enactment of stringent laws → that specifically criminalizes stalking and eve-teasing such as Section 354D of Indian Penal Code for stalking.
- For immediate assistance → Police Helpline (100) and Women's Helpline (181)
- Setting up dedicated police units to handle cases of stalking and eve-teasing.
- CCTV surveillance in public places to deter potential offenders and to provide evidence in case of incidents.
- Public awareness campaigns to educate the public on the seriousness of these offences and encouraging bystanders to intervene or report incidents.

### Public Assaults

About: Public assaults refer to physical attacks or violent behaviour directed at someone in a public place.

- It varies in terms of severity → Physical beatings or attacks + Mugging or robbery with a violent component + Group assaults or mob lynching.

Measures to Counter:

- IPC Sections 323, 325, and 326 → addresses various degree of assault and prescribe punishments.
- Emergency Response Support System (ERSS) 112: A pan-India helpline for immediate police assistance.
- Self Defence Training Program through various NGOs, government bodies to empower to protect themselves.

## Acid Attacks

About: Acid attacks involve deliberate throwing of acid or another corrosive substance onto women's body with intention to disfigure, maim, torture or kill.

→ It causes → Permanent physical and psychological damage, blindness if acid comes in contact with eyes. Long-term medical and psychological treatment needs.

Measures to Counter:

- IPC Section 326A: Specifically addresses acid attacks and prescribes stringent punishment.
- The Criminal Law (Amendment) Act, 2013: Strengthens the laws against acid attacks.
- Supreme Court has directed states to regulate the sale of acid → only to be sold to individuals with a valid ID and a stated reason for purchase.
- National Acid Attack Victim Assistance Program: Provided immediate medical assistance and legal support to victims.
- Financial assistance of Rs. 1 lakh is provided to the female acid attack victims from the Prime Minister's National Relief Fund.
- More Deployment of Police Personnel in Public Spaces.

## Prostitution

→ Supreme Court (2022) used its unique authority granted to it by Article 142 of Constitution, to recognise sex work as a "profession" and stated that those who engage in it have a right to respect and equality legal protection.

→ National Human Rights Commission (NHRC) acknowledged sex workers as unorganised labour in 2020.

→ According to National AIDS Control Organisation → over 8000 female sex workers are employed in India and more than 6000 of them have reported experiencing physical abuse or other types of maltreatment.

→ Justice Verma Commission (2012-2013) agreed that there is a difference between adult, consenting women who engage in sex work of their own free will and women who are trafficked for commercial sexual exploitation.

→ Supreme Court ruled in the Budhadev Karmaskar v. State of West Bengal (2011) case that sex workers have a right to dignity.

## Reasons to De-criminalize Sex Workers

→ Respect women's dignity and human rights → it is prohibition that puts sex workers at the greatest risk.

→ Decriminalization helps guard against violence and abuse.

→ Improve Access To Justice: When sex workers are afraid of being prosecuted, police surveillance, stigma and discrimination → less likely to disclose crimes.

→ Enhance Access To Health Services → having more financial support makes it possible to perform health outreach.

## Sexual Harassment at Workplace

About: Vishaka Guidelines defined sexual harassment; imposed three keys obligations on institutions → prohibition, prevention, redressal and mandated institutions to establish Complaints Committee.

→ POSH Act, 2013 gave legislative backing to Vishaka Guidelines laid down by Supreme Court in 1997.

→ NCRB reported 422 cases related to sexual harassment at workplace in 2022.

Measures Taken to Counter:

- SHe-Box: To facilitate the filling of sexual harassment complaints by giving all women, regardless of their job status, a single point of contact in the event that they work in the public or private, organised or unorganised sectors.
- Nirbhaya Fund a special non-lapsable corpus fund for the purpose of carrying out programs meant to improve women's safety and security throughout the nation.
- Swadhar Greh aims to provide basic requirements to neglected women and girls who are trying to make ends meet, with little help from the government or society.
- Sakhi One Stop Centre → helps victims to have easier access to a comprehensive variety of resources, including police, medical, legal and psychological support, as well as short-term housing.
- Women Helpline Schemes: A 24X7 emergency and non-emergency response in both the public and private domain for incidents of sexual assaults and harassment.

## Key Provision of POSH Act 2013:

»» Definition: Sexual harassment includes any one or more of following unwelcome acts or behaviour (whether directly or by implication) → Physical contact or advances, demand for sexual favours, showing pornography.

»» Definition of workplace: Any place visited by an employee arising out of a during course of employment, including transportation provided by employer for undertaking such a journey.

»» Act covers both organised and unorganised sectors.

- Covers all women → irrespective of their age or employment status.
- It also covers clients, customers and domestic workers as well.

## Discrimination

- Gender Bias in Hiring and Promotion tilted in favour of their male counterparts.
- Pay Inequality: Women are frequently paid less than men for performing the same job with similar qualifications and experience.
- Maternity Discrimination against women due to pregnancy, childbirth or related medical conditions, including denial of maternity leave and termination of employment.
- Glass Ceiling → An invisible barrier that prevents women from reaching the top positions in their careers.

# MEASURES TAKEN TO DEAL WITH VIOLENCE AGAINST WOMEN

## Amendment to Criminal Laws

- Criminal Law (Amendment) Act of 2013 → provided for a wider definition of rape + stringent punishment, introduce new offences such as acid attacks.
- Criminal Law (Amendment) Act, 2018 → death penalty for rape of a girl below the age of 12 years + time bound investigation and trial in 2 months
- Information Technology (Intermediary Guidelines and Digital Media Ethics Code) Rules 2021 → Social Media Intermediaries to remove or disable objectionable content such as morphed images on complaint of women within 24 hours.
- Satish Chander Ahuja vs Sneha Ahuja Case → Estranged wife's right to claim residence even in a shared household under provisions of Protection of Women from Domestic Violence Act, 2005.
- National Commission for Women (1992): To review Constitutional and legal safeguards for women + recommend remedial legislative measures + facilitate redressal of grievances and advise Government on all policy matters affecting women.

## Schemes/Initiatives

- Mahila Police Volunteers → act as a public-police interface with a mandate to report incidents of violence against women.
- Cyber Police Stations and Cyber Crime Cells → set up in each State to tackle cybercrimes against women.
- Ujjawala Scheme → Prevention of Trafficking and Rescue, Rehabilitation and Reintegration of Victims of Trafficking for Commercial Sexual Exploitation.
- Fast Track Special Courts → Central Government Scheme for setting up of 1023 FTSCs for time bound trial and disposal of pending cases related to rape and POCSO Act.

- Universalisation of Women Helpline to provide 24x7 hours immediate and emergency response to women affected by violence.

## State Level Initiative

- Himmat app by Delhi Police → allows women to send a distress call along with real time location to Police Control.
- Samman Campaign by Madhya Pradesh Police → Women's public awareness campaign that uses interactive techniques like 'Guddi' the mascot to raise awareness about crimes against women.
- Aparajitha is Online by Kerala Police → Women can report cybercrimes and complaints of domestic abuse.
- Operation Durachari by Uttar Pradesh → Special drive to pin down eve-teasers, accused of crime against women and habitual offenders in cases of sex related crimes through name shaming.

# WAY FORWARD TO TACKLE VIOLENCE AGAINST WOMEN

## Administrative, Legal and Judicial reforms

- Increasing number of female officers in police departments and post female officers to decision making roles.
- Improving data collection on all forms of violence + increase monitoring and oversight of case registration for police.
- Enhancing coordination through appropriate training programmes should be conducted for public prosecutors and police officers who investigate cases.
- Address capacity constraint in Judiciary → hiring more judicial officers and establishing special courts.
- Amend, harmonize or enact laws protecting women and girls from all forms of violence like criminalizing marital rape.

## Enhancing Support System to Survivors

- Gender sensitization of Personnel → To change patriarchal mindsets.
- Community level platforms (like SHGs) should be strengthened to provide awareness on legal and safety mechanisms for women.
- Legal and Psychological Support Services → In collaboration with civil societies and public health organisations.
- Protecting Privacy, identity and dignity of victims by establishing robust witness and survivor protection programmes.

- Redressal against Cyber-Violence → To uphold women's safety in online spaces + provide accessible and transparent reporting.
- Upholding reproductive rights as basic Human rights → should be the fundamental basis for government and community sponsored policies and programs.

## Changing Societal Norms

- Women Empowerment → Effective implementation of laws related to women's rights to property, inheritance + training and education to women to enhance employment and income.
- Rationalised intervention with Men → Social programmes should incorporate front-line workers to sensitize men and boys on gender related issues.
- Reclaiming public spaces for women through political & economic participation and diversifying their engagement in non-traditional sectors.
- Use of technology and emerging concepts such as smart city in urban policy for ensuring safer and gender friendly infrastructures & spaces.
- Deconstruct and Dismantle patriarchal ideologies → through implementation of age-appropriate human rights education programmes in schools → to sensitize children on all sexes on the unacceptability of violence.
  - Design of school textbooks must be revised to ensure that they do not perpetuate stereotyped views of women and girls.
- Work with community and religious leaders who possess the capacity and legitimacy to mobilize their communities for dialogue and reformation of harmful norms.

## Women Movements

**Gender equality, employment opportunities, amending legislations that only partially benefited women and creating a society free from intellectual physical, or emotional discrimination against women were among the progressive post-independence goals.**

| Movement | Purpose |
|---|---|
| **Telangana Movement (1946 – 1951)** | • To inspire and encourage women's political consciousness, **communist party** founded a **women's association.**<br>• It published a women's periodical named **Andhra Vanitha.**<br>• **Dubala Salamma**, **Regulla Achamma**, **Chityala Ailamma**, and **Ch. Kamalamma** were among the women who actively took part in the movement. |
| **Anti-Dowry Movements** | • In **Delhi**, **"Dahej Virodhi Chetna Manch"** was a coalition of progressive organizations, including **feminist ones**, that was founded in the 1980s.<br>• The **1984 Dowry Prohibition (Amendment) Act** was finally passed after much debate.<br>• The Act restricts the amount that can be given in dowry but does not outright forbid it. |
| **Chipko Movement** | • In **December 1972**, illiterate Adivasi women in the **Tehri Garhwal** region of **Uttar Pradesh's Advani hamlet** on a small slope began the initiative.<br>• They were shot at by police in **February 1978**, and as a result, they actively sought capture.. |
| **Anti-Rape Movements** | • Women activists forced government to review **Rape Laws.**<br>• Women's organisations and legal and social activists efforts→ to amend into **Criminal Law (Amendment) Act was, 1983.** |
| **Narmada Bachao Movement** | • Leadership was provided by **Medha Patkar**, who got its start as a demonstration against inadequate rehabilitation and resettlement for those who had been uprooted during construction of the **Sardar Sarovar Dam.** |
| **Me Too Movement** | • **Gained momentum** in India, 2018 → associated with sexual harassment and abuse of women at workplace.<br>• **Prominent Cases** included allegations against Bollywood actor **Nana Patekar**, filmmaker **Vikas Bahl**, and journalist-turned-politician **M.J. Akbar.**<br>• **Journalist Sandhya Menon** played a pivotal role in **Indian #MeToo movement** by sharing her own experiences and encouraging others to do the same. |

## Role of Women Organisations

### Pre-Independence Women Organisations

| | |
|---|---|
| **Mahila Mandals** | • Mainly by **Arya Samaj** and **Brahmo Samaj.**<br>• **Bharat Stree Mandal** was founded by **Sarala Devi Chaudhari** in 1910.<br>• Focused on fight against the **Purdah system.** |
| **Women's India Association, 1917** | • Founded in **Adayar, Madras** in **1917** by **Annie Besant, Margaret Cousins, Jeena Raja Dasa.**<br>• Focused on fight against child marriage, illiteracy & Devadasi system. |
| **National Council of Women in India (NCWI)** | • Advocacy of women rights.<br>• Education, Health, Legal rights, Economic empowerment, Violence, Political participation. |
| **All India Women's Conference (AIWC)** | • Working on women's rights, education, child health, reproductive rights, violence against women. |
| **Sathya Sodhak Samaj** | • Started by **Mahatma Jyothirao Phule.**<br>• Upliftment of lower caste communities, fought against caste-discrimination.<br>• Focus to **Social equality** and **access to education**, employment and other opportunities for all castes |

| Post-Independence Women Organisations | |
|---|---|
| **Indian Association of Women's Studies, 1981** | • It was founded as a group of academic and activist women.<br>• It conducts research and offers instruction.<br>• It actively publishes feminism-related books and publications. |
| **Swadhina (Self-esteemed Women),1986** | • It is primarily a civil society organisation with a focus on development of children and women via sustainable development and appropriate livelihood. |
| **Bharatiya Grameen Mahila Sangh,1955** | • A **non-political**, non-sectarian national organisation having branches in 14 states and union territories. |
| **All India Democratic Women Association (AIDWA), 1981** | • A pan-Indian women's organisation and is dedicated to advancing women's independence, equality, and democracy. |
| **Self-Employment Women's Association (SEWA), 1972** | • The first women's trade union was established in 1972 with the goal of enhancing the situation of women employed in the unorganised sector. |
| **Annapurna Mahila Mandal, 1975** | • Founded as recognised organisation and trust of urban poor, illiterate, self-employed women.<br>• It developed out of the requirements and issues faced by the wives of textile mill workers |

**Women Organisations: Were they able to achieve the desired results?**

Women organisations played a pivotal role in emancipation of several women issues but there peak achievement is yet not realised which can be observe in prevalent women issues like:

- **Domestic Violence:** Despite the enactment of the Protection of Women from Domestic Violence Act, 2005 → domestic violence remains widespread. Cases go unreported due to social stigma, fear of retaliation, and lack of support systems.
- **Sexual Harassment:** Sexual harassment in public spaces and workplaces continues to be a major issue, despite legal protections like the Sexual Harassment of Women at Workplace Act, 2013. Rape and Sexual Assault remain alarmingly high.
- **Workplace Inequality** → Discrimination in hiring, pay disparities and limited career advancement opportunities. The gender wage gap and glass-ceilings in leadership positions.
- **Educational Inequality** → Access to education is considerably low for women in higher education and STEM fields.
- **Maternal mortality rates** are still high especially in northern parts of India, particularly in rural areas.
- **Informal Sector Vulnerability:** Women mainly work in the informal sector → Lack job security, benefits and protections.
- **Child Marriage:** Despite legal prohibitions, child marriage remains prevalent, particularly in rural and impoverished areas → further impacting girls' health, education, and future prospects.
- **Patriarchal norms and cultural practices** → Like dowry, honor killings, and female foeticide, continue to undermine women's rights and status.
- **Political Underrepresentation: 18th Lok Sabha will have 74 women MPs (declined from 17th Lok Sabha)** despite so much advancement and affirmative measures.
  - **Enactment of Nari Shakti Vandan Adhiniyam, 2023 (Women Reservation Act)**

## PYQs Corner

*(Write the Answer and Get Free Evaluation)*

1. Explain why suicide among young women is increasing in Indian society. **(2023)**
2. "Empowering women is the key to control population growth". Discuss. **(2019)**
3. What are the continued challenges for women in India against time and space? **(2019)**
4. How does patriarchy impact the position of a middle class working woman in India? **(2014)**
5. Why do some of the most prosperous regions of India have an adverse sex ratio for women? Give your arguments. **(2014)**
6. Male membership needs to be encouraged in order to make women's organisations free from gender bias. Comment. **(2013)**

CHAPTER 07

# Poverty and Developmental Issues

## CONCEPT OF POVERTY

- UN Human Rights Council defines poverty as "a human condition characteristics by the sustained or chronic deprivation of the resources, capabilities, choices, Security and power necessary for the enjoyment of an adequate standard of living and other civil, cultural, economic, political and social rights.

| Traditional View (Uni-Dimensional) | Present View (Multi-dimensional |
|---|---|
| • Lack of financial resources and unable to fulfill even its basic necessities of life.<br>• Emphasis on minimum standard of living rather than reasonable level of living. | • Poverty goes beyond monetary deprivations by including access to social infrastructure - Health, education etc and basic essential services such as Sanitation, drinking water etc. |

## Multi-dimensional Poverty Index

- Global MPI is a poverty measure that reflects the multiple deprivations poor people face in the areas of education, health and living standards

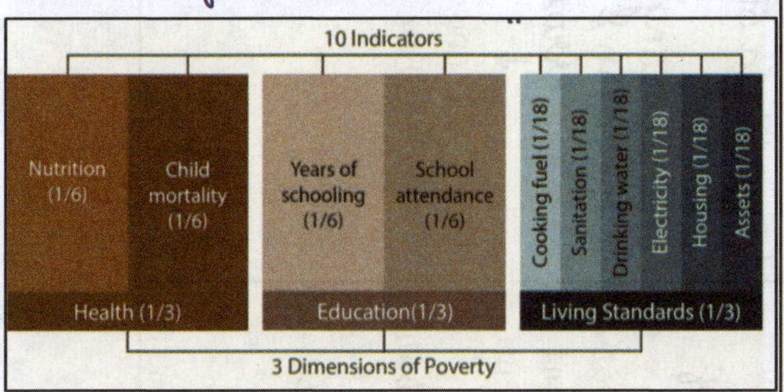


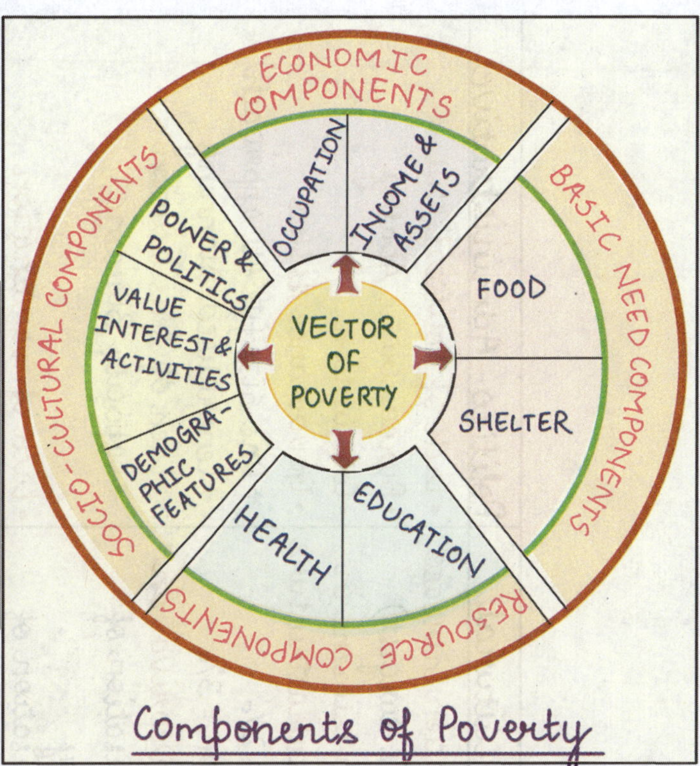


Components of Poverty

- First launched in 2010 by UNDP and Oxford Poverty Human Development Initiative.
- A person is multidimensionally poor if he/she is deprived in one third or more of the weighted indicators.
- Reflects both the incidence of multi-dimensional poverty and its intensity

## National MPI, 2023

- It is an important Public Policy tool which monitors multi-dimensional poverty & leads to evidence based policy making.
- It captures multiple deprivations & thus its broader in nature
- 2nd edition of MPI is published by NITI Aayog based on National Family Health Survey - NFHS 5 (2019-21)
- 3 Equally weighted dimensions and 12 indicators (2 more than Global MPI.
- India's population in multi-dimensional poverty decreased to 14.96% in 2019-21
- Rural Poverty > Urban Poverty (19.20%) (5.27%)
- Uttar Pradesh saw the largest decline in the number of poor individuals.

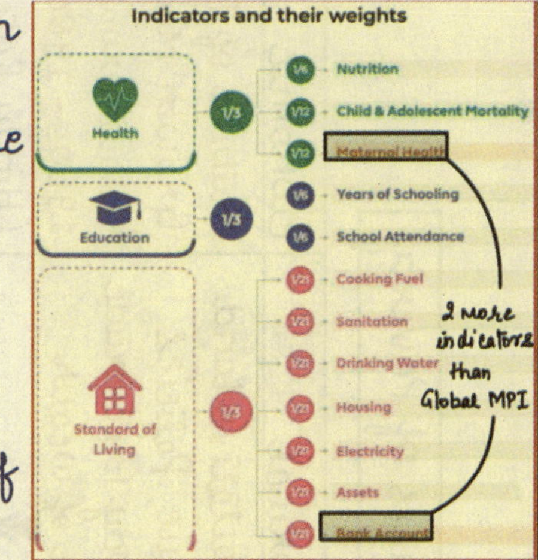

## Causes of Poverty

| Historical | Economic | Socio-cultural | Politico-Administrative |
|---|---|---|---|
| • Exploitative Land Revenue Policies<br>• One way Free trade<br>• Drain of wealth<br>↓<br>Deindustrialisation<br>↓<br>Increased Unemployment<br>↓<br>Overburdened Agriculture Sector<br>↓<br>• Low productivity<br>• Disguised Unemployment<br>↓<br>High Poverty | • Failure of Trickle-Down Growth Model<br>• Slow Growth rate during 1960s-1980s (Hindu Rate of Growth ≈ 3.5%)<br>• Tertiarisation of Economy + Stagnant manufacturing Sector.<br>↓<br>Jobless Growth (Reduced Employment Elasticity)<br>• Slow Pace of Inclusive Growth<br>• Low productivity in Agriculture<br>• Informalisation of Labour<br>• Inadequate and ineffective social security schemes | • Population increase (World's largest)<br>• Low investment in Social infrastructure<br>Health = 2%<br>Education = 3%<br>• Social Deprivation<br>→ Feminisation of Poverty<br>→ Ruralisation of Poverty<br>→ Castetisation of Poverty<br>• Systemic Deprivation of certain sections<br>• More Pressure on resources<br>• Persistent regional disparities<br>• Digital Divide | • Lack of Political will.<br>• Bureaucratic Apathy<br>• Corruption<br>• Governance Issues<br>→ One-Size-fits-All approach<br>→ Centralised planning<br>→ Lack of Sensitisation<br>→ Capacity Building.<br>• Lack of Coordination (working in Silos)<br>• Mistargeting of Beneficiaries (Inclusion & Exclusion error<br>↓<br>Leakages and Misutilisation of public funds |

# Types of Poverty

| Parameters | Absolute measure of Poverty | Relative Measure of Poverty |
|---|---|---|
| Definition | • Refers to a condition when household income is below a necessary level to maintain basic living standard such as food, clothing or shelter | • Defined from social perspective i.e. living standards compared to economic standard of population living in sorroundings |
| Purpose | • Assessing the number of people living below the poverty line and monitoring changes over time. | • Analyzing income inequality trend, comparing poverty levels across region/countries & evaluating the impact of economic growth and policies on income distribution. |
| Measurement | • Fixed Poverty line is calculated based on the cost of a basket of essential goods and services. | • Measured using Gini coefficient calculated through Lorenz curve. |
| Income Inequality | • Does not consider income inequality within the society. | • Consider income inequality & the distribution of resources within society |
| Policy Implication | • Helps in targeting resources and interventions to alleviate absolute poverty. | • Highlight disparities & the need of redistributive policies to address relative poverty. |

# Poverty line Estimation (PLE)

- Poverty estimation in India is carried out by NITI Aayog's Task Force through the calculation of poverty line based on the data captured by National Statistics office under the Ministry of Statistics and Programme Implementation (MoSPI).
- Poverty line estimation in India is based on consumption expenditure and not on the income levels.
- Consumption Expenditure is required on the basket of goods and services necessary to satisfy basic human needs known as 'Poverty line Basket (PLB)'
- Price levels for consumption of goods & services in PLB varies from state to state and therefore, official poverty lines are higher in some states than in others.

## Various Committees

- Dadabhai Naoroji (Poverty and Un-British Rule in India) made the earliest estimation of poverty line. The poverty line proposed by him was based on the cost of a subsistence or minimum basic diet.

- **National Planning Committee, 1938**: It was based on a minimum standard of living perspective in which nutritional requirements were implicit.
- **Planning Commission Working Group (1962)**: Poverty line in India was quantified for the 1st time in terms of minimum requirement of individuals but excluded the expenditure on health and education (It was assumed that it will be provided by the state)
- **Dandekar and Rath (1971)** It made the 1st Systematic assessment of poverty in India based on National Sample Survey data.
  - It was the first to establish the consumption levels required to meet a minimum calorie requirement, normally of an average of 2250 Calories per capita per day.
- **Alagh Committee (1979)**: Official poverty counts began for the 1st time in India based on the approach of this task force.
  - This Committee constructed a separate poverty line for rural and urban areas on the basis of nutritional requirement and related consumption expenditure.
  - Caloric Requirement: Rural (2400 calories per day) and Urban (2100 calories per day)

↓

Higher calorie requirement because rural people do more physical work.

| Criteria | Lakdawala Committee | Tendulkar Committee | Rangarajan Committee |
|---|---|---|---|
| Constituted | 1993 | 2004-05 | 2012. |
| Criteria | • Caloric intake based on consumption expenditure<br>• Presumption of provision of health & education by the state only | • Shift from calorie consumption to nutritional outcomes<br>• Incorporation of private expenditure on health and education. | • Consumption basket that includes food components such as calorie, protein & fat intake & essential non-food item groups (Education, Clothing, Health, Housing & Transport. |
| Poverty Line | • Separate Poverty line Basket for rural and Urban India | • Uniform all India Poverty Line Basket across rural and Urban India | • Separate Consumption Basket for rural and Urban India |
| Data Collection Poverty | • Uniform Reference Period<br>• State-specific Poverty lines using CPI-IW in urban areas and CPI-AL in rural areas. | • Mixed Reference Period<br>Daily per-capita expenditure of Rs 27 and Rs 33 in rural & urban areas | • Modified mixed reference period.<br>• Daily per capita expenditure of Rs 32 and Rs 47 in rural and urban areas. |

## Reason for Estimation of Poverty Line

1. Identification of poor population. This helps in better targeting of resources.
2. Allocation of expenditure on various poverty alleviation measures taken by the government.
3. Tracking the performance of Welfare schemes.
4. Helps in fulfilling SDG-1.
5. Fulfilling the constitutional goal of Justice-Economic.

## Parameters in the Poverty Line Estimation

- Poverty line Basket (PLB) → It consists of Goods and Services which needs to be consumed, based on that whatever expenditure has been incurred, that is known as consumption Expenditure.
  - Earlier consists of minimum Subsistence level of diet
    - Now → Multi-dimensional poverty

**Food Components**

1. Calorie requirement
2. Nutrition requirement

**Non-Food Components**

Health, Education, Conveyance, Rent, Transport, Clothing.

## Reduction in Poverty levels over time with respect to Rural and Urban Poverty

- Based on the estimation of Tendulkar committee, there has been a decline in poverty level from 45.3% in 1993-94 to 21.9% in 2011-12.
- Rural poverty witnessed a significant decline in poverty from 50.1% in 1993-94 to 25.7% in 2011-12 while urban poverty declined from 31.8% to 13.7% in the same period.

| Year | Lakdawala | | | Tendulkar | | | Rangarajan | | |
|---|---|---|---|---|---|---|---|---|---|
| | R | U | T | R | U | T | R | U | T |
| 1993-94 | 37.3 | 32.4 | 36.0 | 50.1 | 31.8 | 45.3 | – | – | – |
| 2004-05 | 28.3 | 25.7 | 27.5 | 41.8 | 25.7 | 37.2 | – | – | – |
| 2009-10 | – | – | – | 33.8 | 20.9 | 29.8 | 39.6 | 35.1 | 38.2 |
| 2011-12 | – | – | – | 25.7 | 13.7 | 21.9 | 30.9 | 26.4 | 29.5 |

- As per Global MPI Report 2022, the incidence of poverty fell from 36.6% in 2015-16 to 21.2% in 2019-21 in rural areas and from 9.0% to 5.5% in urban areas
- According to the update by World Bank of Indian poverty using the new poverty line of $2.15 per day, 10% of Indians were poor in 2019, down from 22.5% in 2011. Rural India had more poor than the urban: 11.9% in rural areas and 6.4% in urban areas.
  - Extreme poverty is 12.3% points lower in 2019 than in 2011, with greater poverty reductions in rural areas.

# POVERTY ALLEVIATION MEASURES

## Trickle down Growth Model

- Big Farmers / (Green Revolution)
- Big Industries (Nehru-Mahalanobis Strategy)

↓

Increased GDP / Increased Economic Growth

↓

Employment Generation

↓

Benefits trickle down to lowest strata

↓

Unsuccessful (Benefits did not adequately Trickle Down)

## Directly Targeted Poverty Alleviation

- "Garibi Hatao" Slogan
- Employment Generation programmes

↓

Emphasis upon → Self Employment / Wage Employment

↓

Employment Generation

↓

Increased Income

↓

Poverty Reduction

Eg: Swarn Jayanti Shehri Rojgar Yojana

- Integrated Rural Development Program

## Basic-Needs Approach

- Focus on providing basic needs to the people.

Eg: Integrated Child Development Scheme

- Mid-Day Meal
- PDS
- Sarva Shiksha Abhiyan
- 'Food For Work' program

- People = Passive Beneficiaries
- Government's policies to lift people out of poverty

## Rights-Based Approach

- Similar to Amartya Sen's Capability Approach
- Change towards People's Rights.
- People = Active Participants (Rights / Entitlements of people)
- Government has a natural obligation of Poverty Alleviation

Eg - National Food Security Act.

- Right to Education
- MGNREGA
- PM Jan Dhan Yojana

- Empowering people so that they themselves lift out of poverty

## Change in Poverty Alleviation Measures in the Post-LPG Era

While earlier poverty alleviation measures have resulted in the reduction of poverty levels, there has been faster reduction in poverty in post-LPG era

In the post reform period, poverty declined faster in 2000s than in 1990s.

Also, India lifted as many as 415 million people out of multi-dimensional poverty between 2005-06 and 2019-21.

Poverty declined by 1.36% points per annum after 1991, compared to that of 0.44% points per annum prior to 1991.

- This has been due to various changes in policies adopted in post-LPG Era

☛ Shift from Welfare to Rights-Based Approach:

- MGNREGA generated over 279-crore person-days of employment, benefitting more than 12 crore households since its inception (Ministry of Rural Development)
- The Right to Education (RTE) ensured free and compulsory education for children aged 6-14 years, benefitting over 22 crore children (Ministry of Education)

☛ Emphasis on Skill Development and Entrepreneurship: Government initiated several programs to enhance vocational training and promote self-employment. Eg: Skill India Mission, Start up India, Stand Up India.

☛ Shift towards Inclusive Growth in the post-LPG era as a means to alleviate poverty. Eg: XI and XII FYPs explicitly mentioned about achieving Inclusive Growth

☛ Targeted Programs and Identification of Beneficiaries: Eg: Antyodaya Anna Yojana (AAY) identified the poorest households and provided them with heavily subsidized food grains, benefitting over 2.5 crore families (Ministry of Consumer Affairs)

☛ Focus on Human Development and not just Growth:

- National Health Mission (NHM) improved access to healthcare services, resulting in the decline of Maternal Mortality Rate (MMR) from 301 in 2001-03 to 97 in 2023 (Ministry of Health and Family Welfare)
- The Sarva Shiksha Abhiyan (SSA) achieved significant progress in achieving universal elementary education, with the Gross Enrolment ratio in primary Education reaching 97.4% in 2022 (Ministry of Education)

☛ Financial Inclusion and Social Security: Pradhan Mantri Jan Dhan Yojana (PMJDY) facilitated financial inclusion, with over 43.04 crore bank accounts opened and deposits worth more than ₹1.46 lakh crore (Ministry of Finance)

☛ Asset creation and Employment Generation: PM Awas Yojana aimed to provide affordable housing to all by 2022, with over 1.12 crore houses sanctioned and 77 lakh houses completed (Ministry of Housing and Urban Affairs)

- Climate change and Vulnerability: Climate change impacts, such as extreme weather events, natural disasters, & agricultural challenges, disproportionately affect the poor and vulnerable communities.
- Digital Divide: Poor are not able to reap the benefits of digital technologies.
- Other factors like Jobless growth, high inflation etc.

## NITI Aayog Strategy to Combat Poverty

- Sustained rapid growth that is also employment intensive
- Making anti-poverty programs effective

1. Employment-Intensive Sustained Rapid Growth: First, by creating jobs that pay steadily rising real wages which directly dents poverty and secondly, it leads to growth in government revenues which in turn allow the expansion of social expenditures at faster pace.
   Eg: Emphasis on labour intensive sectors such as Apparel, footwear, food processing, electronic and electrical appliances, other light manufactures, construction and retail trade.
2. Making Anti-poverty Programs more effective such as Public Distribution System (PDS), Midday Meal Scheme, MGNREGA and Housing for All.
   Eg: MGNREGA can be made more effective by allowing it to impart skills.

# FEMINISATION OF POVERTY

About: 'Feminisation of Poverty' term coined by Diana Pearce in 1976 → refers to a phenomenon in which women are disproportionately represented among the world's poor and highlights the trend that women are more likely to experience poverty as compared to men.

- About 19.7% of people living in female-headed households live in poverty compared with 15.9% in male-headed households.
- World Economic Forum's Global Gender Gap Report 2021 India's gender pay gap is around 20-30% as per wage index.
- Agricultural Census 2015-16 → In India women own only about 12.7% of agricultural land.

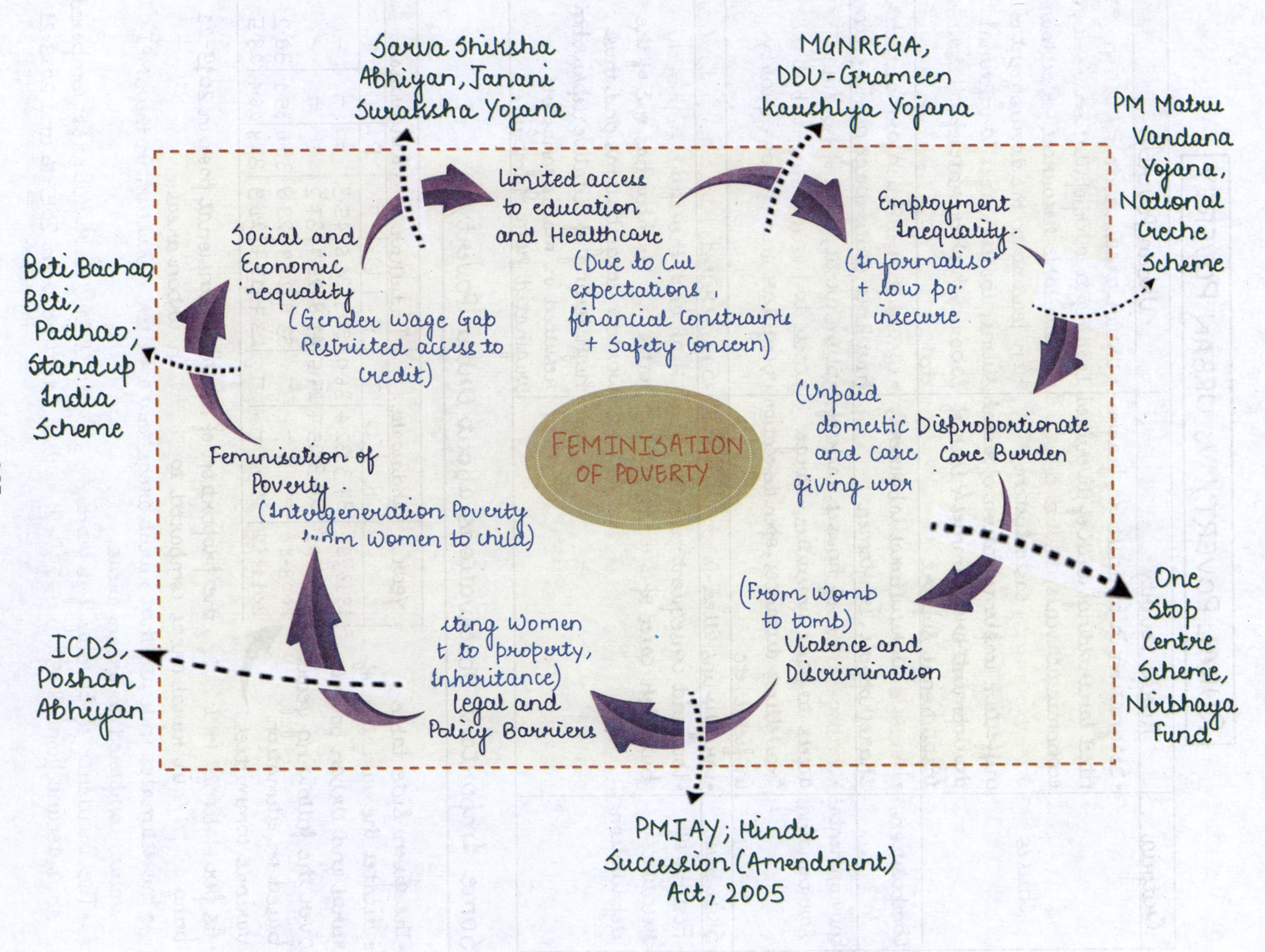
FEMINISATION OF POVERTY
Limited access to education and Healthcare
(Due to Cul expectations, financial constraints + Safety concern)
Sarva Shiksha Abhiyan, Janani Suraksha Yojana
Employment Inequality
(Informaliso + low pa insecure
MGNREGA, DDU-Grameen Kaushlya Yojana
(Unpaid domestic and care giving wor
Disproportionate Care Burden
PM Matru Vandana Yojana, National Creche Scheme
(From Womb to tomb)
Violence and Discrimination
One Stop Centre Scheme, Nirbhaya Fund
iting Women t to property, Inheritance)
Legal and Policy Barriers
PMJAY; Hindu Succession (Amendment) Act, 2005
Feminisation of Poverty
(Intergeneration Poverty from women to child)
ICDS, Poshan Abhiyan
Social and Economic Inequality
(Gender wage Gap Restricted access to credit)
Beti Bachao, Beti Padhao; Standup India Scheme

# RURAL POVERTY vs URBAN POVERTY

| Criteria | Rural Poverty | Urban Poverty |
|---|---|---|
| Causes | • Stagnation in agriculture, fragmented landholdings, lack of diversified economic activities, disguised unemployment, caste system, ineffective implementation of rural development programmes & lack of institutional support. | • Urban areas invite migration leading to overpopulation vis-a-vis the available resources for exploitation leading to the development of slums, lower wages to informal labour, higher rate of inflation etc. |
| Composition | • Landless agricultural labourers, sharecroppers, craftsmen | • Casual labour in informal sector, hawkers, daily wage earners, etc. |
| Environmental Sorroundings | • Shabby nature of houses, lack of access to basic amenities - large travelling distances, open defecation in fields, etc. | • Slum areas, lack of housing, access to basic amenities but is irregular and of poor quality. |
| Skill level | • Largely unskilled - labour intensive | • Semi-skilled; less labour intensive. |
| Feeling of relative deprivation | • Low and consequent lesser crime but high cases of suicides. | • High and therefore higher crime rates. Eg: Mumbai has one of the world's largest slums and thus high feeling of relative deprivation resulted in many gangsters originated from Mumbai. |

## Some Important Observations about Urban Poverty

• The given side table indicates the variation of rural and Urban poverty over the following years based on estimation various committees:

| Year | Lakdawala | | | Tendulkar | | | Rangarajan | | |
|---|---|---|---|---|---|---|---|---|---|
| | R | U | T | R | U | T | R | U | T |
| 1993-94 | 37.3 | 32.4 | 36.0 | 50.1 | 31.8 | 45.3 | – | – | – |
| 2004-05 | 28.3 | 25.7 | 27.5 | 41.8 | 25.7 | 37.2 | – | – | – |
| 2009-10 | – | – | – | 33.8 | 20.9 | 29.8 | 39.6 | 35.1 | 38.2 |
| 2011-12 | – | – | – | 25.7 | 13.7 | 21.9 | 30.9 | 26.4 | 29.5 |

• As per National MPI 2023, the proportion of multi-dimensional poor in 2019-21 being 19.28% in rural areas compared to 5.27% in urban areas.

- The estimates indicate that rural areas saw a faster reduction in their MPI value, compared to urban areas.
- The incidence of poverty fell from 32.59% to 19.28% in rural areas compared to a decline from 8.65% to 5.27% in urban areas between 2015-16 and 2019-21.

- Today one in every six of India's urban households live in slums, a number forecast to rise exponentially over the coming years.
  - Most slum dwellers do not have access to clean water, sanitation and healthcare facilities. They face a constant threat of eviction, removal, confiscation of goods and have virtually no social security cover.
  - Some 54% of urban slums do not have toilets; public facilities are unusable due to lack of maintenance.
- Migration towards urban centres has increased, indicating that economic reforms have not been effective in creating jobs in small and medium towns as well as rural areas.

## Reasons behind the increasing Urbanisation of Poverty

01 Push-Pull Factors: The causes of urban poverty can be linked to the lack of infrastructure in rural areas (push factor), forcing inhabitants of these regions to seek out work in India's mega-cities (pull factor).
- The urban poor is largely the overflow of rural poor who migrate to urban areas in search of alternative employment and livelihood.

02 Lack of Skills to participate in the emerging employment opportunities in different sectors of urban economy.

03 Indebtness: Unemployment or underemployment and the casual nature of work in urban areas lead to indebtedness, that in turn, reinforces poverty.

04 Informalisation of Labour: Jobless growth witnessed after LPG Reforms led to increased informalisation of labour which created irregular income among the urban workers.

05 Increasing Gig Economy: Recent boost to gig economy while generated employment opportunities have also posed challenges for gig workers such as no fixed employment terms, uncertain income according to the whims & fancies of employer and many more. Eg: Blinkit Gig worker protest in 2023 against the reduction in fee per delivery

06 Inflation intensifies the hardship and deprivation of lower income groups.

07 Unequal distribution of income and assets has also led to persistence of poverty in urban India.

# FORMS OF INEQUALITIES IN INDIA

- **Income Inequalities**: Oxfam India's report, "Survival of the Richest: The India Story," Says that between 2012 and 2021, 40% of the wealth created in India has gone to just 1% of the population and only a mere 3% of the wealth has gone to the bottom 50% (Total number of billionairs in India increased from 102 in 2020 to 166 in 2022)
- **Extreme hunger**: India's ranking in Global Hunger Index 2023 declined to 111 out of 123 countries.
- **Financial Exclusion**: Bank Savings are there for 62% upper caste households whereas this is 49% for SC households. Hence, ability to invest in technology is lower for SC households.
- **Educational Inequalities**: The rapid shift to e-learning prompted by the pandemic has resurfaced long standing issues of inequality and digital divide in India that must be addressed by future economic, education and digitalization policies.
- **Gender Inequalities**: India stood at rank 122 out of 191 countries with a score of of 0.490 in the Gender Inequality Index 2021.
  - Female LFPR in India (Based on PLFS 2022-23) stands around 37% also there is a considerable gender wage gap which contribute to gender inequality in country.
- **Caste Inequalities**: Higher poverty levels among SC (42.93%) & ST (42.7%) compared to other groups.
  - There is a significant disparity in graduate percentages among different caste groups, with the general category having the highest (14.54%)
- **Urban poor**: There are large swathes within the informal workforce who would be facing inequalities in health, income and employment.
  - Health-Income-Employment triple insecurity faced by the urban poor has grown exponentially as they live in densely populated urban neighbourhood where diseases spread much faster, generating further income losses & job uncertainities.

## Reasons for increasing Inequality in India

→ **Agricultural Wages**: Stagnation in agricultural wages owing to stagnation yields, crop failures, post harvest damages and climate risks have impacted income level of nearly 50% of the population that draws sustenance from agriculture.

→ **Skewed growth**: A considerable share of economic growth was cornered by the Service Sector that employed nearly a third of the population. On the contrary, agriculture grew at less than 3% in the last few decades.

→ **Regional disparity**: Incomes remain subdued in the relatively backward states of Rajasthan, Bihar, Chhattisgarh etc. which have lagged behind in GSDP growth owing to Infrastructure deficit and governance deficit.

→ Failure of Trickle down Effect : Employment grew merely by 0.5% per annum from 2004-05 to 2011-12 → The period that saw the highest growth of GDP by 8.5% per annum.

→ Informalisation of Economy : As per ILO data, 81% of total employment is informal in nature. The contractual labourers remain outside of the ambit of labour laws and are bereft of social security and fair wages.

→ Capital-led growth : Growing economic inequalities due to over-reliance on capital and finance as the drivers of growth and neglect of labour.

→ Inefficient Re-distribution : With only 6 out of 100 individuals paying taxes (Only 5% Indians pay taxes) and tax to GDP ratio being 11% (Economic Survey), India is not efficient at redistribution of wealth. The income gap between rich and poor also worsens due to prevalent tax evasion, black money.

- Heavy reliance on consumption taxes like GST increases inequality and is regressive in nature because poor people pay a larger share of their incomes.

→ Low investment in Public Health : India's investment in public health are among the lowest in the world and most cities lack any kind of public primary health services

→ State's Withdrawal from the welfare expenditure leaving the domain open to private sector which further exacerbated inequality.

## Measures needed to Contain Inequality

☛ Improving the state of Agriculture by investing in irrigation technologies, preventing fertiliser overuse etc., to ensure remunerative prices for farmers - through MSP reforms, eliminating middle men by promoting platforms like e-Rashtriya Kisan Agri Mandi etc and to promote research to improve farm productivity.

☛ Employment Oriented growth : Promoting labour intensive industries such as leather, & apparel as suggested by NITI Aayog, can be instrumental in raising incomes of bottom 50%

☛ Tax Efficiency : India needs to improve tax to GDP ratio and bring it on par with emerging economies (23%). This can be done by lowering income tax evasion and generation of black money, simplifying tax procedures to improve compliance etc.

☛ State to be dominant provider of merit goods such as health, nutrition, Education.

- Public sector spending in these sectors need to increase to around 6% of GDP which currently stands at around 2%.
- Increased social spending has been shown to reduce inequality by 20% across OECD countries.

☛ Preventing deprivation : Enforcing laws against eviction & exploitation such as LARR, Forest Rights Act can also avoid impoverishment of people while also ensuring income security through land and forest resources

☛ Women Empowerment : Higher wages and stronger labour rights - especially for women workers who tend to work in the lowest paid and most insecure jobs - are key to reducing inequality.

## PYQs Corner

*(Write the Answer and Get Free Evaluation)*

1. COVID-19 pandemic accelerated class inequalities and poverty in India. Comment. **(2020)**
2. "The incidence and intensity of poverty are more important in determining poverty based on income alone". In this context analyse the latest United Nations Multidimensional Poverty Index Report. **(2020)**
3. 'Despite implementation of various programmes for eradication of poverty by the government in India, poverty is still existing.' Explain by giving reasons. **(2018)**
4. 'Poverty Alleviation Programmes in India remain mere show pieces until and unless they are backed by political will'. Discuss with reference to the performance of the major poverty alleviation programmes in India. **(2018)**
5. "An essential condition to eradicate poverty is to liberate the poor from deprivation." Substantiate this statement with suitable examples. **(2016)**

CHAPTER 08

# Welfare Schemes for the Vulnerable Sections

- Vulnerability is defined as "proneness to harm or damage originating from external forces".
- Vulnerable sections are that segment of population who are more likely to suffer as a result of flawed or unfair systems, whether they be social, political, cultural, economic, physical, family-oriented.
- Empowering vulnerable sections is key to unlocking India's full potential for an inclusive society.

Different Vulnerable Groups in India
- Scheduled Caste (Discussed in Chapter 1)
- Scheduled Tribes (Discussed in Chapter 1).
- Child
- Elders
- Transgenders
- Disables.

WELFARE SCHEMES

## Rationale Behind Welfare Schemes For Vulnerable Section.

### Constitutional Basis

- Preamble- Seeks to ensure "Justice, social, economic and political" and Equality of status and of opportunity"
- Fundamental Rights:
  - Article 14: ensures Right to Equality
  - Article 15: Allows affirmative action for disadvantaged groups.
  - Article 21: Right to life and liberty → a right to dignified living.

- Directive Principles of State Policy (DPSPs):
  - Article 38 - State to strive to promote the welfare of the people by securing a social order in which justice, social, economic and political, shall inform all the institutions of national life.
  - Article 39(a) - Right to free legal aid - ensures vulnerable groups have access to justice.
  - Article 41 - Right to work, education and public assistance in cases of unemployment old age, sickness and disablement.
  - Article 46 - Promotion of educational and economic interests of SCs, STs and other weaker sections.

## Humanitarian Grounds

- Reducing Suffering by providing basic necessities like food, shelter, and healthcare to those who cannot afford them.
- Promoting Dignity - Ensuring vulnerable groups have access to education and opportunities for a better life
- Protecting Vulnerable - Providing support to children, the elderly, people with disabilities, and those facing discrimination.

| Socio-Economic Necessity | Nation Building |
|---|---|
| → Reduced Inequality - Through education, healthcare and skill training → creation of an equitable and inclusive society.<br>→ Improved Social Mobility of vulnerable groups allows them to contribute to the economy.<br>→ Reduced Crime - Poverty + lack of opportunity → crime. Welfare programs can help break this cycle by providing alternatives.<br>→ Public Health - Addressing issues like malnutrition and lack of access to healthcare can benefit society as a whole. | → Creating a Stable Society - By reducing poverty and inequality, these programs can promote social cohesion and reduce unrest.<br>→ Developing Human Capital - Investing in education and healthcare creates a more productive and skilled workforce.<br>→ Promoting Social Harmony - When everyone has a chance to succeed, it fosters a sense of inclusion and national pride.<br>→ Fulfilling National Aspirations - By creating a just and equitable society welfare schemes contribute to the vision of a developed India. |

# LIMITATION OF WELFARE SCHEMES

## TARGETING ISSUES

- **Inaccurate Identification-** As per Planning Commission estimates → 36% of PDS food grains do not reach intended beneficiaries.
- **Data Reliability-** Inaccurate or outdated data on demographics and income levels lead to inefficiences in targeting.
  - As per NSSO → 10% of households who were eligible for BPL cards did not have them, and about 12% of those who had BPL cards were ineligible.
- **Inclusion Errors** where non-eligible individuals benefits due to corrupt practices or errors in the identification process.
  - CAG reported that in Pradhan Mantri Fasal Bima Yojana → significant number of non-eligible farmers received insurance claims due to incorrect data.

## IMPLEMENTATION CHALLENGES

- **Corruption and leakages-** Corruption at various levels of administration leads to significant leakages of funds meant for welfare schemes.
  - CAG reported → substantial leakages, ghost beneficiaries and misappropriation of funds in MGNREGA.
- **Bureaucratic Inefficiencies-** Delays and inefficiencies in the bureaucratic processes hinder the timely delivery of benefits.
  - World Bank highlighted bureaucratic delays in the implementation of the Swachh Bharat Mission- slower than expected increase in number of functional toilets.
- **Lack of Accountability** and transparency in the implementation processes, making it difficult to track and rectify issues.
  - Mid-Day Meal Scheme has faced multiple cases of food contamination and irregularities in meal distribution → no one held accountable.
- **Infrastructure Deficiencies, especially** in rural areas, hampers effective implementation.
  - As per NITI Aayog report → 44% of government schools lack proper sanitation facilities → hinders realisation of actual vision of Sarva Shiksha Abhiyan.
- **Coordination Problems** among different government departments and agencies can lead to duplication of efforts and resources, and gaps in service delivery.
  - Pradhan Mantri Gram Sadak Yojana is the prime victim of it.

## BENEFICIARY PARTICIPATION.

- **Lack of Awareness**- Beneficiaries are not aware of schemes or how to access them due to poor outreach and communication efforts.
  - According to Ministry of Rural Development, nearly 30% of eligible rural households were unaware of Pradhan Mantri Awas Yojana - Gramin.
- **Complex Procedures**- Complex application and verification processes deter participation, especially among the uneducated and rural populations.
- **Social and Cultural Barriers**- such as gender discrimination, can limit the participation of certain groups.
- **Inadequate feedback and grievance redressal** mechanisms prevent beneficiaries from voicing their concerns and issues.
  - Absence of effective grievance redressal systems in the National Social Assistance Programme (NSAP) has led to delays and denials of old-age pensions.

## SCHEME DESIGN ISSUES.

- **One-Size-Fits-All Approaches** do not consider diverse needs of different regions, communities, and individuals, leading to ineffectiveness in addressing specific local challenges.
- **Rigid and Inflexible Structures** that do not adapt to changing needs and circumstances can limit their impact.
- **Overlapping Schemes**- can lead to confusion among beneficiaries and inefficient use of resources.
  - Ex- Ayushman Bharat overlaps with state-level health initiatives → non-judicious use of resources.
- **Lack of Monitoring and Evaluation** mechanisms to assess the impact and efficiency of schemes and make necessary adjustments.
  - NITI Aayog highlights → Integrated Child Development Services lacks a robust monitoring system → poor quality of services delivery.

## FINANCIAL AND RESOURCE CONSTRAINTS

- **Digital Infrastructure Challenges**- Direct Benefit Transfers (DBTs) can face last-mile delivery issues due to inadequate digital infrastructure in rural areas.
- **Insufficient Funding** limits schemes reach and effectiveness
  - India's expenditure on Health is 2.1% of GDP → limiting effectiveness of Health schemes.
- **Delayed Disbursement** from central government to state governments → and then to beneficiaries disrupt smooth functioning of schemes.

- **Resource Allocation** - Misallocation or inefficient use of resources can lead to wastage and reduced effectiveness of welfare schemes.
- **Capacity Constraints** - Limited capacity of implementing agencies in terms of human resources, skills and infrastructure hampers effective delivery.
  - Ex- FCI has struggled with inadequate storage facilities, leading to wastage of food grains meant for distribution under PDS.

## Overcoming limitations of Welfare Schemes : A decisive Step Towards Social Justice

### GENDER EQUALITY

is first a matter of social justice allowing equal access to rights, resources and opportunities.

Gender equality is a condition of development, and a matter of sustainable peace and security

### HUMAN RIGHTS

Human rights and social justice are two sides of same coin. They can't exist apart from each other. For a society to be just, it must ensure the protection of everyone's civil, political, economic, cultural and social rights.

### EQUITY

To achieve social justice and ensure equal opportunities for success, it is important to provide equitable resources that focus on the specific needs of communities and the individuals within them.

### PROMOTION OF PEACE

Peace is the fruit of justice and is dependent upon the respect and cooperation between peoples and nations.

Social workers promote peace and the general welfare of society from local to global levels.

### PARTICIPATION

Social justice requires that individuals have the opportunity and platform to participate in making the policies that affect their well-being

## Policy and Institutional Reforms

- Streamlined Policy Framework to reduce overlapping and redundant schemes like streamlining of Pradhan Mantri Awas Yojana with state housing schemes.
- Decentralized Decision-Making empower local governments like Rashtriya Krishi Vikas Yojana (RKVY) → to tailor schemes in accordance to regional needs and conditions → enhancing responsiveness and effectiveness.
- Regular Review and Adaptation of policies on ground realities and feedback from beneficiaries.
  Ex: Atal Pension Yojana (APY) undergoes regular reviews to adapt in accordance with changing demographic needs.
- Improved Data Management → Regular update in Socio-Economic Caste Census data → to create accurate beneficiary lists for schemes like PMAY and Ujjwala Yojana, improving targeting and reducing errors.

## Governance Reforms

- Enhanced Transparency such as public dashboards displaying real time data on scheme implementation, fund implementation, fund allocation and beneficiary details.
- Strengthened Accountability:
  - Introduce strict accountability norms for officials at all levels, with clear consequences for corruption and inefficiencies.
- Effective Grievance Redressal like Centralized Public Grievance Redress and Monitoring System (CPGRAMs) → allows citizens to lodge complaints about welfare schemes and track their resolution online.
- Third-Party Audits – Conduct regular third-party audits and social audits to ensure judicious use of funds and effective implementation of schemes.

## People's Participation

- Increased Awareness Campaigns using mass media, social media, and local networks to educate people about available schemes and how to access them.
  - Ex- Beti Bachao Beti Padhao and Swachh Bharat Abhiyan
- Simplified Application and Verification processes to make them user-friendly particularly for illiterate and semi-literate populations.
- Inclusive Participation from marginalized groups, such as women, tribal communities, differently-abled individuals, in planning and implementation.

## Technological Intervention

- Digital Integration - like Jan Dhan- Aadhar- Mobile trinity uses digital platforms to link bank accounts, Aadhaar numbers, and mobile numbers → facilitating DBT → reducing leakages.
- Mobile Applications like UMANG app → to provide information about schemes, enable applications, and track status of benefits, leveraging widespread use of smartphones.
- Biometric Verification to ensure accurate identification of beneficiaries and prevent fraud.
- Use of Blockchain Technology to enhance transparency and security of transactions and records in welfare schemes.
  Ex: Andhra Pradesh used blockchain technology for a trial period in highway transport and registrations department.

# DISABILITY

According to The Rights of Persons with Disabilities Act, 2016, "Person with disability" means a person with long term physical, mental, intellectual or sensory impairment which, in interaction with barriers, hinders his full and effective participation in society equally with others. ("Person with benchmark disability" means a person with not less than forty per cent of a specified disability.)

## Disability and India

- 2·68 Cr persons (2·21% of total population) are 'disabled'.
- 55% of disabled are illiterate.
- 44% of the disabled persons are women.
- 69% of the disabled persons live in rural areas.
- Only 36% are workers.
- Highest in the age group 10-19 years (46·2 lakh people)

## Provisions for Persons with Disabilities (PWDs) in India.

| Constitutional Safeguards | • Preamble- It guarantees social justice, equality of status, and opportunity for all, including PwDs,<br>• Fundamental Rights - Ensures their dignity as individuals. FR are available to all.<br>• Directive Principles-<br>∘ Article 41- State to provide PwDs with right to work, education, and public assistance during unemployment old age, sickness, and disability. |
|---|---|

- Article 46- State to promote education and economic well-being of weaker sections, protecting them from social injustice and exploitation.
- Seventh Schedule- Relief of Disabled is a State Subject (Entry 9 in List II)
- 11 & 12 Schedule- Welfare of the Disabled and mentally retarded.

**Legislative Framework**

- Rehabilitation Council of India (RCI) Act, 1992: Established RCI to regulate and monitor disability services, standardize syllabi, and maintain a register of qualified professionals.
- National Trust for the Welfare of Persons with Autism, Cerebral Palsy, Mental Retardation and Multiple Disabilities Act, 1999: Established a national body to provide comprehensive care and promote independent living for PwDs with specific disabilities.
- Rights of Persons with Disabilities (RPwD) Act, 2016: Disability is defined as an evolving and dynamic concept.
  - Number of recognized disabilities has increased from 7 to 21.
  - Education- Every child with a benchmark disability will receive free education from age 6 to 18.
  - Reservation- in education and government jobs has increased from 3% to 4%.
  - Infrastructure- Mandatory time limits for making ex' infrastructure.
  - Fund- National a e Funds will be created to ide financial support to persons with disabilities.
  - Special Courts will be designated in each district to handle cases concerning the violation of rights of persons with disabilities (PwDs).

**Types of Disabilities have been increased from existing 7 to 21**

| | |
|---|---|
| Blindness | Muscular Dystrophy |
| Low-vision | Acid Attack victim |
| Leprosy Cured persons | Parkinson's disease |
| Locomotor Disability | Multiple Sclerosis |
| Dwarfism | Thalassemia |
| Intellectual Disability | Hemophilia |
| Mental Illness | Sickle Cell disease |
| Cerebral Palsy | Autism Spectrum Disorder |
| Specific Learning Disabilities | Chronic Neurological conditions |
| Speech and Language disability | Multiple Disabilities including deaf blindness |
| Hearing Impairment (deaf and hard of hearing) | |

## Issues Faced by Persons with Disabilities In India

| Issues | Description |
|---|---|
| Accessibility | • Buildings, transportation systems, and access to services often lack necessary infrastructure to accomodate people with disabilities |

| | |
|---|---|
| Healthcare | • Affordable issues- struggle to afford proper healthcare, assistive devices, and rehabilitation services.<br>• Limited Rural Access- Healthcare system lacks proactive measures to address disability.<br>• Inadequate Training- Healthcare facilities and rehabilitation centres often lack staff trained to address the specific needs of people with disabilities. |
| Education | • Non-Inclusive System- The education system struggles to effectively integrate children with mild to moderate disabilities into mainstream schools.<br>• Resource Scarcity- Shortages of special schools, accessible facilities, trained teachers, and specialized educational materials create further barriers.<br>• Unfulfilled Reservations- Reservation quotas for students with disabilities in higher education are often not met. |
| Employment | • Low Employment Rates- 36% of disabled are unemployed.<br>• Private Sector Disparity- They employ far fewer people with disabilities than public sector<br>• Only five out of NIFTY 50 companies have more than 1% people with disabilities on their rolls.<br>• Public sector companies: Reserve 4% of all jobs for disabled people (RPD Act, 2016) |
| Discrimination and Social Exclusion | • Negative Attitudes- Negative societal and familial attitudes can hinder social participation and workforce inclusion for people with disabilities.<br>• Stigma and Exclusion- People with disabilities, particularly those with mental illness or intellectual disabilities, face significant social stigma and exclusion. |
| Data and Statistics | • Difficult in Defining Disability- The lack of a clear definition for disability makes data collection challenging.<br>Data Coverage Gaps- Data collection efforts often have limited scope, failing to capture the full picture of disability prevalence.<br>• Under-reporting- The stigma associated with disabiliby can lead to under-reporting in data collection efforts. |
| Weak Enforcement | • Act provides for reservation in government jobs for persons with disabilities but this target is often not met. |

| Limitation of the Rights of Persons with disability Act (RPWD Act, 2016: | • Uneven Implementation- Many states haven't adopted necessary rules, hindering consistent application.<br>• Accessibility Gaps- The Act mandates accessible infrastructure and services, but public spaces, transportation, and communication technology often lack accessibility, creating a disconnect between policy and reality.<br>• Weak Penalties- The Act's penalties for violations might not be strong enough. The low maximum fine (₹10,000) may not deter entities from discriminatory practices. |
|---|---|

## POVERTY AND DISABILITY

1. High Poverty Rates Among Disabled Individuals: The World Bank estimates that globally, 20% of the world's poorest have some kind of disability.
   - Inequality in Poverty: Disabled people are six percentage points more likely to be in poverty than non-disabled people (26% vs. 20%).

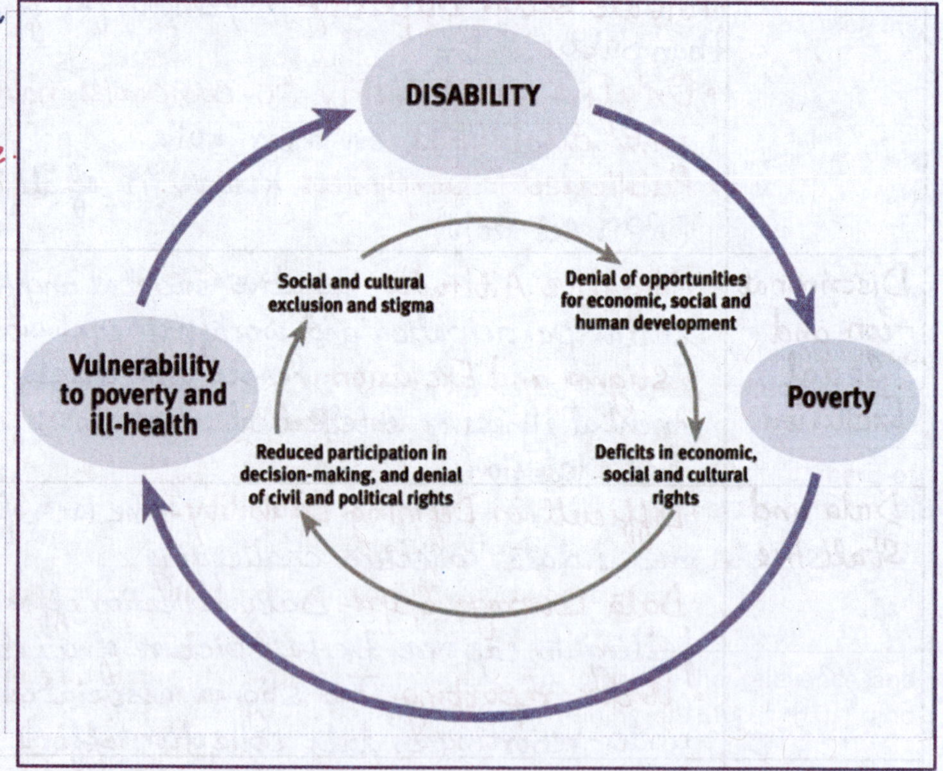


2. Household Impact: Research also suggests that disability can lead to a broader form of poverty beyond just income.
   Ex- Disability can lead to increased costs for healthcare, assistive technology and potential loss of income if the disabled person cannot work.
3. Benefits and Poverty: Benefits do not fully protect disabled people against poverty.
4. International Perspective: Globally, people with disabilities have a labour force participation rate of just over 50% compared to more than 80% for people without disabilities.

# Indian Government Initiatives for Persons with Disabilities (PwDs)

## Government Initiatives

- Accessible India Campaign (Sugamya Bharat Abhiyan): Aims to create a barrier-free environment for PwDs in built environments, transportation, and ICT.
- Deendayal Disabled Rehabilitation Scheme (DDRS): Provides financial aid to NGO's for running projects like special schools, rehabilitation programs etc.
- Assistance to Disabled Persons for Purchase (ADIP)- For acquiring assistive devices to improve their independence and economic potential.
- Scholarships for Higher Education (RGMF Scheme) + Indian Sign language Research and Training Centre (Promotes the use of sign language and trains professionals).

## Legislative and Policy Framework

- Right to Education (RTE Act): Guarantees free education for PwD children upto 18 yrs.
- Supreme Court Ruling on Reservations (2020): Extends reservation rights to promotions for PwDs in government jobs.
- National Education Policy (NEP 2020): Promotes inclusive education with accessibility for all children with disabilities.
- National Fund for PwDs- Supports various programs and initiatives for PwDs.
- Unique ID for PwDs Project: Provides PwDs with a special identification card.
- CCPD recently directed PayTM (digital payments application) to make it mobile applications accessible for Persons with disabilities. The PayTM application ultimately became more inaccessible.

## Global

- Signatory to Biwako Millennium Framework working towards an inclusive, barrier-free and rights based society.
- Incheon Strategy to "Make the Right Real" for Persons with Disabilities in Asia and the Pacific.
- Ratified United Nations Convention on the Rights of Persons with Disabilities (UNCRPD), 2006.
- UN Principles for People with Disabilities:
  - PwD shall not be denied access to justice + right to free or affordable legal assistance.
  - Facilities and services must be universally accessible without discrimination
  - Appropriate procedural accomodations.
  - Right to report concerning human rights violations and crimes.
  - Sensitisation of all stakeholders involved.

## Reasons for Limited Impact of Disability Initiatives in India

- **Social Stigma** - Negative attitudes and societal biases towards Persons with Disabilities (PwDs) hinder their inclusion and access to opportunities.
  - These biases perpetuate exclusion and limit the effectiveness of initiatives aimed at empowering PwDs.
- **Data Gaps**: failing to accurately estimate the current population of Persons with Disabilities (PwDs) in the country. (Parliamentary Standing Committee).
- **Low Policy Priority** - Disabilities are often not given the priority in government policies.
  - Criticism over dropping of the disability-related questions from the National Family Health Survey (NFHS-6).
- **Implementation Challenges** - measure of issuing Unique Disability ID (UDID) cards is not enough as the department has issued 94.09 lakh UDID cards so far.
- **Inadequate Funding** for meeting the needs of the large disabled population.
- **Corruption and mis-management** of funds allocated for schemes lead to poor implementation.

## Futuristic Measures

- **Strengthen Preventive Measures** - Implement robust preventive health programs with mandatory newborn screening (like Kerela's CNS program) to identify and address potential disabilities early.
- **Promote Community-Based Rehabilitation - (CBR)** - Integrate CBR programs to empower PwDs by maximizing their abilities, ensuring access to essential services, and facilitating community inclusion.
- **Increase Public Awareness and Understanding** - Launch social campaigns utilizing media (like the positive portrayals in "Taare Zameen Par" and Barfi") to challenge stigma and promote disability rights.
- **Foster Inclusive Education** - Move away from labeling schools as "special needs" to promote inclusivity. Develop a smooth transition plan to integrate students from special schools into mainstream education.
- **Strengthen Central-State Collaboration** - Provide fiscal decentralization to state governments to improve health care infrastructure and prenatal care, particularly in rural areas. This will reduce preventable disabilities.
- **The Inclusion of persons with disabilities** - into the economy can help boost global GDP between 3% to 7% (International Labour Organization (ILO))

# CHILD

- According to the Convention on the Rights of the Child (UNICEF), a child is defined as a person male or female who is below 18 years of age.
- Child and Adolescent Labour (prohibition and regulation) Act 1986 → defines the child as a person who has not completed the age of 14 years.
- Protection of Children from Sexual Offences (POCSO) Act, 2012 defines a child as someone below the age of eighteen.
  - It also defines a juvenile as a person who has not yet reached the age of eighteen years.
- According to the World Health Organisation (WHO), an adolescent is defined as any person between the ages of 10 and 19 years.
- According to the Juvenile Justice (Care and Protection of Children) Act, 2015 → a "juvenile" or "child" is a person who has not completed 18 years of age.

## Constitutional Provisions Related to Child

- Article 14: Equality before law and equal protection of laws for all children, regardless of caste, religion, or other factors.
- Article 15(3): Allows the state to take affirmative action for the benefit of children.
- Article 21- Protects children's right to life and liberty, including freedom from torture or cruel, inhuman or degrading treatment.
- Article 21A- State shall provide free and compulsory education to all children of the age of six to fourteen years.
- Article 24: Prohibits employing children below 14 years old in factories mines, or hazardous occupations.
- Article 39- Directs the state to ensure children have opportunities for healthy development, protection from exploitation and freedom from material abandonment.
- Article 38- State strives to promote a social order that secures the welfare of the people, including children.
- Article 39(f)- Specifically emphasises children's right to healthy development protection from exploitation, and freedom from material abandonment.
- Article 45- States the state's endeavour to provide free and compulsory education for all children until they complete the age of fourteen.
- Article 243G- Empowers Panchayats (local. village governments) to take care of children's welfare within their jurisdiction.

## Important Facts

- Number of Children (Census 2011): 472 million.
- Child Abuse - According to MoWCD study in 2007 → 53.22% children reported having faced one or more forms of sexual abuse.
- Malnutrition - According to NFHS 5, 2019-2021 →
  - Stunting stands at 35.5% Wasting stands at 19.3% Underweight accounts for 32.1%.
- Poor learning outcomes: Only 42.5% of children in grade three can read a grade one text.
- Child Marriages - According to International Centre for Research on Women → prevalence of girl child marriages in India has declined from 49% in 1993 to 22% in 2021.
- Drop-out rate of students: The all-India average dropout rate of primary students is 4.13% while it is 17.06% in secondary levels (Educational Statistics at a Glance, 2018).
- Cyber bullying - As per 2019 UNICEF U-Report poll, one in three children in India reported that they experienced cyberbullying.
- Child Pornography - At least 25000 images of child sexual abuse are uploaded every day from India (U.S. National Centre for Missing & Exploited children).
- Child labour - Census 2011 reported 10.1 million working children in the age group of 5-14 years, out of whom 8.1 million are in rural areas mainly engaged as cultivators (26%) and agricultural labourers (32.9%).
  - According to ILO, 2016 → 12.9 million child labourers exist in India.

## Key Child Issues

Key child Issues

- Child Labour
- Child Marriage
- Malnutrition
- Child Abuse
- Child Mortality
- Juvenile Delinquency

### Child Labour

- Child labour refers to the employment of children in any work that deprives them of their childhood, interferes with their ability to attend regular school ie mentally, physically, socially dangerous and harmful.
- Census data shows a 2.6 million decrease in child labour, with a larger decline in rural areas than in urban areas.
  - SDG Target 8.7 → end child labour in all forms by 2025.

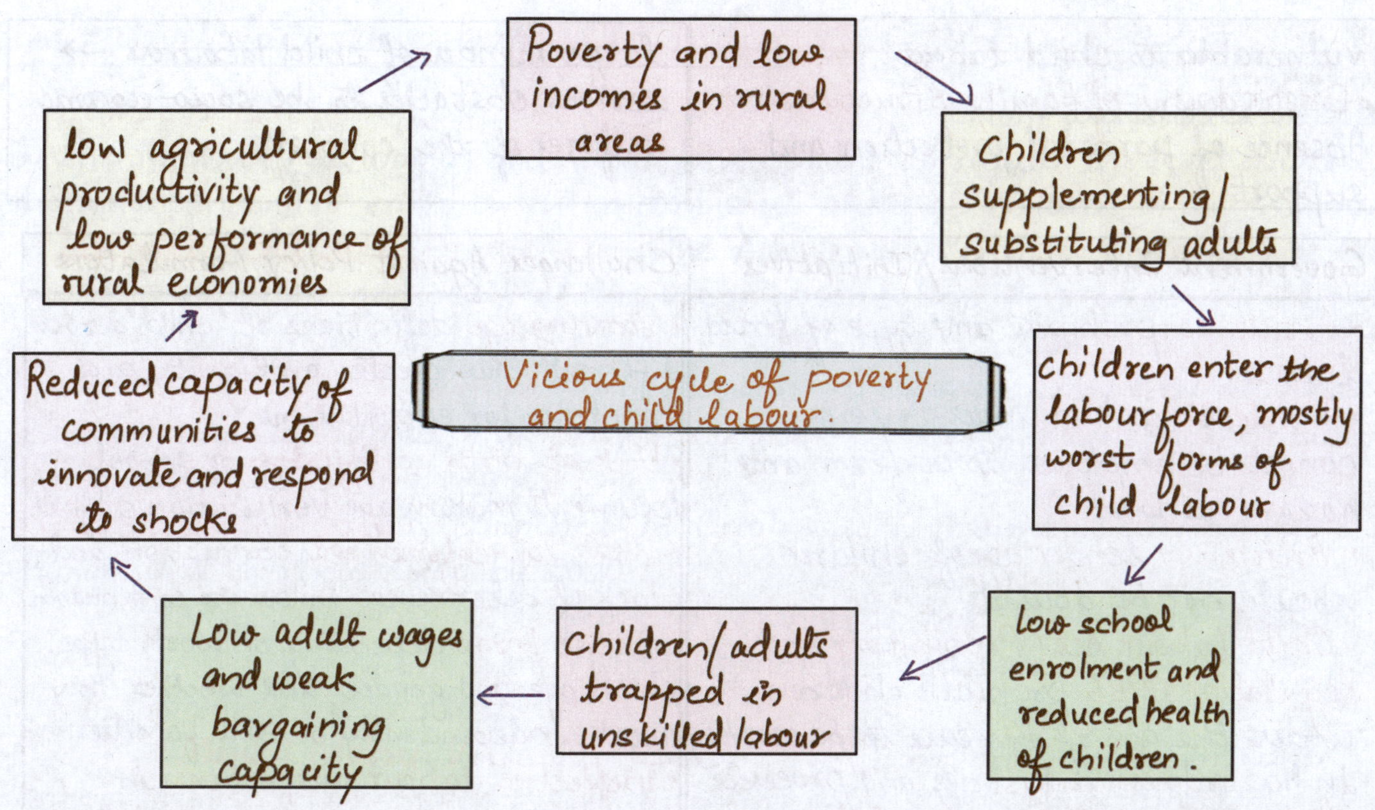


## Factors leading to Child labour

- **Poverty** is the biggest driver of child labour in India
- **Lack of Access to Quality Education** → Children perceived as an economic asset rather than students
- **Demand for Cheap Labour** - creates a market for child workers, like agriculture small-scale manufacturing, and informal service sectors.
- **Weak Enforcement of Child labor laws** + lack of resources for proper inspection make it difficult to crack down on offenders.
- **Normalization of Child labour** as a way to teach children responsibility or skills
- **Migration and Displacement** - towards urban slums → children are more

## Impact of Child Labour

- **Physical health** - Exposure to hazardous work environments → increased risk of accidents → stunted growth, injuries and even death.
- **Mental and Emotional Health** - The psychological trauma, low self esteem and potential for abuse take a heavy toll, causing anxiety, depression and hindering emotional well-being.
- **Social Development** - limited social interaction + perpetuation of poverty cycles + social stigma isolate children and hinder their development.
- **Education** - Forced to work → childrens lose access and acquire skills → limiting their future prospects.
- **National Impact** - Existence of a

| | |
|---|---|
| vulnerable to child labour.<br>• Breakdowns of Family Structures → Absence of parental protection and support. | large number of child labourers → serious obstacles to the socio-economic welfare of the country. |

| Government Interventions/ Initiatives | Challenges Against Policy Formulators |
|---|---|
| • Article 23- prohibits any type of forced labour.<br>• Article 24- a child under 14 years cannot be employed to perform any hazardous work<br>• Article 39- tender age of children should not be abused.<br>• Child Labour Act (Prohibition and Regulation) 1986 prohibits children under the age of 14 years to be working in hazardous industries and processes.<br>• Ratification to International Labour Organization Conventions- Indian government have demonstrated its commitment towards elimination of child labour. | • Varying age definitions of "child" across different laws creates ambiguity and loopholes for exploitations.<br>• Lack of birth certificates- or school documents making age verification difficult.<br>• Weak law enforcement corruption and lack of deterrence → allow its continuation.<br>• Diverse Forms depending on work type, child's age and gender, and whether they work independently or with families.<br>• Ineffective labour inspections in informal economy.<br>• Around 71% of working children are concentrated in the agriculture sector |

## Child Marriage

» Special Marriage Act, 1954 and Prohibition of Child Marriage Act, 2006 sets the minimum age for marriage at 18 years for women 21 years for men.

| Status: | Government Interventions/ Initiatives |
|---|---|
| » As per UNICEF estimates → every year at least 1.5 million girls under 18 get married in India.<br>» Child marriage is in rural areas (48%) is more than urban areas (29%)<br>» As per NFHS 5 → 23.3% of women and 17.7% of men surveyed in India were married before the legal age.<br>» 39% of child marriages in India take place among Adivasis and Dalits. | » Hindu Marriage Act (1956)- A young woman can have marriage declared void if it happened before she turned 15 + challenged it in court before reaching 18.<br>» Prohibition of Child Marriage Act, 2006: defines a child to mean a male below 21 years and female below 18 years.<br>» It attracts punishments of rigorous imprisonment for two years and/ or fine of Rs 1 lakh. |

| Factor leading to Child Marriage | Impact of Child Marriage |
|---|---|
| » Educational Disparity - As per NFHS4 → 45% of women with no education and 40% with primary education married before the age of 18.<br>» Poverty - Over 30% of women in two poorest wealth groups are married by 18, compared to just 8% in the wealthiest group.<br>» Vulnerability to Trafficking - Poverty → families tempted to sell their daughters into marriage or prostitution.<br>» Geographical Disparity - Child marriage is more prevalent in rural areas compared to urban centers | » Poor state of health and wellbeing - because of early pregnancy and childbirth.<br>» Disruption in Education - limits future opportunities and earning potential → perpetuating a cycle of poverty.<br>» Hinders women empowerment → women became dependent on their husbands.<br>» It restricts a girl's social interaction and limits her agency → deteriorates her personal growth.<br>» National Development - Child marriages cost economics at least 1.7% of their GDP. |

## Way Forward

» Education as a Shield to empower the child → fosters a shift in community attitudes towards their potential.

» Strengthening Child Protection → through essential healthcare services + counselling

» Gender Sensitive Informed and Responsive System → through gender sensitivity programs for police, NGOs and government officials.

» Effective law enforcement, including hotlines like Odisha's Child Marriage.

» Community Engagement - Working with community leaders, promoting public pledges, and utilizing traditional media + Social Media + civil Society organizations.

» Integrating programs across different sectors, like education and social welfare strengthens their impact.

- Government initiatives like "Beti Bachao Beti Padhao" and Sukanya Samriddhi Yojana" are positive steps.

» Incentivizing Change through conditional cash transfer schemes like Dhanalakshmi, SABLA to discourage child marriage.

## Malnutrition.

➤ Global Hunger Index (GHI) 2023 ranks India 111 out of 125 countries for childwasting

➤ According to statista, prevalence of undernourishment in India decreased from 21.6% between 2004 and 2006 to 16.5% between 2020 and 2022.

➤ As per NFHS 5, 2019-2021:

- Stunting stands at 35.5%, Wasting stands at 19.3%, Underweight accounts for 32.1%.

| Causes of Malnutrition | Government intervention |
| --- | --- |
| » Poor Mother health:<br>• As per NFHS 5, 57% women aged 15-49 were anaemic.<br>• 10% of women have a low body mass index.<br>• 41.3% of women are obese in India.<br>» Patriarchy and Social Inequality: Girl children are more likely to be malnourished than boys.<br>• Low-caste children are more susceptible to malnutrition than upper-caste children.<br>» Lack of Diversified food- Limited food in take (less than 3 food items) significantly increases the risk of stunting.<br>» Lack of Nutritional Security- Dietary pattern of Indian household, heavily relies on Cereals → led to development of nutritional micronutrient deficiency persistence of malnutrition with obesity<br>» Poverty- leads to malnutrition by limiting access to diverse, nutritious foods and healthcare.<br>» Corruption system- ICDS and National Health Mission → plagued by inefficiency and corruption → intended beneficiaries were still deprived. | » Pradhan Mantri Matru Vandana Yojana → Rs 6000 is transferred directly to the bank accounts of pregnant women for availing better facilities for their delivery.<br>» POSHAN Abhiyaan- aims to reduce stunting, under-nutrition, anaemia and low birth weight babies.<br>» National Food Security Act (NFSA) 2013 → aims to ensure food and nutrition security for the most vulnerable through its associated schemes and programmes, making access to food a legal right.<br>» Mid-day Meal (MDM) scheme aims to improve nutritional levels among school children<br>» Integrated Child Development Services (ICDS)- with its network of 1.4 million Anganwadi Centres, reaching almost 100 millions beneficiaries who include pregnant and nursery mothers and children up to 6 years.<br>» NITI Aayog has worked on a National Nutrition Strategy (NNS), isolated the 100 most backward districts for stunting and prioritized those for interventions.<br>• NNS has set ambitious targets for 2022 and the Poshan Abhiyaan has also specified three-year targets reduce stunting, under nutrition and low birth weight by 2% each year & to reduce anaemia by 3% each year |

## Impact of Malnutrition

- Stunted Growth & Development hinders physical growth and cognitive development in children
- Perpetuation of Poverty: Malnutrition can trap families in a cycle of poverty, as it reduces their ability to earn a living and care for themselves
- Higher Mortality Rates among children.
- Reduced Productivity because of lower energy levels and difficulty in learning → loss of human resource.
- Weakened Immune System makes children more susceptible to infections and illnesses.
- Increased Risk of Chronic Diseases like diabetes and heart diseases later in life.

## Way Forward

- Improved maternal health and nutrition through better access to prenatal care, nutritious food and education.
- Address social inequalities through girl's education, women's empowerment programs, and ensuring equal access to resources for all children.
- Improve sanitation and access to clean water to prevent diseases that hinder nutrient absorption.
- Promote diverse and nutritious diets through education, agricultural practices that that encourage a wider range of crops, and food fortification programs.
- Strengthen food security by improving food distribution systems, reducing food waste, and addressing poverty.
- Strengthen existing programs like ICDS and the National Health Mission to ensure wider reach, efficient delivery, and reduced corruption.
- Improve healthcare access for children including vaccinations, treatment for common illnesses, and early detection of malnutrition.
- Develop region-specific plans that address local availability, cultural practices, and resource limitations.

## Child Abuse

» About Child Abuse is defined as "injury, sexual abuse, sexual exploitation, negligent treatment or maltreatment of a child".

- According to WHO → Child abuse can be in form of physical, mental, emotional, psychological or in the form of neglect or exploitation.

» Status

- As per NCRB: In 2022, India witnessed a staggering 8.7% increase in child abuse cases.

- According to Child Rights and You (CRY)
  - Kidnapping and abduction constitute 46% of crimes against children.
  - Sexual offences against children has surged by 96% from 2016 to 2022.
- As per NCPCR, nearly 55% of children in India experienced some kind of abuse

## Constitutional Provision to Safeguard Children from Abuse

» Article 14: Ensures that every citizen - man, woman and child is equal in the realm of law.

» Article 15: provides for prohibition of discrimination and along with that it empowers the state to make special provisions for women and children.

» Article 39(e)- Ensure that health and strength of workers, men and women and the tender age of children are not abused.

» Article 39(f)- directs the state to ensure that children develop in a free and dignified environment and that their childhood and youth is protected against exploitation and against moral and material abandonment.

| Impact of Child Abuse | Government Initiative and Interventions |
|---|---|
| • Low Self-Esteem- As per NIMHANs study → 85% of abused children's → reported feelings of worthlessness and inadequacy.<br>• Difficult with Trust: CRYou survey found that 60% of abused children reported difficulty forming trusting relationships with adult later in life.<br>• Delinquency and Substance Abuse- Abused children are 5 times more likely to become involved in criminal activity.<br>• School Difficulties: NCPCR report revealed that abused children are likely to have lower academic performance and higher dropout rates.<br>• Stunted Growth- National Institute of Nutrition study → abused or neglected children are likely to experience stunted growth and developmental delays. | • Protection of Children from Sexual Offences (POCSO) Act, 2012 address the crimes of sexual abuse and sexual exploitation of children through stringent legal provisions.<br>• POCSO e-Box- Online complaint management system for easy and direct reporting of sexual offences against children and timely action against offenders.<br>• National Commission for Protection of Child Rights (NCPCR)- Policies and Programmes are in consonance with the Child Rights perspective (Indian Constitution + UN Convention on the Rights of the child).<br>• Integrated Child Protection Scheme Aims at building a protective environment for children in difficult |

| | |
|---|---|
| • Cycle of Abuse- As per AIIMs research- abusive children are more likely to become abusers themselves, perpetuating the cycle of violence in future generations. | circumstances through Government-Civil Society Partnership. • Operation Smile, also called as Operation MUSKAAN is an initiative of the Ministry of Home affairs to rescue/rehabilitate missing children. |

## Child Mortality

» Status-

- According to NFHS 5:
  - Neonatal mortality rate (per 1000 live births): 24.9.
  - Infant mortality rate (per 1000 live births): 35.2.
  - Under-five mortality rate (per 1000 live births) 41.9.

| Causes of Child Mortality | Government Initiatives |
|---|---|
| • Preterm Birth and Low Birth Weight babies due to Lack of adequate prenatal care and maternal nutrition + anaemia → high risk of mortality.<br>• Infectious Diseases like Pneumonia Diarrhoea, Malaria → leading cause of child mortality, often exacerbated by poor living conditions and lack of access to healthcare.<br>• Under-nutrition → weakens children's immune systems → makes them more susceptible to infections.<br>• Limited access → to quality healthcare services and skilled birth attendants, especially in rural areas.<br>• Poverty limits access to nutritious food, clean water, sanitation and healthcare. | • Janani Suraksha Yojana and Janani Shishu Suraksha Karyakram- Promotion of Institutional deliveries through cash incentives.<br>• Strengthening of delivery points: Through establishments of Special Newborn Care Units, Newborn Stabilization Units and Kangaroo Mother Care units.<br>• India Newborn Action Plan, 2014 → aims at attainment of goals of "Single Digit Neonatal Mortality Rate" and "Single Digit Stillbirth Rate" by 2030.<br>• Mothers Absolute Affection (MAA) programmes, 2016, for promoting and revitalizing breastfeeding practices across the country's healthcare system.<br>• Universal Immunization Programme → to provide vaccination to children against life threatening diseases such as Tuberculosis, Diphtheria, Pertussis, Polio, Tetanus, Hepatitis B and Measles. |

# Juvenile Delinquency

» **Juvenile:** According to Juvenile Justice (Care and Protection of Children) Act, 2015 any person below the age of 18 years.

- Post Nirbhaya Incidents → Juveniles aged between 16-18 years who committed heinous crimes, as defined by the JJA and Indian Penal Code (IPC), may be tried as adults.

» **Statistics:**

- NCRB, 2022, data → highlights a surge in juveniles criminal activities in Delhi upto 2430 criminal cases.
  - Gravity of situation can be observe in nature of crimes such as murders, attempts to commit murder, rape, outraging the modesty of women, kidnapping and abduction.
- Recent Pune Porsche Car incident and subsequent legal proceedings sparks the debate over Juvenile Delinquency.

| Causes of Juvenile Delinquency | International and National Legislation |
|---|---|
| • Poverty- forced Juveniles into delinquent acts in order to meet and satify the primary wants of their life.<br>• Family- Delinquents families are characterized by discord, desertions and indulge in unethical ways.<br>• Mental Health- various mental health factors contributes to increasing juvenile delinquency.<br>• Substance Abuse- is directly proportional to juvenile delinquency.<br>  • It is associated with both violent and income-generating crimes by youth.<br>• Bad Peer Group- Juvenile delinquency is caused or worsened by peer pressure. | • Convention on the Rights of the Child (CRC)- sets out international standards for protection and well-being of children, including juvenile delinquents.<br>• Beijing Rules- Non-binding guidlines for juvenile justice administration adopted by the United Nations.<br>• Havana Conventions- UN Rules for the Protection of Juveniles Deprived of their liberty.<br>• Juveniles Justice Act, 2015:<br>  ◦ Classifies offences committed by juveniles into three categories: petty, serious and heinous.<br>  ◦ Juvenile Justice Boards at district level to handle cases of juveniles in conflict with law.<br>  ◦ Child Welfare Committees at district level for the care and protection of children. |

## Issues with Juveniles Justice

- Sentence Length- One-size-fits all approach to rehabilitation, with a maximum sentence of three years.
- Aftercare Challenges- India's large population make it difficult to ensure continued therapy and followup with parole officers, potentially hindering successful reintegration.
- Misplacement in a Adult Jails of juveniles either due to police actions that violate the Juvenile Justice Act or due to difficulty in determining a minor's age.
- Problems in Juvenile Homes- like lack of essential resources → staff shortage + financial mismanagement + lack of vocational training & counselling → hinders rehabilitation efforts.

## Court Verdicts

- Subramanian Swamy vs Raju (2014)- Court dismissed challenges to the Juvenile Justice Act and upheld the requirement under the Act that all persons under 18 yrs of age are to be treated as juveniles subject to the Act.
- Sampurna Behura vs. Union of India (2018)- Supreme Court held that the State needs to make sure that the JJ Act is implemented in a proper manner in order to cater to the needs of the children in the society.

## Way Forward

- The court should adopt reformative approach towards the child delinquency rather than the punitive one. The state should try to create such an environment so as to reintegrate the delinquent with the mainstream of the society.
- State should not given so much power so as to make the law regarding the Juvenile Justice Act, rather more power should be given to the international Conventions and CrPc, so that the purpose of the JJA should be attained.
- The Juvenile Justice board is of great importance and hence a special training programme in child psychology should be conducted for the members of the JJB including the Magistrate.

# TRANSGENDER

- According to the World Health Organization (WHO), transgender is an umbrella term for people whose gender identity and expression does not conform to the norms and expectations traditionally associated with the sex assigned to them at birth
- They are referred to as transsexuals if they desire medical assistance in order to make the transition from one biological sex to another.
- The Transgender Persons (Protection of Rights) Act, 2019 defines a Transgender person as one whose gender does not match the gender assigned at birth.
  - **Components:** Trans-men and trans-women, persons with intersex variations, gender-queers, and persons with socio-cultural identities, such as Kinnar and Hijra.
- Current status - Overall calculated population of transgenders is approximately 4.8 lakh (Census 2011), In Lok sabha elections 2019, only 23% of transgenders were eligible to vote.
  - There were more than 54,854 transgender children who were under the age of (Census 2011).

## Constitutional Safeguards

- Article 14 - Guarantees equality before the law and the protection of laws for all individuals, including transgender persons.
- Article 15 - Prohibits discrimination based on sex, religion, caste, or place of birth, including gender identity.
- Article 16 - Ensures equal opportunity for all citizens in public employment regardless of gender identity.
- Article 19(1) - Protects the right of transgender persons to express their gender identity freely.
- Article 21 - Safeguards the right to life and dignity, encompassing the right of transgender persons to live authentically.

## Legal Developments and Frameworks for Transgenders

### Yogyakarta Principles - 2006

- **About** - It is a document outlining how existing international human rights law applies to sexual orientation and gender identity.
- It was created in response to documented human rights abuses faced by LGBTQ+ people around the world.

- Yogyakarta Principles plus 10 emerged in 2017 as a supplement to the Yogyakarta Principles to address new developments in human rights, law and emerging understandings of the challenges faced by LGBTQ+ individuals.

→ **National Legal Services Authority v. Union of India (NALSA) Judgement 2014**

- This landmark judgement by the Supreme Court recognized transgender persons as a "third gender" and guaranteed them fundamental rights.
- It directed the government to create mechanisms for recognizing their gender identity and prohibiting discrimination against them.

→ **Transgender Persons (Protection of Rights) Act, 2019**

- Define a transgender person and someone whose gender does not match with one assigned at birth.
- Prohibits discrimination against a transgender person, including denial of service or unfair treatment in relation to education, employment, healthcare, access to or enjoyment of goods, facilities, opportunities available to the public.
- Right to identity- Allows self-declaration of gender identity without requiring medical procedures.
    - It mandates their recognition on the basis of a 'Certificate of identity' issued by a District Magistrate.
- Right of residence- Every transgender person shall have a right to reside and be included in his household.
- Educational institutions- funded or recognised by government shall provide inclusive education, sports and recreational facilities for transgender persons, without discrimination.
- Health care- The government must take steps to provide health facilities to transgender persons including separate HIV surveillance centres, and sex reassignment surgeries.
- Established National Council for Transgender persons (NCT).
    - The Council will advise the central government as well as monitor the impact of policies, legislation and projects with respect to transgender persons. It will also readdress the grievances of transgender persons.

**Criticism of Transgender Persons (Protection of Rights) Act, 2019.**

- Non-Alignment with NALSA Judgements:
    - Self Declaration- Certificate of identity is against the principles of self-determination of gender identity.
    - It does not provide reservation quotas for transgender people in education or employment.

- Criminalises Begging- A common source of income for some transgender people, without offering alternative social security measures.
- Unequal penalties- The Act prescribes lighter punishments for discrimination and assault against transgender people compared to similar crimes against cisgender people.
- Focus on vulnerability- The Act portrays transgender people solely as victims, neglecting their agency and rights.
- Uncertain rights- The Act remains silent on issues like marriage, divorce, and adoption rights for transgender individuals, as raised by the Standing Committee.
- Right to Residence Concerns- The Act's requirement to live with parents or seek court approval is seen as a violation of the right to freedom of residence under Article 19 of the Constitution.
- No provision penalising rape or sexual assault of transgender person.

## Challenges faced by the Transgender Communities

➡ Social Rejection- It includes marginalisation, discrimination based on factors like racism, sexism and homophobia.

Ex- Nearly 6 out of 10 transgender persons surveyed in Kerala in 2015 had dropped out of school due to "severe harrassment" and gender-related negative experiences.

➡ Limited Education- Poverty and insensitive educational environment can hinder access to education for transgender individuals.

- Census 2011 observes a troubling literacy rate of 56.1% among transgenders notably lower than the national average of 74.04%.

➡ Health care Barriers: Lack of qualified healthcare providers, inadequate clinic facilities etc make it difficult for transgender people to access necessary medical care.

- According to a UNAIDS 2021 report, HIV prevalence among transgenders in India is 3.8%.

➡ Workplace Discrimination- In 2017, just 6% of transgender people were formally employed in either the private or non-governmental organisation (NGO) sector.

- As per NHRC, about 5% engaged in sex work and domestic labour respectively.

➡ Transphobia and Violence- make it harder for them to integrate into society.

- India recorded 102 registered murders against transgender persons between 2008 and 2021.

➠ Violation of rights- Ambiguity surrounding their legal identity → leading to violation of basic rights like limited participation in elections.
- Ex- In 2024 General Elections, no major political party fielded an openly LGBTQ candidate.

## Reasons for Negative Attitudes Towards Transgender People in India

| | |
|---|---|
| Social Stigma | ➔ Limited Understanding about transgender identities and experiences. Equating Gender identity and sexual orientation as same → creates a barrier to acceptance towards the third gender.<br>➔ Prejudice: Stereotyped as beggars, associated with sex work, or seen as a threat to social norms. |
| Marginalisation | ➔ Economic Disadvantage- Most transgender people come from lower castes and socio-economic backgrounds → social exclusion.<br>➔ Family Rejection- Societal pressure and stigma can lead families to disown or ostracised transgender children.<br>➔ Educational Barriers- Rigid gender norms and a lack of understanding in schools can force transgender children to drop out of education. |
| Violence | ➔ Workplace Discrimination- Transgender people often face harassment and violence in workplaces due to their gender identity.<br>➔ Vulnerability to Abuse- Social marginalization makes transgender people vulnerable to sexual assault, rape, and exploitation. |
| Misconception | ➔ Choice vs Identity- Transgender is a choice that creates a barrier to acceptance.<br>➔ Motives and Misunderstanding- Some people mistakenly believe transgender people transition for sexual reasons. |

## Initiatives For the Transgender Community in India

### Government Programs

- National Council for Transgender Persons: Advises on policies for the transgender community, monitors their welfare programs, and addresses their grievances.
- Ministry of Social Justice and Empowerment offers Ayushman Bharat Transgender Plus scheme → provides benefits such as-
  - Rs 5 lakh per year in insurance coverage
  - Coverage for transition-related healthcare.

- Hormone therapy
- Sex reassignment surgery, including post-operation formalities

- SMILE Scheme (2021): To provide holistic support for the welfare of transgender people.
- National Portal for Transgender Persons allows transgender individuals to apply for a Certificate and Identity card without needing to visit a government office
- Garima Greh: Provides shelters with basic amenities like food, medical care and recreation, along with skills training to help transgender people achieve self-sufficiency.
- Pension for Transgender Person- Rs 1000 to transgender pensioners who have little or no source of income.

**Kerala Transgender Policy 2015**

- Pioneer- First state policy in India specifically aimed at transgender rights.
- Legal Recognition- Upheld the right to self-identification of gender as male, female or transgender.
- Combatting Discrimination- Aimed to end discrimination against transgender people in various aspects of life, including education, employment and healthcare.
- Social Inclusion- Provided measures for social welfare, rehabilitation, and skilling to empower the transgender community.
- Monitoring Mechanism- to oversee the policy's implementation and address any issues faced by transgender individuals.

## Way Forward

### Public Awareness

- Comprehensive strategy that includes public awareness campaigns to dismantle social stigma surrounding transgender people
- School-level Education- large scale sensitization programs starting from schools can promote acceptance of transgender individuals as an integral part of society.

### Law Enforcement

- Sensitisation of Agencies about the challenges faced by the transgender community.
  - To improve the ability to protect transgender rights
- Stricter Penalties- Stringent criminal and disciplinary actions should be taken against perpetrators of violence against transgender people.

## Policy and Social Change

- Inclusive Approach - Policy changes need to be coupled with an inclusive approach.
- Breaking Barriers - Understanding the negative attitudes held by the public can help identity barriers to acceptance.
- Problem-Focused Solutions - A better understanding of the problems and challenges faced by the transgender community will guide policy changes and ensures they receive their rightful place in society.
- Reservation - Job reservations for transgender people under the OBC category.
  - Inclusion of transgender people in the armed forces.

### PYQs Corner

*(Write the Answer and Get Free Evaluation)*

1. Child cuddling is now being replaced by mobile phones. Discuss its impact on the socialisation of children. **(2023)**

2. "Development and welfare schemes for the vulnerable, by its nature, are discriminatory in approach." Do you agree? Give reasons for your answer. **(2023)**

3. Despite the consistent experience of high growth, India still goes with the lowest indicators of human development. Examine the issues that make balanced and inclusive development elusive. **(2019)**

4. Performance of welfare schemes that are implemented for vulnerable sections is not so effective due to absence of their awareness and active involvement at all stages of the policy process. Discuss. **(2019)**

CHAPTER

# 09 Education

India boasts a rich intellectual heritage, with a long history of learning. Ancient centers like Takshashila and Nalanda flourished as renowned universities, attracting scholars from across the globe. Tradition of knowledge transmission, initially through Guru-Shishya Parampara has continuously evolved. Today, India embraces cutting-edge Ed-Tech solutions transforming educational landscape from its ancient roots to a dynamic, tech driven future.

**Prominent Views on Education**

- "The true teachers are those who help us think for ourselves" - Sarvepalli Radhakrishnan.
- Learning gives creativity, creativity leads to thinking, thinking provides knowledge, knowledge makes you great. - Dr APJ Abdul Kalam.
- Literacy is a bridge from misery to hope - Kofi Annan.
- With guns you can kill terrorists. With education you can kill terrorism. Malala Yousafzai.
- Education is the most powerful weapon for changing the world. - Nelson Mandela.

# CONCEPT OF QUALITY EDUCATION

▶ A quality education is about nurturing well-rounded individuals prepared to thrive in a complex world.

→ It encompasses students, instructors, the learning environment, relevant curriculum captivating pedagogy, learning outcomes, ongoing formative assessment and sufficient student support.

## Aspect of Quality Education

### 01 Learners:

- Health and Wellbeing of students to actively participate and learn effectively.
- It includes access to nutritious food, healthcare services, and a supportive environment. Ex- Mid-Day Meal Scheme in India provides nutritious lunches to millions of students.
- Engagement and Motivation- Effective teaching strategies that cater to diverse learning styles and ignite curiosity are crucial.
  - Ex- "Eklavya Model Residential Schools" focus on activity based learning and sports, catering to diverse learning styles and keeping tribal students engaged.

### 02 Content and Curriculum:

- Relevance and Balance- The curriculum should be relevant to student's lives and future aspirations, while also providing a solid foundation in core subjects.
  - National Education Policy (NEP) 2020 emphasizes skill development alongside core subjects, making education more relevant to future careers.
- Critical Thinking and Problem-solving Skills- The focus should go beyond rote memorization to develop critical thinking, problem solving and analytical skills.

### 03 Teachers and Teaching:

- Qualified and Competent Educators: Teachers should be well-trained, passionate about their subjects, and possess strong pedagogical skills to effectively deliver the curriculum and guide students.
  - Paramarsh Scheme → to mentor National Accreditation and Assessment Council (NAAC) accreditation aspirant institutions for promoting quality assurance in higher education.
- Supportive and Inclusive learning Environment - where all students feel valued and respected, regardless of background or ability.
  - "Sarva Shiksha Abhiyan" program promotes inclusive education

## 04 Learning Environment

- Safe and Secure and conducive to learning. It includes access to proper infrastructure, sanitation and resources.
  - Swachh Bharat Abhiyan also aims to improve sanitation facilities in schools.
- Technology Integration - can be a powerful tool for learning when used effectively.
  - During Covid 19 pandemic distance education, on-line education, virtual education were effective tools of knowledge dissemination.

## 05 Learning Outcomes and Assessment:

- Clear Learning Objectives ensure that educators and students are working towards same goals.
  - Continuous and Comprehensive Evaluation system in India outlines specific learning goals at each stage, helping track student progress.
- Assessment for learning should be used not just to measure achievement, but also to identify areas where students need additional support and tailor instructions accordingly.

## 06 Equity and Access-

- Equal opportunities: Quality education should be accessible to all, regardless of socioeconomic background, gender, disability, or location.
  - "Right to Education Act" 2009 guarantees free and compulsory education for children aged 6-14, promoting access for all.
  - Reservation for backwards and disabled in Educational institutions highlights India's commitment to equitable and inclusive education

## 3-TIER EDUCATION SYSTEM OF INDIA

- In India, Central and State boards of school education follow the "10 + 2 = 3" education system pattern ⟶ consisting of Primary, Secondary, Senior Secondary Education and Higher Education.
- This education system in India is based on the recommendations of the Kothari Commission (1964-66).

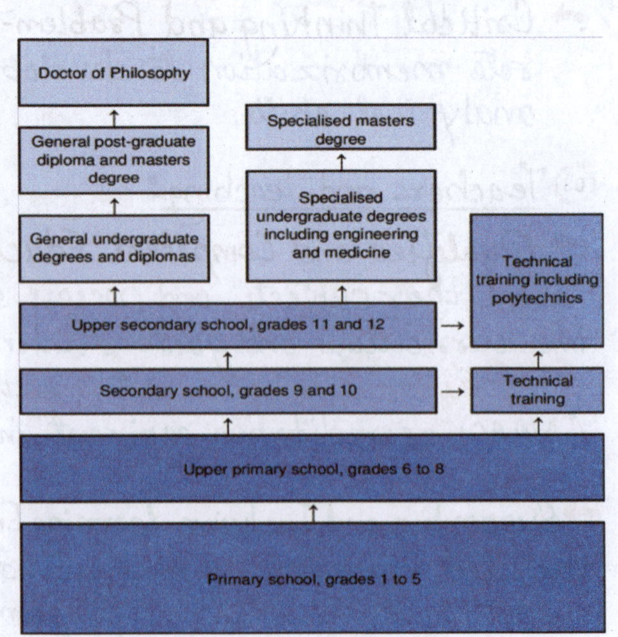

## Primary School and Secondary School Education System.

| Divisions | Characteristics |
|---|---|
| Pre-primary education | • Includes Playgroup, Nursery and Kindergarten |
| Primary education (or elementary education). | • Lower primary (class I-IV)<br>• Upper primary (class V-VIII)<br>• 6-14 years. |
| Secondary education | • Consists of Class VIII to class XII<br>• 14-18 years<br>• Final two years of secondary school are called higher secondary or senior secondary. |

## Institutional Framework For School Education System

☛ **Central Advisory Board of Education (CABE)** - Highest advisory body to advise Central and State Governments in field of education.

• **Objectives:**

- Providing recommendations and ideas to all the educational bodies of India for designing the syllabus.
- Providing a platform for the governments to express their opinions and ideas for enhancing the quality of education in India.
- Guiding in resolving any query or issue related to education.

☛ **National Council of Educational Research and Training (NCERT)** - An autonomous body established in 1961 to assist and advise Central and State Governments on policies and programmes for qualitative improvement in school education.

• **Objectives:**

- Conducts research in school education, like curriculum development, pedagogy and student psychology
- Develops National Curriculum Framework (NCF) which sets to overall vision and guidelines for school education in India.
- Creates model textbooks, syllabi, and teaching-learning materials aligned with NCF.
- Publishes a range of educational materials like journals, newsletters, and digital resources.

☛ **State Council of Educational Research and Training (SCERT)**: A Nodal agency for implementation of the National Policy on Education in the states.

• **Objectives:**

- Educational research and teacher training in the states.

☛ National Council for Teacher Education - An advisory body for central and State Governments on all matters pertaining to teacher education.

• Objectives:

• Planned and coordinated development of teacher education system throughout the country.

• Regulation and proper maintenance of norms and standards in teacher education system.

☛ Central Board of Secondary Education (CBSE) - is a national level board of education in India for public and private schools, controlled and managed by the Government of India

• Objectives:

• Affiliation of Schools across India that meet its standards for curriculum, infrastructure, and teacher qualifications.

• Conducting Final Examinations for school students of class 10th and class 12th

• Prescribes Syllabi and Guidelines for Affiliated Schools.

• Conducts Teacher Training Programs.

## SCHOOL EDUCATION

→ According to Performance Grading Index (PGI), Indian School Education System comprises nearly 14.9 lakh schools, 95 lakh teachers, and 26.5 crore students.

→ As per Unified Digital Information for School Education Plus (UDISE+) → 57 crore students enrolled in 2021-22 as compared to 25.38 crores in 2020-21.

→ As per UDISE+ →

• Gross Enrollment Ratio (GER) in higher secondary schools has increased from 53.8% in 2020-21 to 57.6% in 2020-22.

• GER for primary section has improved from 101.3% in 2018-2019 to 104.8% in 2021-22.

→ As per Gender Parity Index, more than 12.29 crore girls were enrolled in primary to higher secondary in 2021-22.

### Lacunae/Challenges in School Education system

→ Accessibility issue - As per Annual Status of Education Report (ASER) 2023 report 3.9% of 14-year-olds and 32.6% of 18-year-olds children are not enrolled in schools.

➡ Regional Disparity- As per (UDISE+) 2019-20 report → Net Enrollment Ratio (NER) at the secondary level is only 51.6% in rural areas compared to 60.2% in urban areas.

- NSSO 75th round report indicates female literacy rate in rural areas is 56.8% compared to 79.5% in urban areas underscoring regional gender disparities in educational access.

➡ Socio-cultural barriers- National Commission for Scheduled Castes 2021 report documented over 5000 cases of discrimination against Dalit students in school.

- Incidences of cooks not allowed to cook meals (under mid day meal scheme) have been reported.

➡ Gender Inequality- According to the National Institute of Aging (NIA) 2023 study, 62% of women in India have no schooling, compared to 31% of men.

➡ Inadequate Funding- Samagra Shiksha Abhiyan, major driver behind reversing learning losses, has registered a mere hike of 0.18% with the allocation of Rs 37,453 crore in 2023-24.

- Economic Survey of India 2020-21- pointed out India's public expenditure on education is around 3.1% of GDP which is lower than the recommeded 6%.

➡ Poor Quality of Education - According to the Annual Status of Education Report (ASER) 2021, only 40% of rural children in Grade 5 can read a Grade 2 level text.

➡ Poor Teacher-Student Ratio:

- State of the Education Report for India: No Teachers, No Class published by UNESCO estimates that 1.1 lakh schools in India are run by a single teacher. There are currently 11.16 lakh or 19% unfilled teaching positions in the nation → 69% of them are in rural areas.

➡ Quality of Teachers: NCERT 2023 survey, found that only 40% of teachers felt adequately prepared to handle the demands of the new curriculum implemented in 2020.

➡ Inadequate Infrastructure- As per UDISE + 2021-22;

- Kitchen Gardens in 27.7% of schools.
- Only 44.85% of schools had computer facilities, and only 34% had an internet connection.

➡ Shift Towards Private School- As per ASER 2022, "proportion of government schools with less than 60 students enrolled" has increased every year over the last decade

➡ Digital Divide and Technological Backwardness: According to Ministry of Education, only 24% of Indian households have internet access with rural areas having as low as 15% penetration → highlights the digital divide.

- UNESCO 2021 report → only 20% of teachers had received any formal training on digital teaching tools.

## Constitutional Safeguards Available for School Education

Article 21A - provide free and compulsory education to all children in the age group of 6 to 14 years.
Article 28 - Freedom of religious worship or instructions in certain institutes
Article 30 - Right of minorities to establish and administer educational institutions.
Article 51 A(K) - A parent or a guardian to provide opportunities for education to his child or, as the case may be, between 6-14 years.

## Government Measures / Initiatives for School education in India

| Category | Initiatives |
|---|---|
| Primary | Mid-Day Meal Scheme 1995 - Improved enrollment, attendance, and nutrition for primary school children. |
| Secondary | Rashtriya Madhyamik Shiksha Abhiyan (RMSA), 2009 - Universal access to secondary education (focus on infrastructure development, additional classrooms, and vocational training). |
| Primary + Secondary | Sarva Shiksha Abhiyan (SSA): 2001 - Universal access to elementary education (focus on infrastructure, teacher recruitment, and community participation).<br>National Scheme of Incentive to Girls for Secondary Education (NSIGSE) 2008 - Increased enrollment and retention of girls in secondary education through financial assistance.<br>Right to Education Act (RTE), 2010 - Free and compulsory education for children aged 6-14. |
| Secondary + Senior Secondary | Sukanya Samriddhi Yojana 2014 - Financial support for girl child's education and future needs.<br>Skill India Mission 2015 - Integration of vocational skills training into secondary and senior secondary education. |
| Primary + Secondary + Senior Secondary | Padhe Bharat Badhe Bharat Mission, 2018 - Reading comprehension + foundational literacy / numeracy skills across all levels.<br>National Education Policy (NEP) 2020: Holistic education reform emphasizing critical thinking, problem-solving, and life skills across all stages.<br>NIPUN Bharat Mission 2021 - Mission to achieve foundational literacy and numeracy for all children by 2025<br>STARs Project (Students Achievement Tracking System) 2023: Monitoring student learning outcomes and providing targeted interventions. |

## Recommendations to Reform School Education System

| Resolving Infrastructure Issue | Policy Measures |
|---|---|
| → Increased Funding closer to recommended 6% by UNESCO and NEP towards education to improve infrastructure.<br>→ Public Private Partnerships (PPP) for infrastructure development and maintenance.<br>→ Focus on Rural Schools which often lag behind urban areas.<br>→ Implementation of School Adoption Program similar to adopt a heritage or village programmes.<br>→ Maintenance and Upgradation of existing school infrastructure. | → Regular Teacher Recruitment Drives to fill vacant teacher positions and improve student-teacher ratio.<br>→ Attracting and retaining teachers market oriented salaries, better working conditions and professional development opportunities.<br>→ Performance-Based Incentives for teachers → to motivate continuous improvement and innovation.<br>→ Curriculum Reform to emphasise critical thinking, problem-solving alongside core subjects.<br>→ Integration of vocational training at secondary and senior secondary levels to equip students with job-ready skills. |
| **Attitudinal and Behavioural Change** | **Emphasis on quantity Education** |
| → Parental Involvement Programs to encourage greater parental involvement in their children's education.<br>→ Promote community engagement initiatives in school activities and infrastructure development to foster a sense of shared responsibility.<br>→ Breaking Stereotypes that hinder girls education or push children towards specific career paths based on caste or background.<br>→ Sensitization of teachers through Teacher Training on Social-Emotional Learning (SEL) techniques promote positive student-teacher relationships. | → Focus on Learning outcomes through a system for effective assessment that goes beyond rote memorization and standardised tests.<br>→ Digital Learning Initiatives - through Increase access to technology and teacher training → to integrate technology effectively into lesson plans for engaging learning experiences.<br>→ Mentorship Programs where experienced teachers can guide and support new teachers → fostering a culture of continuous improvement.<br>→ Collaboration and Exchange Programs between schools within India and internationally → to share best practices and innovative teaching methods. |

# HIGHER EDUCATION SYSTEM

## Institutional Framework For Higher Education System.

| Body | Description |
| --- | --- |
| University Grants Commission (UGC) | • Premier funding organisation established in 1953 and became statutory organisation in 1956.<br>• Provides financial assistance to universities and colleges, set standards for teaching, examination, and research, and maintains a list of recognized universities. |
| National Medical Commission (NMC) | • Established through the National Medical Commission Act, 2019.<br>• Sets standards for medical colleges and courses + conduct entrance exams for medical courses (NEET UG, NEET PG) + Registers medical practitioners |
| All India Council for Technical Education (AICTE) | • National-level Apex Advisory Body for technical education in accordance with the provisions of the AICTE Act 1987. |
| Bar Council of India (BCI) | • Statutory body established through Advocates Act 1961.<br>• It also sets standards for legal education and grants recognition to Universities. |
| National Assessment and Accreditation Council (NAAC) | • Independent body → assesses quality of general universities and colleges.<br>• Grants accreditation to institutions based on established parameters.<br>• Accreditation is crucial for receiving UGC funding and student enrollment. |
| National Board of Accreditation (NBA) | • Independent body that assesses quality of technical programs.<br>• Grants accreditation to technical programs.<br>• Accreditation is crucial for attracting students and enhancing reputation. |

## Status of Higher Education in India

- All-India Survey of Higher Education (AISHE) 2021-22 → registered 1168 Universities/University level Institutions, 45473 Colleges and 12,002 Stand Alone Institutions
  - There are 17 Universities exclusively for Women.
- Total enrolment in higher education has increased to nearly 4.33 crore in 2021-22 from 4.14 crore in 2020-21.

- Female enrolment in Higher Education increases to 2.07 crore (32% increase since 2014-15).
- Scheduled Caste enrolment stands at 15.3%, 6.3% belong to Scheduled Tribe, 37.8% are from Other Backward Classes.
- Female GER continues to be more than male GER for 5th consecutive year as per AISHE 2021-22.
  - Female GER has increased to 28.5% in 2021-22 from 27.9% in 2020-21 and 22.9% in 2014-15.

## Lacunae/ Challenges In Higher Education System

- High Dropout Rates: According to National University of Educational Planning and Administration (NUEPA), dropout rate for higher education in India is 25% → means that one in four students who enroll in college are unable to complete their degree.
- High Proportion of Reserved Seats- In Indian central universities, 49.5% of seats are reserved for historically underprivileged communities.
- Limited Skilled Faculty: As of 2020, central universities in state such as Haryana, Gujarat, Orissa, Rajasthan and Bihar were operating on 52% of sanctioned faculty strength.
- Academic curriculum is not industry aligned → Absence of necessary skills in Youth making them Unemployable workforce.
  - As per India Skills Report 2024 India has a 60-73% of demand-supply gap in key positions like ML engineer, data scientist DevOps engineer and data architect.
  - Aspiring Minds report 2020 found that only 47% of Indian engineering graduates are employable in the IT sector.
- Inadequate Research and Development Expenditure- India's expenditure remains between 0.73% to 0.87% → this is lower than US (2.74%) and Europe (1.85%)
- Fragmentation of the higher education system leads directly to suboptimal various fronts: resource utilization, range and number of programmes and discipline
  - Over 40% of colleges run only a single programme + Over 20% of colleges have enrolment below 100, while only 4% of colleges have enrolment over 3000.
- Lack of teacher and institutional autonomy- Lack of faculty motivation, scope for innovation particularly in affiliated colleges which are required to follow a central syllabus, curriculum, pedagogy and textbooks.
  - Bureaucratic hurdles because of regulations from UGC, AICTE, other bodies can be cumbersome for institutions → hindering their autonomy and ability to innovate and adapt to changing needs.

- **Lacunae with career management and progression of faculty:** Selection, tenure, promotion, pay raise, and vertical mobility system is based on seniority or arbitrariness rather than merit.
- **Governance Paralysis and Political Interference**- Leadership and governance of Higher Education Institutions are heavily influenced and controlled by people and organisations outside of the institution.
  - These outside forces frequently have financial, political or other stakes in the HEIs.
- **Inadequate investments in Higher education**- Governments expenditure on higher education is mere 2.7% of the GDP against the recommended 6% by the Kothari Commission.
  - Interim Budget 2024-25 for Education in India has been reduced by 7% with the allocation for the university Grants Commission slashed by 61%.
- **Regional Disparity** Higher education institutions are uneven across different regions and states in India like Delhi, Tamil Nadu and Maharashtra have a higher concentration of reputed institutions while states in north eastern and central regions lag behind in terms of quality and access.
  - NITI Aayog 2019 report revealed that over 80% of colleges are located in urban areas.
- **Brain Drain**- Talented graduates often seek opportunities abroad, leading to a loss of skilled professionals in India.
  - UNESCO 2021 report estimates that 6 million Indian-origin scientists and engineers work abroad, representing a loss of valuable talent.

## Constitutional Provisions Related to Higher Education

- **Article 15(3):** Special provisions for women and minorities in educational institutions.
- **Article 29(1):** Secure the cultural and educational rights of minorities
- **Article 46** Promotion of educational and economic interests of SC's ST's and other weaker sections
- **Article 66 (Union list)** Standards in institutions for higher education or research and scientific and technical institutions
- **Article 64 & 65 (State list)** Establish and maintain universities and other educational institutions.

## Government Interventions/Measures in Higher Education

### Improving Quality And Access

- Institution of Eminence Scheme - Establish 20 prestigious educational institutions.
  - To empower higher education + implementation of world-class teaching systems to enhance affordable access to high-quality education.
- National Education Policy (NEP) 2020: Roadmap for transforming higher education.
  - Focus: multidisciplinary learning, holistic development, focus on critical thinking and problem-solving skills, and alignment of curriculum with industry needs.
- Technical Education Quality Improvement Programme (TEQIP): To upscale the quality of technical education and enhance capacities of institutions.
- Affirmative Action-reservation of seats in universities and colleges for SCs, STs, Women, OBCs and EWS → Promote inclusion and bridging socio-economic gaps in access to higher education.

### Funding and Financing

- Higher Education Financing Agency (HEFA): Loans to premier higher education institutions for infrastructure development and expansion.
- Rashtriya Uchchatar Shiksha Abhiyan (RUSA): Providing strategic funding to eligible state higher educational institutions.

Funding →
- 60:40 for general category States
- 90:10 for special category states
- 100% for union territories

- University Grants Commission - Grants to universities and colleges for specific purposes → infrastructure development + Research projects + Faculty development programme + Innovation in curriculum design.

### Research and Development

- Prime Minister's Research Fellows (PMRF) Scheme: Attract meritorious students into Ph.D programmes in IITs, IISERs and IISc.
  - Fellowship of Rs 70,000/- per month for the first two years, Rs 75,000/- per month for the 3rd year, and Rs 80,000/- per month in 4th and 5th year.
- Scheme for Promotion of Academic and Research Collaboration (SPARC): Facilitate academic and research collaborations.
  - Thrust Areas: Fundamental Research, Emergent Areas of Impact, Convergence, Action-Oriented Research, and Innovation-Driven research.

- Impacting Research Innovation and Technology (IMPRINT) - Pan - IIT and IISc joint initiative → to develop a new education policy + roadmap for research → to solve major engineering and technology challenges → self-reliance.
- Impactful Research in Social Sciences (IMPRESS): Promoting research in social sciences to address critical national challenges.
- Atal Innovation Mission (AIM) - Foster a culture of innovation and entrepreneurship in higher education institutions by establishing tinkering labs.

## Strengthening Governance and Regulatory Oversight

- Higher Education Commission of India (HECI): Under NEP 2020 as an overarching body for higher education with four independent verticals.
- National Institutional Ranking Framework (NIRF): To rank institutions based on various parameters such as teaching, learning, research and infrastructure.
- National Academic Depository (NAD) - Digital platform for issuing, storing and verifying academic awards to ensure transparency and prevent fraud.
- National Testing Agency (NTA) conducts entrance examinations for higher educational institutions, ensuring standardised and fair assessments.
- Global Initiative of Academic Networks (GIAN) - Engagement of international faculty in Indian institutions to enhance the quality of education and foster global collaboration.
- National Higher Education Regulatory Council (NHERC) for regulation.
- National Accreditation Council (NAC) for accreditation.
- Higher Education Grants Council (HEGC) for funding.
- General Education Council (GEC) for standard setting.

## Recommendations to reform Higher Education System

| Improving Access and Equity | Enhancing Quality and Relevance |
|---|---|
| • Increase Public Funding through budgetary allocations → targeting expansion programs in underserved regions and creating more seats in universities and colleges.<br><br>• Improve Scholarship Targeting through Streamline scholarship schemes → ensuring their reach to students from most disadvantaged backgrounds. | • Industry Collaboration encourages joint research projects internship opportunities, and industry-aligned curriculum development → to prepare an employable workforce.<br>• Implement active learning pedagogies such as problem-based learning, simulations, and project work to develop critical thinking communication and collaboration skills. |

- Promote Online and Open Educational Resources to make education more accessible to students in remote areas or those facing financial constraints.
- Bridge the Digital Divide - Invest in infrastructure and initiatives → to improve internet connectivity + access to digital devices in rural areas.

- Faculty Development Programs to equip them with the latest teaching methodologies and industry knowledge
- Regular Curriculum Review to ensure it stays current with advancements in various fields and meets the evolving needs of the jobs market.

### Promoting Innovation and Research

- Increase Research Funding through alternative funding models like PPP and industry collaborations.
- Create Research Cluster focusing on specific areas of national importance to foster collaborations and accelerate innovation.
- Promote Innovation Hubs within universities, providing students and researchers with access to resources → to develop prototypes and translate research findings into marketable solutions.
- Strengthen Industry - Academia Linkages to encourage joint research projects and commercialization of research outcomes.

### Strengthening Governance and Regulation

- Streamline Regulatory Framework governing higher education institutions, reducing bureaucratic hurdles and empowering institutions with greater autonomy.
- Performance - Based Funding to institutions based on their performance in areas like student learning outcomes, research output, and innovation.
- Strengthen Accreditation processes by National Assessment and Accreditation Council (NAAC) to ensure a robust quality assurance mechanism.
- Promote Institutional Self-Evaluation within institutions for continuous improvement.

## NEW EDUCATION POLICY 2020

- Ministry of Education formed a committee under Dr. K. Kasturirangan to formulate NEP.
- It aims at transforming India into a vibrant knowledge society by making both school and college education more holistic, flexible and multidiscipli-nary and aimed at bringing out the unique capabilities of each student.
- "There is no better investment towards a society's future than the high quality education of our young people".

- NEP 2020 identified "Education as a public good"
- 5 foundational pillars of NEP 2020: Access, Equity, Quality, Affordability and Accountability.

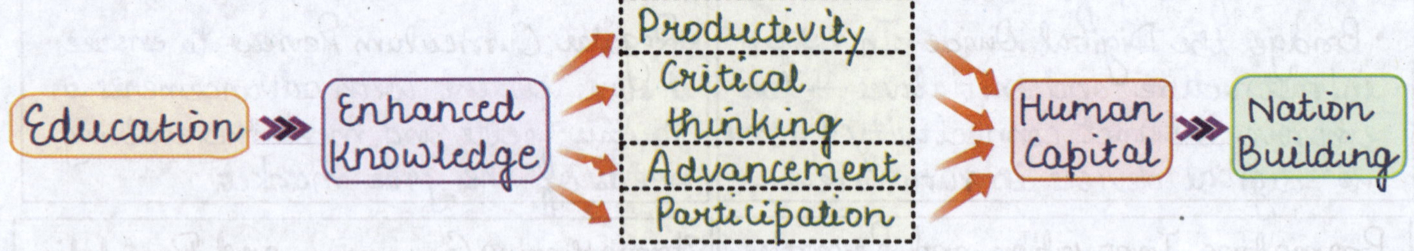


## Features of New Education Policy

ECCE
SE
HE

**Early Childhood Care & Education**
- Universal access
- Integration of Pre-Primary schools.
- Play & activity based learning
- National Curricular

**School Education**
- Reforms in Curricular Structure (5+3+3+4 System)
- Curriculum and pedagogy reform
- Assessment Reforms
- Inclusive Education
- Vocational Education
- Multilingualism

**Higher Education**
- Multidisciplinary Approach
- Multiple entry and exit points
- National Research Foundation
- Inclusive Education
- Light but tight Education.

## Early Childhood Care and Education (ECCE)

- Universal access to high-quality ECCE across India by 2030.
- Integration of pre-primary education with the primary school system to ensure continuity.
- Play and activity-based learning focusing on developing cognitive, affective and psychomotor abilities.
- National Curricular + Pedagogical Framework will be developed by NCERT in consultation with various stakeholders, including state governments.

## 1. School Education

- Reform in Curriculum Structure (5+3+3+4 system)
  - Foundational Stage (3-8 years) consists of three years of preschool/Anganwadi and two years in primary school (grades 1 and 2).
  - Preparatory Stage (8-11 years) covers grades 3-5, focusing on discovery and interactive classroom learning.
  - Middle Stage (11-14 years) includes grades 6-8 with exceptional learning across subjects.
  - Secondary Stage (14-18 years) comprises grade 9-12 → offering a multi-disciplinary study with greater depth and critical thinking.
- Curriculum and Pedagogy reform- Streamlined Curriculum for Holistic Development by reduced content, experimental learning and developing critical thinking.
- Assessment Reforms- Schools are moving towards a more well-rounded evaluation system that includes holistic report cards, revamped board exams, and adaptive assessments.
- Inclusive Education- Bridging the educational gap for disadvantaged groups like SCs, STs, OBCs, Women through Gender Inclusion Fund and Special Education Zones.
- Vocational education will be integrated into mainstream education starting from grade 6.
  - At least 50% of learners will have exposure to vocational education by 2025.
- Multilingualism- Mother tongue or regional language medium of instruction until atleast grade 5, but preferably till grade 8 and beyond.

## 2. Higher Education.

- Multidisciplinary Approach students will have flexibility to choose subjects across various streams.
  - It aims to transition all higher education institutions into large multi-disciplinary universities, colleges, and clusters by 2040.
- Multiple entry and exit points- Certifications after one year (certificate), two years (diploma), and three/four years (degree) of study.
- National Research Foundation will be established to foster a strong research culture and build research capacity across higher education institutions.
- Light but tight regulation: Emphasis on the autonomy of institutions with accountability through a transparent and robust system of regulation.

• Single Regulator: HECI will be established as a single overarching regulator for higher education, excluding medical and legal education.

## Measures taken to Implement NEP

Phased Implementation
With specific timeline
Collaboration between Central and state governments
Implementation Strategy
Essential for successful Implementation
Monitoring and Evaluation
To ensure desired Outcome

➔ National Assessment Centre and PARAKH (Performance Assessment, Review and Analysis of Knowledge for Holistic Development) → aims at improving standards of education through quality assessment

➔ NIPUN Bharat: National Initiative for Proficiency in Reading with Understanding and Numeracy.

➔ PM SHRI: Upgrades schools to offer high-quality education in an inclusive and joyful environment.

➔ NISHTHA (National Initiative for School Heads' and Teachers' Holistic Advancement): An Integrated teacher training programme for different stages of school education.

➔ Academic Bank of Credit in higher education → a national-level digital facility for promoting academic mobility through a formal system of credit accumulation, credit transfer, and credit redemption.

➔ AICTE made provisions for technical education in regional languages

➔ Samagra Shiksha scheme aims at integrating Vocational Education with academic education.

➔ National Digital Education Architecture: Union Budget 2021-22 announced NDEAR with a major emphasis on strengthening country's digital infrastructure for education.

# PRIVATISATION OF EDUCATION SECTOR

## School Education

**Status** - According to Annual Status of Education Report (ASER) 2019:

- Around 30% of all schools in India are privately managed.
- In urban areas, percentage of private schools is higher, and in some cities, it is nearly 70%.

**Benefit** -

- Improved infrastructure and facilities because of better funding → leading to modern classrooms, labs and libraries.
  - As per World Bank report 2018 private schools in India have a higher student-teacher ratio.
- Focus on Innovation and Curriculum - private schools have more autonomy to experiment with teaching methods and curriculum.
  - CBSE allows affiliated private schools to introduce additional subjects beyond core curriculum.
- Accountability and Performance - is key to attracting students → lead to better teacher training and improved student outcomes.
  - NUEPA 2017 study found higher learning levels in Mathematics and Science in private schools compared to government schools.
- Increased Access to Education - Private schools can expand educational options, especially in under-served areas.
  - Department of School Education and Literacy (DoSE&L) 2020 report states that private schools contribute significantly to overall GER in India.
- Vocational and Skill Development - Some private schools offer specialised vocational training programs, preparing students for specific job markets.
  - National Skill Development Mission (NSDM) encourages private participation in skill development initiatives.
- Diversity of Educational Choices - Private schools cater to different needs and budgets, offering parents a wider choice of educational philosophies and environments.
- Government - Private Partnerships - can leverage resources and expertise for better educational outcomes.
  - Public Private Partnerships are being explored in states like Rajasthan for school infrastructure development.

## Concerns

- **Affordability and Exclusion**- High fees in private schools → exclusion of students from low-income families → increasing educational inequality.
    - Only 26.5% of children in India from poorest wealth quintile attend private schools. (RTE forum 2018 report)
- **Commercialization of Education**- Profit motive in private schools may prioritise financial gain over quality education and social responsibility.
- **Uneven Distribution**: Private schools might concentrate in urban areas → regional inequality in terms of accessibility of quality education.
    - Proportion of private schools is significantly higher in urban areas compared to rural areas in India (PRS Legislative Research 2019 report).
- **Teacher Quality and Work Conditions**: Private schools might prioritize cost-cutting measures → leads to teachers salary reduction → decline in teacher quality and motivation.
- **Standardisation and Reduced Focus on Holistic Development** because of competition among private schools → leads to overemphasis on rote learning and standardised test scores.
- **Lack of Regulation and Oversight**- Ensuring quality education standards and preventing malpractices in private schools require strong government regulation and oversight.
    - Regulatory oversight in states like Bihar is so poor that even their topper were accused of cheating.
- **Potential Weakening of Public Education System**- Over-reliance on private schools could lead to a weakened public education system, impacting the most vulnerable sections of society.

## Higher Education

**Status**: As per AISHE 2021-2022:

- Government Universities constituting 58.6% of total Universities, contribute 73.7% of total enrolment, Private Universities account for 26.3% of total enrolment.
- Private (Aided) colleges constituting 13.3% of total colleges account for 20.6% enrolment, whereas the 65.2% Private (Un-aided) Colleges account for only 44.6% of total enrolment.
- Out of 1168 Universities registered, 685 are Government managed (Central Govt 240, State Govt. 445), 10 are Private Deemed (Aided) and 473 are Private (Un-aided).

## Benefits:

➔ Increased Capacity- Private institutions can help meet growing demand for higher education.

➔ Improved Infrastructure- Private universities often boast better infrastructure and facilities due to higher investment, enhancing the learning experience.

- Shiv Nadar University- boasts state of the art facilities including a dedicated research park and a world-class library.

➔ Focus on Industry Needs- Private institutions can adapt curriculums aligned with industry requirements. like Data Science, Biotechnology.

➔ Innovation and Research can be boosted → contributing to advancements in various fields → through collaborations with private companies for research projects

- IIT Bombay, established through PPP mode, has partnered with private companies like Reliance Industries for research projects in arena of renewable energy.

➔ Autonomy and Efficiency in decision-making and resource management → better curriculum reforms.

➔ Improved Faculty - Competitive salaries in private universities can attract better qualified faculty members, potentially leading to better teaching standards.

➔ Diversity of Courses- Private institutions can offer a wider range of specialised courses catering to specific needs like Media Studies, Fashion Design.

➔ Global Collaboration- Private universities might have greater flexibility to partner with international institutions, offering students global exposure and exchange programs

➔ Entrepreneurship culture can be encouraged through incubation centers and relevant courses, fostering innovation. (Examples- startup accelerators within universities).

➔ Accountability and Quality is key to attract students.

## Concerns

➔ Affordability and Equity- High fees in private universities → quality education inaccessible for students from lower socio-economic backgrounds.

➔ Commercialization of Education- Education might be seen as a business, with profit taking precedence over social responsibility.

- Mushrooming of higher educational institutions is result of the same.

- **Uneven Quality-** Not all private institutions are created equal. There is risk of unregulated institutions offering sub-par education, jeopardizing student outcomes.
- **De-emphasis on Public Good Courses-** Prioritising lucrative courses over subject considered less profitable → neglecting crucial fields like social work or rural development.
- **Lack of Transparency-** Higher educational institutions employ opaque and disguised methods to attract students.
- **Erosion of Public Funding-** Increased reliance on private institutions could lead to decreased government funding for public universities, impacting their ability to improve.
- **Erosion of Social Responsibility-** Role of Public universities will be undermined → who play a social role by offering outreach programs and affordable education.
- **Brain Drain-** Highly qualified faculty from public universities might be lured by higher salaries in private institutions, potentially weakening public universities.
- **Regional Imbalance-** Privatization might be concentrated in urban areas, neglecting educational needs in rural areas.
- **Commodification of Knowledge-** Education could become a commodity accessible only to those who can afford it → hindering social mobility.
- **Pressure on Students-** High fees and competition might create undue pressure on students, impacting their well-being and mental health.

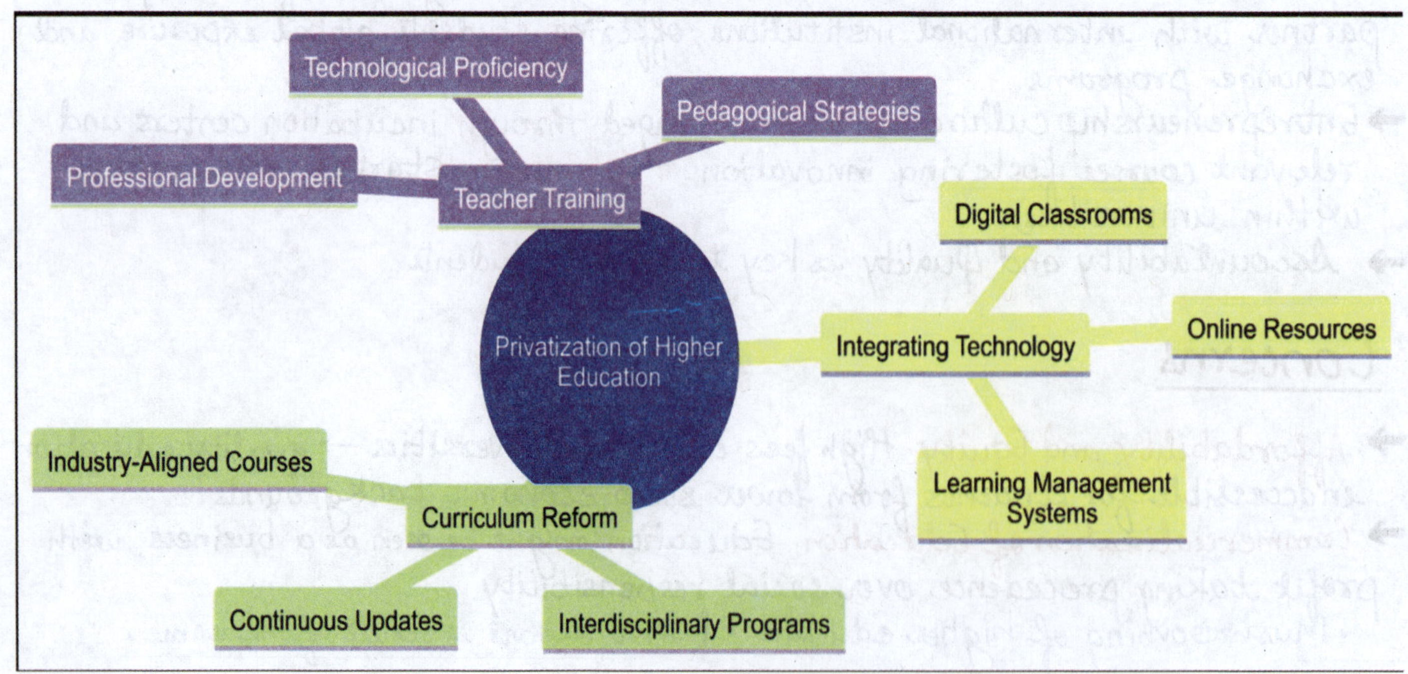

# ED-TECH SECTOR

- Ed Tech is the usage of technology - software and/or hardware, to enhance teaching and learning.
- Indian EdTech sector was valued at US$ 750 million in 2020 and has grown to → US$ 5.8 billion by early 2023, at a CAGR of 43%.
- Market size is estimated to grow 3.7x over the next five years, from the current levels to $ 10.4 billion.
- Growth is driven by rising demand for non-academic courses from Tier II and III cities and the need for personalisation in the EdTech space.

## Benefits to Stakeholders involved in Edtech Sector

### Students

- Personalised learning - EdTech platforms can tailor learning to individual student needs → adaptive learning software adjusts difficulty levels based on student performance, ensuring students are challenged but not overwhelmed.
  - Ex- Dreambox learning adapts maths lessons based on a student's progress.
- Engaging Content can make learning more interactive. Educational games and simulations can transform dry topics into fun experiences.
  - Ex- Minecraft Education Edition allows students to learn about history and science through creative in-game projects.
- Improved Accessibility - Online learning platforms provides flexibility for students with busy schedules or those who need to learn remotely.
  Ex- Unacademy offers high-quality video lectures on a wide range of subjects.
- Deeper Understanding - Technologies like Virtual reality (VR) simulations can immerse students in historical events or scientific phenomena, promoting a deeper understanding.
  - Ex- Google Expeditions allows students to virtually explore Great Barrier Reef or surface of Mars.
- Facilitate Collaboration and Communication on Online forum and discussion boards, Apps → allow students to share ideas and work on project together, even if they are not physically in the same location.
  - Ex- Goodnote facilitates multiple collaboration on same project.
- Immediate Feedback on student performance.
  - Ex- Online quizzes and assessments allows students to gauge their understanding and identify areas needing improvement.
- Self-paced learning - EdTech empowers students to learn at their own pace.
  - Ex. Video lectures + online tutorials can be paused, rewound, and reviewed as needed.

## Teachers

- **Effective Differentiation** - EdTech tools can help teachers differentiate instruction to cater to diverse learning styles and needs.
  - Ex- Interactive presentations with embedded quizzes.
- **Efficient Lesson Planning** - through premade content + interactive activities → saving teachers valuable time in lesson planning.
- **Streamlined & Enhanced Assessment** → provide valuable data on student progress.
- **Real-time Feedback and Data** on student performance → provide insights into areas where students might be struggling.
- **Improved Communication with Parents** - EdTech platforms facilitate communication between teachers and parents.
  - Ex- Remind allows teachers to send text messages and announcements to parents.
- **Professional Development Opportunities** through online courses + resources for professional development.
  - Ex- Edutopia offers a wealth of resources on using technology in the classroom, including articles, webinars, and professional development courses.

## Key Growth Drivers

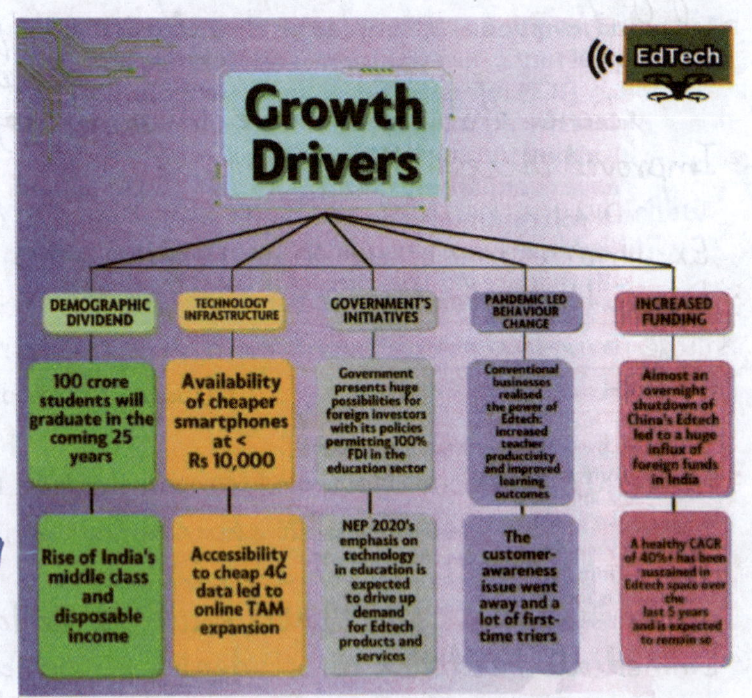


- **Demographic Dividend** - About 300 million kids in kg-12, out of whom 85-90 million have internet access.
  - Current penetration of EdTech among kids with internet access stands at just 5%.
- **Technology Infrastructure** - Government's initiatives to expand digital infrastructure, such as National Broadband Mission, Digital India and BharatNet, along with the telco-led digital revolution have made it easier for EdTech to reach out to remote areas.
- **Government Initiatives** - Government has launched various programmes and initiatives to promote digital education, such as SWAYAM, DIKSHA, and ePathshala.
  - Union Budget 2022 announced National Digital University (NDU), a

virtual university that will offer a wide range of courses across disciplines using digital technology.

- Pandemic-led Behavioural Changes accelerated the adoption of online education in India and across the world.
- Increased Funding from venture capitalists and private equity firms, which have enabled EdTech companies to expand their offering and reach a larger user base.

## Challenges associated with EdTech Sector

- Psychological and Social Effects of Online Digital Education- Lack of face-to-face interaction and socialization opportunities → affect mental health and social skills of students.
- Perception of Parents about effectiveness of EdTech and may prefer traditional classroom-based education for their wards.
- Low Pupil-teacher Ratio has to be maintained in online education programmes to ensure that students receive personalized attention, support, and mentorship from teachers.
- Digital Divide Accessibility- Unequal access to internet connectivity + devices across urban and rural areas creates a digital divide
- Affordability- High costs of devices and data plans make it difficult for low-income families to afford online education tools.
- Localization- Content needs to be tailored to regional languages and cultural contexts, which requires substantial investment and effort.
- Uneven Quality- A lack of stringent quality control measures can lead to students encountering sub-par educational content.
- Teacher Training- Integrating technology effectively requires proper training for teachers → A lack of such training → hinder successful implementation of EdTech tools in classrooms.
- Engagement and Retention Student Engagement- Keeping students engaged in an online environment is more challenging than in a traditional classroom.
  - High dropout rates in online courses can be problematic, as students might lose interest or face difficulties in self-paced learning.
- Accreditation- Ensuring that online courses and certifications are recognised and valued by educational institutions and employers is crucial.
- Data Privacy Concerns- Protecting students personal data is critical and breaches can erode trust in EdTech platforms.

→ Cybersecurity- Ensuring robust security measures to protect against cyber threats is a continuous challenge.

→ Winter Funding- A Significant decrease in the amount of venture capital (VC) funding flowing into Ed Tech startups → hindering growth potential and innovation.

## PYQs Corner

*(Write the Answer and Get Free Evaluation)*

1. Right of Children to Free and Compulsory Education Act, 2009 remains inadequate in promoting incentive-based systems for children's education without generating awareness about the importance of schooling. Analyse. **(2022)**

2. National Education Policy 2020 is in conformity with the Sustainable Development Goal-4 (2030). It intends to restructure and reorient the education system in India. Critically examine the statement. **(2020)**

3. How have digital initiatives in India contributed to the functioning of the educational system in the country? Elaborate your answer. **(2020)**

4. Professor Amartya Sen has advocated important reforms in the realms of primary education and primary health care. What are your suggestions to improve their status and performance? **(2016)**

5. The quality of higher education in India requires major improvements to make it internationally competitive. Do you think that the entry of foreign educational institutions would help improve the quality of technical and higher education in the country? Discuss. **(2015)**

# CHAPTER 10
# Health Sector

- India's healthcare system has evolved significantly from ancient to modern times. Ancient texts like Charaka Samhita and Sushruta Samhita laid the foundation, focusing on holistic and surgical treatments.
- Over centuries. Ayurveda, Siddha and Unani systems flourished.
- Colonial era introduced Western medicine, leading to a hybrid system.
- Good health extends beyond the mere absence of disease or infirmity → encompasses physical, mental, and social well-being → enabling individuals to lead fulfilling and productive lives.
- Public Health → Entry 6 of State list in Seventh Schedule → Health is core domain of state → obliged to provide for public health and sanitation, hospitals and dispensaries.

| | Constitutional Provision Related to Health |
|---|---|
| Article 21 | Right to health is an integral component of the Right to live with dignity. |
| Article 38 | Promotion of welfare, Providing affordable healthcare is integral to welfare. |
| Article 39 (e) | Health and strength of workers, men and women and the tender age of children are not abused. |
| Article 41 | State to provide public assistance in cases of unemployment, old age sickness and disablement, etc. |
| Article 42 | Protect the health of infant and mother by maternity benefits. |

| Article 47 | State to raise the levels of nutrition and the standard of living and to improve public health. |
|---|---|
| Article 48A | State shall endeavour to protect and improve the environment so as to maintain pollution free environment for good health. |

## Structure and Status of Health Care System in India

- Cost Competitive - The cost of surgery in India is about one-tenth of that in the US or Western Europe.
- As per Economic Survey 2022-23 health care expenditure touched 2.1% of GDP in FY23 and 2.2% in FY22, compared to 1.6% in FY 21.
- According to National Health Accounts Estimates for India 2019-20 → households out-of-pocket expenditure (OOPE) on health is 47.07%
- Merely 37% of people in India were covered under health insurance schemes in 2021.
  - Nearly 400 million individuals in India have zero access to health insurance.
  - Around 70% of population is estimated to be covered under public health insurance or voluntarily private health insurance.



- Immunization coverage among 12-23 month old children → estimated at 76% in 2019-2020
- As per World Malaria Report, 2022 → India achieved a reduction of 85.34% in malaria morbidity and 94% in malaria mortality between the year 2000 and 2020.
- As per Sample Registration System (2020)
  - Neonatal Mortality Rate: 20 per 1000 live births in 2020
  - Infant Mortality Rate: 28 per 1000 live births in 2020.
- As per NFHS 5 (2019-21)
  - Sex Ratio (females per 1000 males): 1020
  - Neonatal Mortality Rate: 24.9.
  - Infant Mortality Rate: 35.2.
  - Institutional Births: 89%

## Challenges in the India's Healthcare System.

| Policy and Governance Challenges | Infrastructural Challenges |
|---|---|
| • Poor Health Investment: India's expenditure on health care touched 2.1% of GDP in FY23.<br>• Existing Inter state variation in health expenditure like Kerala, Delhi spend more than poorer states such as Jharkhand, Bihar.<br>• Poor governance leads to Malpractices like overbilling, unnecessary diagnostic tests and surgical procedures etc are prevalent in hospitals. | • Lack of Basic Infrastructure - As per NITI Aayog report 2021 50% of India's population has access to 35% of hospital beds.<br>• Regional Divide - As per Rural Health Statistics from MoH&FW 2021 → Urban areas have 5439 PHCs and 3966 PHCs in the tribal area.<br>• Beds per 1000 people is 0.5 compared to China 2.6, USA 3.2.<br>• WHO standard for under developed countries is 1. |

| Resource Constraints | Service Delivery Challenges |
|---|---|
| • Shortage of doctors: Doctor population ratio in the country stands at 1:834.<br>• Regional disparities - 80% shortage of specialists in rural community health centers<br>• Poor penetration of Insurance - Only 18% in Urban and 14% in Rural areas have some kind of health insurance<br>• OOPE - As per National Health Accounts Estimates for India 2019-20 it stands at 47.07%. | • Low quality care is prevalent due to misdiagnoses + under trained health professionals + prescription of incorrect medicines.<br>• Barriers of access due to both social and financial inequality.<br>• Dominance of Private Hospitals - 70% of hospital market share was controlled by private sector in financial year 2020.<br>• 63% of hospital beds were provided by private sector hospitals. |

## GOVERNMENT INTERVENTIONS IN HEALTH SECTOR

| | |
|---|---|
| **National Health Mission, 2013** | • An overarching mission aims to provide equitable, affordable, and quality healthcare services across rural and urban India, with a special focus on **Maternal** and child health, **Reproductive** health, **Communicable** and **non-communicable disease.**<br>• It encompasses two sub-missions:<br>○ **National Rural Health Mission (NRHM)** focuses on improving healthcare access and quality in rural areas.<br>○ **National Urban Health Mission (NUHM)** addresses healthcare needs of the urban population. |

| | |
|---|---|
| **National Health Policy, 2017** | • A guiding document outlining the government's vision to achieve universal health coverage by:<br>• Increasing access to quality healthcare services<br>• Making healthcare affordable<br>• Focusing on preventive and promotive care |
| **Ayushman Bharat** | • A flagship program to improve access to quality and affordable healthcare services for secondary and tertiary care, while strengthening preventive and primary care.<br>○ **AB Pradhan Mantri Jan Arogya Yojana (PM-JAY)**: Provides cashless and affordable secondary and tertiary care services at public and private hospitals for low-income families.<br>○ **Up to ₹5 lakh per family per year** for secondary and tertiary hospitalization.<br>○ **ABHealth and Wellness Centres (AB-HWCs):** Focus on comprehensive primary healthcare at the village level. |
| **National Digital Health Mission 2020** | • It aims to create a digital health ecosystem in India to facilitate:<br>○ Secure electronic health records (EHRs) for individuals<br>○ Telemedicine services<br>○ Improved healthcare delivery through technology. |
| **Rogi Kalyan Samiti** | • To make cancer treatment more affordable and accessible for low-income patients → provides financial assistance to cancer patients for treatment.<br>○ **Up to ₹7 lakh** for financial assistance to help cover treatment costs |
| **E-Rakt Kosh** | • An online platform for blood donation management → to streamline process of finding blood donors and ensure a readily available blood supply for patients. |
| **Janani Suraksha Yojana** | • Aims to promote institutional deliveries and improve maternal health outcomes.<br>• Provides financial assistance of ₹6,000 for normal delivery and ₹10,000 for caesarean delivery. |
| **PM Matru Vandana Yojana** | • A cash transfer scheme to provide financial support to pregnant women and lactating mothers. |
| **Mission Indradhanush** | A national immunization mission to prevent childhood deaths and morbidity by ensuring complete immunization against preventable diseases. |
| **National Ayush Mission** | • To integrate **AYUSH** systems of medicine into the mainstream healthcare system and provide a wider range of treatment options.<br>• It focuses on promoting traditional Indian systems of medicine like **Ayurveda**, **Yoga** & **Naturopathy, Unani, Siddha**, and **Homeopathy**. |

| National Pharmaceutical Pricing Authority | National Policy for Rare Diseases, 2021 | National Organ Transplant Programme, 2021 |
|---|---|---|
| Main aim of NPPA is to ensure affordable and accessible medicines.<br>• Regulating the prices of drugs.<br>• Monitoring the availability of drugs.<br>• Taking steps to prevent drug shortages. | • Prevent rare diseases whenever possible.<br>• Improve access to diagnosis and treatment for rare diseases.<br>• Provide financial support to patients with rare diseases. | Aims to increase availability of organs for transplantation in India.<br>• Promoting organ donation awareness.<br>• Strengthening the organ donation infrastructure.<br>• Simplifying the organ transplant process. |

## Futuristic Measures

### 1. Inclusive and Affordable Healthcare

- Increase public health spending: Invest more in government hospitals and clinics to improve affordability and access for low-income populations
- Expand health insurance coverage- Initiatives like Ayushman Bharat can be further strengthened to reach more people, especially in rural areas.
- Address geographic disparities- to build and strengthen healthcare infrastructure in underserved regions.
- Focus on preventive care to lower healthcare costs in the long run.
- Regulate drug prices effectively- Ensure the National Pharmaceutical Pricing Authority (NPPA) effectively regulates drug prices to keep them affordable.

### 2. Improve Infrastructure

- Increase government health expenditure to 2.5% of GDP.
- Upgrade existing government hospitals facilities + clinics with updated equipment and technology.
- Build new hospitals and clinics in rural and underserved areas to improve access to quality health care.
- Invest in medical colleges and training institutions → to increase capacity to train more doctors, nurses, and other healthcare professionals
- Develop telemedicine infrastructure- to provide remote consultations and improve access to specialists in remote areas.
- Invest in R&D to boost indigenous medical innovation.

### 3. Improve Service Delivery

- Improve doctor-patient ratio by incentivizing doctors to work in rural areas and streamlining medical education.
- Emphasize quality of care through robust quality control measures + training programs.
- Enhance patient communication to ensure informed consent and improve patient experience.
- Promote public-private partnerships to leverage their expertise and expand service delivery options.
- Improve sanitation and hygiene to prevent infections and improve overall health outcomes.
- Enhance mental health services- Increase funding for mental healthcare, train healthcare professionals to identify and manage mental health issues and reduce stigma.

## 4. Meet SDG Goals

- Prioritize Maternal and child health → To meet SDG 3.1 to end preventable deaths of newborns and children & SDG 3.2 to end preventable deaths under five
- Combat communicable diseases- Invest in vaccination programs → to meet SDG 3.3: End the epidemics of AIDS, tuberculosis, malaria and neglected tropical diseases and combat hepatitis, water-borne diseases and other communicable diseases systems.
- Promote healthy lifestyles, diet and exercise → to meet SDG 3.4 By 2030 reduce by one third premature mortality from non-communicable diseases through prevention and treatment and promote mental health and well-being.
- Focus on universal health coverage- Continue to expand health insurance schemes and work towards providing quality heathcare services to all citizens.

## UNIVERSAL HEALTH COVERAGE (UHC)

- UHC makes right to health a reality for everyone. It ensures people can get the full range of quality healthcare they need, "at the right time and place, without worrying about the cost."
- 3 Key Aspect of UHC:
  - Access to health services- Everyone who needs services should get them, not only those who can pay for them.
  - Quality of services- Services should be adequate and effective.
  - Financial risk protection- People should not fall into debt paying for treatment and care.

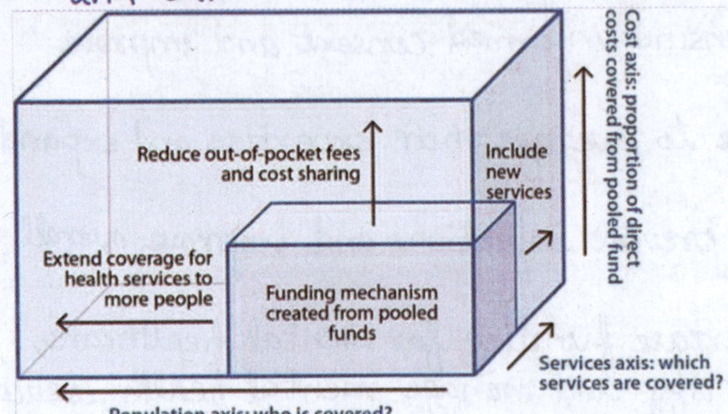


### Evolution of the idea of UHC

- The idea of UHC originated at the WHO **Alma Ata Conference in 1978,** where Health for All was agreed upon by all the participant countries.

- Achieving UHC was made one of the targets under **2030 UN Sustainable Development Goals (SDGs)** in 2015. In the SDG's, **progress on UHC is tracked using two indicators:**
  - Coverage of essential health services **(SDG 3.8.1)**; and
  - Catastrophic health spending (and related indicators) **(SDG 3.8.2).**

- **Global Action Plan for Healthy Lives and Well-being for All (GAP)** was signed in 2019 in the first-ever UN High-Level Meeting on UHC held in 2019.
- **GAP** jointly support countries in delivering on the **SDG 3.8 targets (achieveing UHC).**

## UHC Contribution to National Development

- Human Capital Development - keeping people healthy → allows them to learn + work productivity → pursues better careers → more empowered and skilled workforce.
- Overall Well-being - Affordable and accessible healthcare → Eradicate preventable deaths + illnesses like HIV-AIDS, cancer and heart disease
- Breaking Poverty Cycle - UHC is a lifeline for the poor especially in a country where OOPE stands at 47.07%.
    - Health expenses push 17% of people in low- and middle-income countries into poverty.

**How absence of UHC may push people into poverty?**

- **High out-of-pocket health care cost** (such as consultations, tests, medicine, transportation, etc.)
- Considerable **loss of income due to illness**
- Kins may have to **drop out of school/ workforce** to take care of an ill relative
- Poor families **borrow at high interest rates** for paying medical bills
- Poor families might be forced to **sell assets to cover medical expenses**

- Creating Jobs: A well-functioning UHC system requires a robust healthcare workforce, generating a demand for both skilled and unskilled jobs in health sector.
- Economic Growth Engine - Investing in health today pays off in the future.
    - Every dollar invested can yield up to \$20 in economic growth within a generation.
- Resilience in Crises - COVID-19 pandemic highlighted importance of robust healthcare → "If one person's needs are unmet, everyone is at risk".
    - Countries with strong UHC systems like Japan, were better equipped to handle the crisis.
- Achieving Sustainable Development - Good health is essential for a sustainable future. UHC is a key indicator of progress towards the UN's Sustainable Development Goals (SDGs), particularly SDG 3 (Good Health and well-being).

### Sustainability of UHC

→ Health sector is a major emitter of environmental pollutants.
- Globally, health sector is responsible for nearly 5% of total GHG emissions.

→ UHC may aggravate the situation so understanding the situation and addressing on it becomes an urgency.

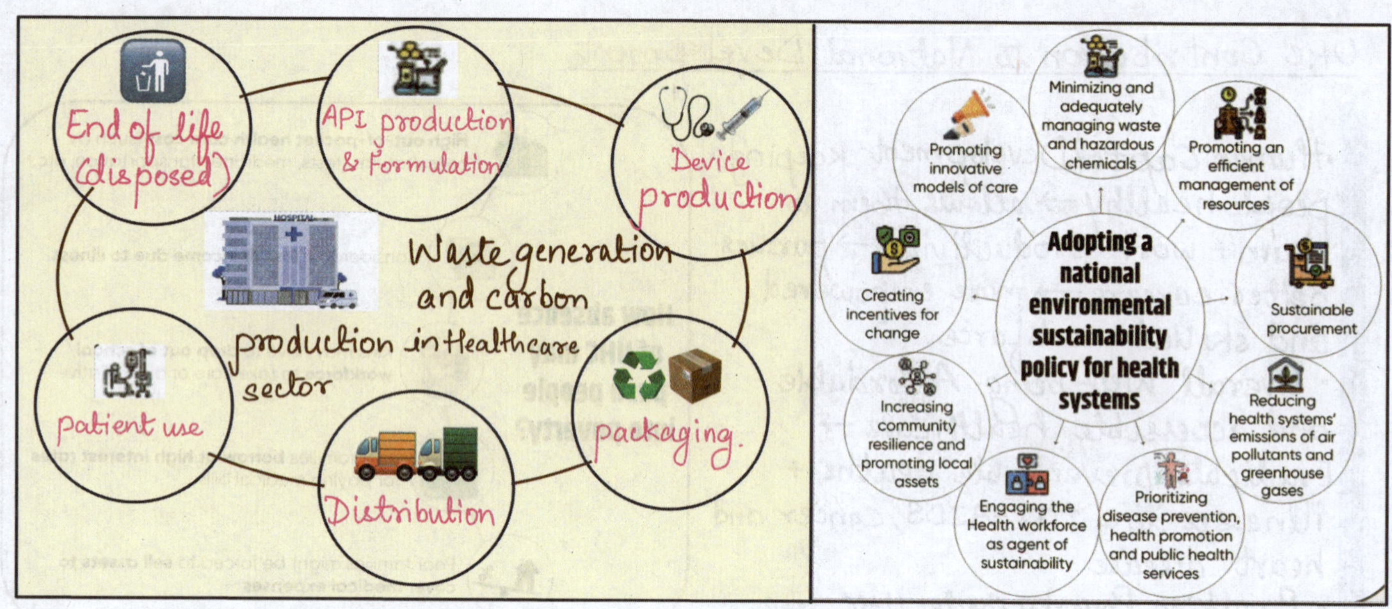


## Policies / Programmes / schemes guiding India's UHC

- Ayushman Bharat Yojana is an attempt to move from a selective approach of health care to deliver a comprehensive range of services spanning preventive, promotive
- National Health Policy, 2017 aims at achieving universal health coverage and delivering quality health care services to all at affordable cost through private sector collaboration.
- Other key initiatives like
  - NMHP to improve the mental well-being of the citizens.
  - National Programme for Health Care of Elderly to make healthcare more inclusive.
  - Pradhan Mantri Swasthya Suraksha Yojna (PMSSY) - to correct regional imbalances in the availability of tertiary healthcare services.
  - Shaksham Angawadi and Poshan 2.0 to address the challenges of malnutrition.
  - Fit India Campaign, Eat Right movement to make fitness an integral part of peoples daily lives.

### Roadblocks in the adoption of UHC

- Chronically underfunded as so far public healthcare expenditures is less than 3% of GDP.
- Unregulated Private Sector leading to high cost of treatment as well as illegal practices.

### Way Forward to achieve UHC

- Roadmap to enhance budgetary allocation to 5% of GDP + leveraging public, private partnership. philanthropic capital etc.
- Moving from Sick care to healthcare by facilitating wellness of patients, improving services at PHCs.

- Poor Quality of Healthcare including at PHCs.
- Rural urban divide in terms of infrastructures as well as availability of health workers.
- Inadequate human resource including doctors, nurses, etc.
- Inadequate health insurance → 30% of the population is devoid of any financial protection for health).
- Lack of accountability due to the absence of grievance redressal mechanism or standard guidelines, etc.
- Low health awareness and inadequate preventive healthcare.

- Improving access and infrastructure in underserved areas → establishing medical colleges in rural areas.
- UHC must be inclusive of all age, gender, caste and creed.
- Judicious use of medicines which account for more than half of the total out-patient spending.
- Enforcing accountability through a clear definition of desirable goals, assessment of goals.

## ONE HEALTH APPROACH

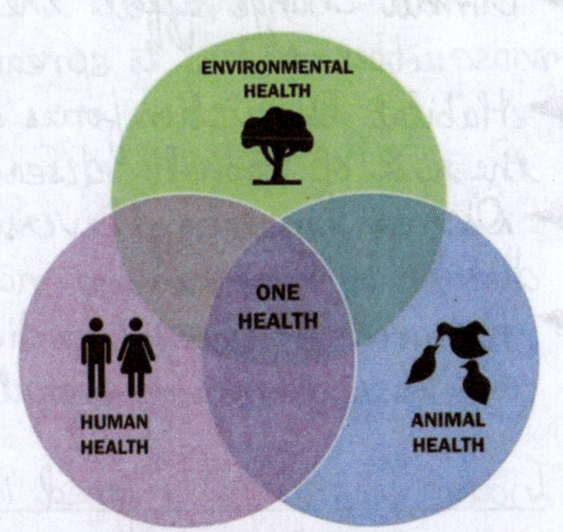


- One Health approach is a collaborative effort that recognizes the interconnectedness between the health of humans, animals and environment.
- It derives its inspiration from One-Health Joint Plan of Action of Quadripartite- FAO, UNEP, WHO and World Organisation for Animal Health (WOAH).

### Collaboration
It brings together experts from various disciplines, such as human health, animal health and environmental science.

### Disease Prevention
It aims to prevent diseases at source, considering their zoonotic nature and means of spread.

### Addressing Global Health Threats
One Health is particularly important for tackling zoonotic diseases like rabies, avian influenza and COVID-19.

### Promoting Sustainability
By addressing the health of ecosystems, One Health approach helps ensure a healthy environment for all living things.

## Need of One Health Concept

- **Emerging Infectious Zoonotic Diseases**- Over 60% of emerging infectious diseases are zoonotic, meaning they are transmitted from animals to humans.
  - Ex- Ebola, SARS, and COVID-19.
- **Disease Surveillance**- Integrating human, animal and environmental health monitoring helps in early detection and control of outbreaks.
- **Antimicrobial Resistance (AMR)**- Coordinated efforts in all sectors are required to develop and implement effective AMR mitigation strategies.
- **Food Safety and Security**- Healthy livestock and poultry are essential for safe and sufficient food supplies.
  - Sustainable farming and responsible use of pesticides + fertilizers → translates into one health.
- **Pollution and Contamination** in environment can affect both human and animal health.
- **Ecosystem Health** supports diverse species, which can prevent the spread of certain diseases by maintaining ecological balances.
- **Climate Change** affects the distribution and behaviour of disease vectors such as mosquitoes → lead to spread of diseases like malaria and dengue fever.
- **Habitat Disruption** forces animals into closer contact with humans, increasing the risk of zoonotic disease transmission.
- **Disease Regulation**- Diverse ecosystems can help regulate the spread of infectious diseases by maintaining natural predators and ecological balances.
- **Resource Efficiency**- Coordinated efforts can optimize the use of resources and expertise, improving overall health outcomes.

## Indian Initiatives Aligned With One Health Concept

- **Standing Committee on Zoonoses, 2006**: Purpose of this committee was to provide the Union and the State governments guidance and recommendations on challenges related to zoonoses.
- **Consortium on One Health, 2021** launched by Department of Biotechnology.
  - It brings together 27 organisations from several ministries and plans.
  - Focus on assessing burden of five transboundary animal diseases and 10 select zoonotic diseases.
- **One Health pilot project, 2022**- launched by Department of Animal Husbandry and Dairy (DAHD) + in partnership with Bill & Melinda Gates Foundation and the Confederation of Indian Industry from Karnataka and Uttarakhand.
  - It intends to strengthen intersectoral collaborations through capacity-building → for improving livestock health, human health, wildlife health and environmental health.

→ National One Health Mission- is currently under consideration to be spearheaded by the Office of the Principal Scientific Advisor.

- The idea behind this mission is to coordinate, support and integrate all existing One Health initiatives in the country.

## MENTAL HEALTH

- Good mental health is a key part of overall health. It empowers us to cope with challenges, reach our full potential and build strong relationships. It allows us to make sound decisions, shape our world, and contribute to society.
- SDG 3.4 emphasises on promoting mental health and well-being.

### Key Components of Mental Health

Environment
Personal Growth
Purpose in life
Self Acceptance
Strong Social Connection
Autonomy

- Environmental Mastery refers to one's ability to manage his surroundings and feel comfortable in your environment.
  - It includes feeling safe, having control over your space, and possessing skills to navigate different situations effectively.
- Personal Growth emphasizes one's desire to learn and develop throughout your life.
  - It involves embracing new challenges, setting goals, and continuously striving to improve yourself as a person.
- Purpose in life provides direction and motivation in life.
- Self-Acceptance towards oneself for who you are, flaws and all.
  - It helps in recognizing one's strengths and weaknesses → treating yourself with kindness.
- Strong social connections are crucial for mental well-being.
  - It includes having healthy and supportive relationships with family, friends and loved ones → fosters emotional well-being.
- Autonomy refers to "sense of independence" + control over your own life.
  - It involves feeling empowered to make your own decisions, set your own goals, and pursue your own path in life.

### Status of Mental Health in India

- As per WHO estimates → age-adjusted suicide rate per one lakh population is 21.1.
- The economic loss due to psychological health conditions, between 2012-2030 is estimated at USD 1.03 trillion.

- As per NMHS 2025-16 prevalence of mental disorders among children between ages 13-17 stands at 7.3%.
- As per NCRB 2022-23, Suicides because of mental illness stands at 18.4%.
- As per NCRB 2020-21, number of suicides among students has steadily increased from 7696 students (2011) to 13,089 students (2021).

**Factors affecting Mental Health among School Children**

**Academic Pressure**
Excessive academic demands, such as homework, exams, and competition, can lead to stress and anxiety.

**Family Dynamics**
Issues like divorce, domestic violence, and parental conflict.

**Childhood Trauma**
Experiencing trauma, such as physical or emotional abuse, neglect, or loss.

**Environmental Stressors**
Factors like pollution, overcrowded living conditions, and exposure to violence in the community.

**Digital Stressors**
The use of social media and the internet can expose children to cyberbullying, and online harassment.

**Genetic factors**
A family history of mental health disorders can increase the risk.

**Peer Relationships**
Social interactions with peers, including issues like bullying, peer pressure, and feelings of social isolation.

**Economic Status**
Factors such as poverty and financial instability.

## Reasons for Poor Mental Health

| | |
|---|---|
| Biological Makeup | • Family History - Having a close relative with a mental health condition can increase one's risk.<br>• Chronic illnesses and neurological conditions can affect one's mental well-being. |
| Early Experiences | • Childhood Trauma - Experiences of abuse, neglect or trauma can contribute to mental health issues later in life.<br>• Personality Traits - Certain personality characteristics can make you more susceptible to mental health challenges. |
| Environment | • Socioeconomic Status - Poverty, unemployment, and financial stress can take a toll on mental health.<br>• Social Support and networking can protect one, while isolation can worsen mental health.<br>• Exposure to Trauma - Experiencing violence, accidents, or natural disasters can have a significant impact.<br>• Access to Healthcare - limited access to mental health services can make it harder to get treatment. |
| Lifestyle Choice | • Substance Abuse - Drug and alcohol abuse can worsen or trigger mental health disorders.<br>• Negligence towards Diet and Excercise - contribute to poor mental well-being.<br>• Sleep Habits: Sleep disturbances and disorders can affect mood and cognitive function.<br>• Chronic Stress - Ongoing stress from work, relationships or other sources can take a toll on mental health. |
| Socio-Cultural Norms and Beliefs | • Cultural Beliefs - Cultural norms and expectations can influence how mental health issues are percived and addresed.<br>• Discrimination Experiencing stigma with respect to race, gender, sexual orientation → may distort one's psychological health. |

## Role of Social Media and Mental Health

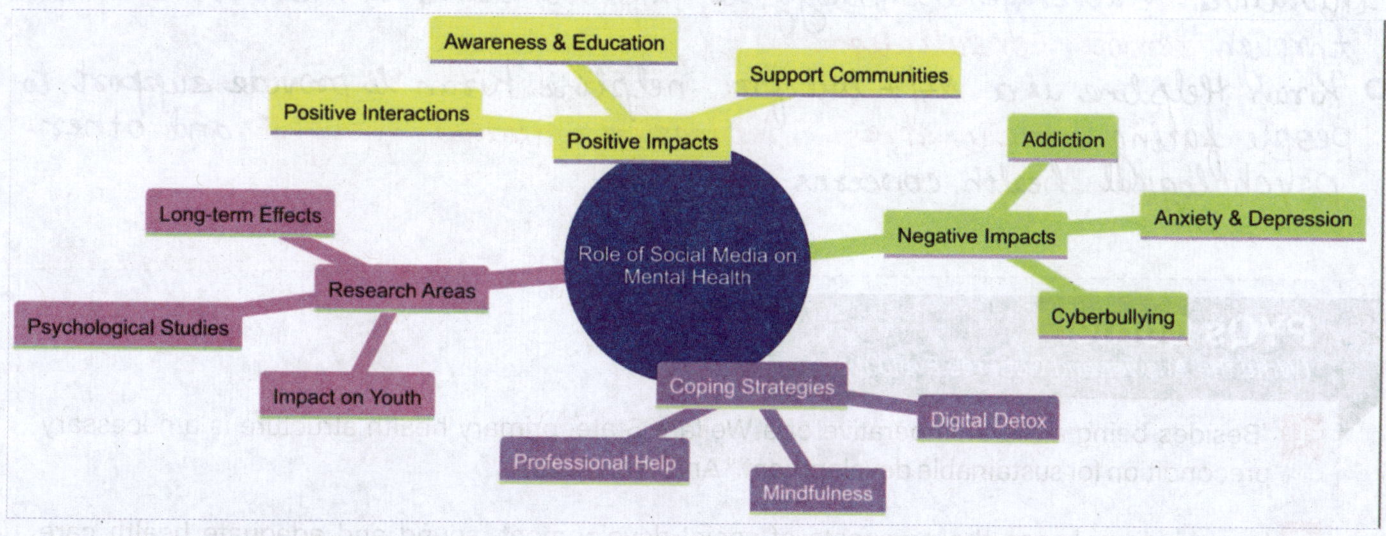


## Government Initiative / Intervention to Address Mental Health Issue

- National Mental Health Program (NMHP) aims to ensure availability and accessibility of essential mental healthcare for all, particularly focusing on underserved and disadvantaged populations.
- District Mental Health Program (DMHP) a subprogram under NMHP based on 'Bellary Model' → focused on strengthening mental health services at district level.
  - Integrate basic mental health services into the existing primary healthcare system.
  - Train primary healthcare workers to identify and manage common mental health conditions.
- Mental Health Care Act 2017-
  - Rights of Individuals: It guarantees the right to access psychological healthcare for mental illness.
  - It allows individuals to make advance directives about treatment preferences.
  - It decriminalizes suicide and prohibits use of electroconvulsive therapy without anesthesia.
  - Psychological Health Review Boards to safeguard the rights of individuals with mental illness.
  - It mandates insurance companies → to provide insurance coverage for psychological health treatment.

  The Act prohibits the use of seclusion and chaining of mentally ill individuals.

- Tele Mental Health Assistance and Networking Across States (Tele-MANAS) initiatives → leverage technology to improve access to mental health care through remote consultation.
- Kiran Helpline is a 24/7 toll-free helpline 'Kiran' to provide support to people facing anxiety, stress, depression, suicidal thoughts and other psychological health concerns.

## PYQs Corner

*(Write the Answer and Get Free Evaluation)*

1. "Besides being a moral imperative of a Welfare State, primary health structure is a necessary precondition for sustainable development." Analyse. **(2021)**
2. In order to enhance the prospects of social development, sound and adequate health care policies are needed particularly in the fields of geriatric and maternal health care. Discuss. **(2020)**
3. Appropriate local community level healthcare intervention is a prerequisite to achieve 'Health for All' in India. Explain. **(2018)**
4. Public health system has limitations in providing universal health coverage. Do you think that the private sector could help in bridging the gap? What other viable alternatives would you suggest? **(2015)**

CHAPTER 11

# Human Resources

- About- A nation's human resources refer to the collective skills, knowledge, talents and abilities of its population that are available for economic development and social progress.
  - India has more than 66% of the total population under 35 years old.
  - It can be a vital asset and human resource → through investments in education healthcare and skill development.

## COMPONENTS

- Knowledge is the foundation → It includes learning through education, training and experience.
- Skills and Capabilities refers to the ability to solve problems, innovate and contribute meaningfully to society by application of skill and knowledge.
- Health- A healthy population has the physical and mental capacity to be productive and contribute.

Health and Education components have been discussed with sufficient depth in Chapter Health Sector and Education Sector

## Statistics:

- India's Demographic Dividend- India has 62.5% of its population in age group of 15-59 years → will be at a peak of around 2036 when it will reach approximately 65%.
- According to Economic Survey 2018-19, India's demographic dividend will peak around 2041, when share of working-age, i.e 20-59 years, population is expected to hit 59%.
- As per Periodic labour Force Survey (PLFS) 2022-23, India's labour force participation rate (LFPR) is 57.9% (78.5% for males, 37% for females).
- The 2015 Report on National Policy on Skill Development and Entrepreneurship estimated that only 4.7% of the total workforce in India had undergone formal skill training compared with 52% in US, 80% in Japan and 96% in South Korea.
- According to the India Skill Report 2019, only 45.6% of youth graduating from educational institutions are employable.
- India has been ranked 116 out of 195 countries in Human Capital Index, 2023.
- Around 85% of workspace in the unorganized sector does not imbibe any form of skill development.

## Need of Human Resource Development

- Productivity Enhancement- Developing human resources through education + training + skill development → increases productivity → economic growth.
- Attracting Investment- Countries with a highly skilled workforce attract more foreign investment, boosting economic development.
- Demographic Dividend- The 'demographic window' is only a span of a few decades. The skilled youth is required to save demographic dividend from becoming a demographic disaster.
- Demand for Skilled Workforce- Confederation of Indian Industry (CII) had projected Incremental Human Resource Requirements till 2022 at 201 million, making total requirement of the skilled workforce by 2023 at 300 million.
- Outsourcing of skill- India could become supplier of talent and skills, if its workforce is equipped with employable skills that keep pace with exponentially changing technological ecosystem.
    - Over the next two decades, labour force in the industrialized world is expected to decline by 4%, while in India it will increase by nearly 20%.
- Changing nature of work- Rising role of technology in background of fourth Industrial Revolution and emerging technologies like IoT, cloud computing, artificial intelligence → making old skills obsolete.

- Huge manufacturing base- COVID-19 pandemic → disrupted the global supply chain + dependent on China's manufacturing industry.
    - It offers an opportunity for India to become a leading supply chain hub.
- China's Slowdown: Companies vacating its factories from China → due to rising Chinese wages + an appreciating Yuan + internal demographic challenge → India has an opportunity to become a factory of the world.
- Sectoral mobilization- As productivity improves → less number of people will be required to work in farming → transition from agriculture to secondary and tertiary activities.
- Poverty Reduction- Improving human resources → Enhance employability with higher income → reducing poverty levels.
- Social Mobility- Education + skill development → opportunities for upward social mobility → different socio-economic groups.
- Environmental Sustainability- An educated and aware population is more likely to adopt and promote sustainable practices + contributing to environmental conservation.
- Social Cohesion- Education + employment opportunities → reduce social unrest → national stability.
- Cultural Exchange- Education and skill development promote cultural understanding and exchange, fostering international cooperation and goodwill.
- Knowledge Economy- Developing human resources in research and development is crucial for a knowledge-based economy, leading to new discoveries and innovations.
- Digital Transformation by preparing workforce to handle digital tools and technologies is essential in modern era, where technology is rapidly evolving.
- Future Skills- Preparing the workforce for future skills required in emerging industries such as artificial intelligence, renewable energy and biotechnology.

## Bottlenecks in Human Resource Development

- Absence of Basic Education- difficult to upskill younger population for higher-end jobs.
    - A 2020 NSO survey revealed that one out of every eight students enrolled in a school or college drops out before completing education.
    - Less than 40% of students pursued higher secondary and/or higher education.
- Insufficient Training Facilities- As per NSSO, there is a lack of training facilities in as many as 20 high-growth industries such as logistics, healthcare, construction hospitality and automobiles.
    - India has 5500 public (ITIs) and private (ITC) institutes as against 5,00,000 similar institutes in China.

- Lack of Awareness- about government-run skill development programs → hinders accessibility of training facilities
- Changing demands under Industry 4.0 overhaul has resulted in creation of new types of jobs that require special skill sets; the highest-end jobs which require more 'human' skills such as networking, creativity, problem-solving etc.
- Lack of Focus on Upskilling/Reskilling- As per World Economic Forum → Half of global labour force might need reskilling by 2025.
  - Due to emergence of Fourth Industrial technologies such as Artificial Intelligence (AI), Data Analytics challenge of reskilling and upskilling is becoming prominent.
- Absence of Job skill: India Skills Report 2021 → only 45.9% of young people would be considered employable.
  - As per UNICEF, more than 50% of Indian youth are not on track to have employment ready education and skills by 2030.
- Unawareness & Apathy Towards Entrepreneurship- About 70% of Indian youth is not aware of schemes, according to a recent study "Young India and Work" by the Observer Research Foundation and World Economic Forum (WEF).
- Low industry Participation- Industries or firms may be reluctant to spend on in-house training or upskilling staff since those trained may quit jobs to join other firms seeking better prospects thus benefiting the latter firm and not the firm that incurred the training cost.
- Gender Inequality- Discrimination + limited access to education + training → low level of female participation in the labour force.
- Inadequate Monitoring and Evaluation (M&E) with little third-party monitoring of quality and outcomes.
  - Absence of formal and active feedback mechanism in place to capture learning experiences of and 'outcomes' for beneficiaries.

## Way Forward

- Reversing Dropouts Trend- Irrespective of rural or urban setting, public school system must ensure that every child completes high school education + imparting appropriate skills, training and vocational education in line with market demand.
- Deploying new technology like virtual classrooms together with Massive Open Online Courses (MOOCS) to yield at a higher educated workforce.
- Employability of Workforce by inculcating General, professional and vocational education at school level.
  - Cutting-edge technologies like robotics, artificial intelligence, machine learning, nanotechnology have to be included in curriculum of Polytechnics, ITI and engineering institutions.

- Incorporation of Upskilling in Goals in an already employed workforce could lead to greater productivity in economy, higher incomes for workers, and higher profitability for firms.
  - PMKVY could equally prioritise upskilling initiatives in the PPP mode on line of UK, Germany and Australia.
- Involving Corporate Sector- Investing in skill development is a win-win solution for the corporate sector as well as government.
  - According to a NASSCOM Report in 2021, investing in skill training programmes resulted in more than 600% return on outlays.

## Government Initiatives

| Measures | Description |
|---|---|
| **Skill India Mission** | • To empower youth of country with skill sets which make them more employable and more productive in their work environment. |
| **National Policy on Skill Development and Entrepreneurship, 2015:** | Aimed to provide an umbrella framework to all skilling activities being carried out within the country, to align them to common standards and link the skilling with demand centres. It emphasized working upon:<br>• **Inhibiting factors:** Addresses key obstacles to skilling, including low aspirational value, lack of integration with formal education, lack of focus on outcomes, low quality of training infrastructure and trainers, etc.<br>• **Demand and Supply gap:** The policy seeks to align supply and demand for skills by bridging existing skill gaps, promoting industry engagement, operationalizing a quality assurance framework, leverage technology and promoting greater opportunities for apprenticeship training.<br>• **Equity:** The Policy targets skilling opportunities for socially/geographically marginalized and disadvantaged groups and especially women.<br>• **Entrepreneurship:** The Policy seeks to educate and equip potential entrepreneurs, both within and outside the formal education system. It also seeks to connect entrepreneurs to mentors, incubators and credit markets, foster innovation and entrepreneurial culture, improve ease of doing business and promote a focus on social entrepreneurship. |
| **Pradhan Mantri Kaushal Vikas Yojana** | • To encourage aptitude towards employable skills and to increase working efficiency of probable and existing daily wage earners, by giving monetary awards and rewards and by providing quality training to them. |
| **Deen Dayal Upadhyaya Grameen Kaushalya Yojana** | • To transform rural poor youth into an economically independent and globally relevant workforce |

| | |
|---|---|
| **SANKALP** | • **Skill Acquisition and Knowledge Awareness for Livelihood Promotion:** To improve short term skill training qualitatively and quantitatively through strengthening institutions, bringing in better market connectivity and inclusion of marginalised sections of the society |
| **SVEP** | **Start-up Village Entrepreneurship Program:** Launched by the Ministry of Rural Development, it aims to promote rural entrepreneurship.<br>• It focuses on marginalized communities, including women, Scheduled Castes and Scheduled Tribes, by providing them with training, financial assistance and mentorship to start their own micro-enterprises |
| **National Career Service (NCS)** | • The NCS is an online platform developed by the Ministry of Labour and Employment. It provides a variety of services, including job matching, career counseling, skill assessments, and training programs. |
| | • The platform aims to facilitate equal opportunities and accessibility to employment resources for all individuals, irrespective of their background. |
| **Mahila E-Haat** | • This initiative by the Ministry of Women and Child Development provides an online platform for women entrepreneurs to showcase and sell their products.<br>• It aims to promote women's economic empowerment and create opportunities for them to participate in the mainstream economy. |
| **Future Skills Prime** | • It is a skilling ecosystem focused on emerging technologies, powered by a partnership between MeitY, NASSCOM and the IT industry.<br>• It seeks to propel India to become a global hub of talent in emerging technologies. |
| **Mandatory CSR Expenditure in Skilling** | • Since the implementation of mandatory CSR spending under the Companies Act, 2013, corporations in India have invested over ₹100,000 crores in diverse social projects.<br>• Of these, about ₹6,877 crores were spent on skilling and livelihood enhancement projects. Maharashtra, Tamil Nadu, Odisha, Karnataka, and Gujarat were the top five recipient States. |
| **Establishment of Training Institutes** | • Over time, a fairly vast institutional system for training and skills has evolved.<br>• This includes 15,154 Industrial Training Institutes (ITIs) (including 11,892 private institutes); 36 Sector Skills Councils, 33 National Skills Training Institutes, and 2,188 training partners registered with National Skill Development Corporation (NSDC). |
| **AI for All** | • Ministry of Education joined hands with the chip-making giant Intel and Central Board of Secondary Education (CBSE) to announce the launch of - 'AI for All' - an initiative that aims to create a basic understanding of Artificial Intelligence (AI) |
| **Operation Digital Board** | • To utilise emerging technologies in promoting quality education in India. |
| **STRIVE Project** | • **Skills Strengthening for Industrial Value Enhancement:** To improve the relevance and efficiency of skills training provided through Industrial Training Institutes (ITIs) and apprenticeships. |

## PYQs Corner

*(Write the Answer and Get Free Evaluation)*

1. The crucial aspect of the development process has been the inadequate attention paid to Human Resource Development in India. Suggest measures that can address this inadequacy. **(2023)**

2. Why did human development fail to keep pace with economic development in India? **(2023)**

3. Skill development programmes have succeeded in increasing human resources supply to various sectors. In the context of the statement analyse the linkages between education, skill and employment. **(2023)**

4. "Earn while you learn" scheme needs to be strengthened to make vocational education and skill training meaningful." Comment. **(2021)**

5. Despite the consistent experience of high growth, India still goes with the lowest indicators of human development. Examine the issues that make balanced and inclusive development elusive. **(2019)**

# CHAPTER 12 Hunger

About - Hunger happens when people do not have enough food to eat.

| | |
|---|---|
| Acute Hunger | • It designates undernourishment over a definable period.<br>• Causes: Droughts from El Niño, wars etc. |
| Chronic hunger | • It designates a state of long-term undernourishment<br>• The body absorbs less food than it needs.<br>• It usually arises in connection with poverty. |
| Hidden hunger | • It is a form of chronic hunger due to an unbalanced diet.<br>• Lack of important nutrients, such as iron, iodine, zinc, or vitamin A. |

## Status of Hunger in India

- Food Security and Nutrition Report 2023: 74% Indians could not afford healthy diet in 2021.
- Hunger in India - As per the National Family Health Survey (NFHS)-5 (2019-21) stunting among children under five years of age has reduced marginally from 38.4% (NFHS-4) to 34.7%
- India's Global Hunger Index score 2023 stands at 28.7, categorized as "serious"
- Regional disparity - Bihar, Uttar pradesh, and Madhya Pradesh have higher prevalance rates compared to Kerala and Tamil Nadu.

## Causes of Hunger in India

- **Poverty** - Poor living conditions and limited food access lead to malnutrition in children, especially in rural areas with overpopulation.
- **Ineffective Food Policy Implementation** - Programs like the integrated Child Development Services (ICDS) and the National Health Mission (NHM) do not provide adequate coverage.
    - Ex- Corruption in the Public Distribution System (PDS)
- **Food Wastage** - India's per capita food waste 55 kg/yr (UN).
- **Issues with Agriculture** - shift from multi-cropping to mono-cropping systems reduces the diversity of agricultural products.
- **Unidentified hunger** - Inaccurate classification of household as above or below the poverty line, coupled with poor quality grains, leads to a decline in food consumption.
- **Gender Bias** - The nutritional needs of a girl children and the elderly are different and are often inadequately addressed in society.

> - Availability - Despite high grain production, 233.9 million people in India are undernourished.
> - Affordability - 74.1% of Indians cannot afford a healthy diet due to stagnant income levels.

- **Lack of maternal knowledge** - Inadequate understanding of nutrition, breastfeeding and parenting among mothers is another area of concern.
- **Climate Change** - led to an increase in uncertainty over agriculture production.
- **Natural disaster** - Weather extremes lead to hunger crises. Droughts and floods destroy harvests and leave the poor vulnerable.
- **Declining income levels** - Periodic Labour Force Survey (PLFS) 2017-18 has revealed that rural unemployment stood is at 6.1 percent, which is the highest since 1972-73.

## Manifestation of Hunger

- **Vicious Cycle of Poverty and Hunger**
    - Poverty → Hunger → Poverty

limits access to nutritious food → Food insecurity and malnutrition → lead to health issues + increasing household expenses

Hunger → Poverty: Hunger weakens individuals physically and mentally. reducing their ability to work effectively or attend school.

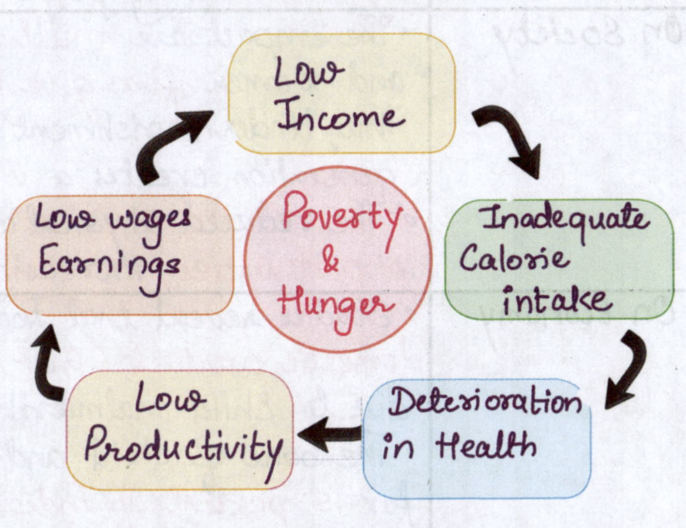

- Micronutrient deficiency (hidden hunger) due to poor dietary intakes, prevalence of diseases & non-fulfilment of increased micronutrient needs during pregnancy and lactation.
- Limited Education- Children are forced to stay home for chores or work.
- Health Issues- Malnutrition has long been linked to poverty as higher rates of malnutrition are found in areas with chronic poverty.
- Lower Productivity: Poor diet on the job costs countries up to 20% in lost productivity (ILO).

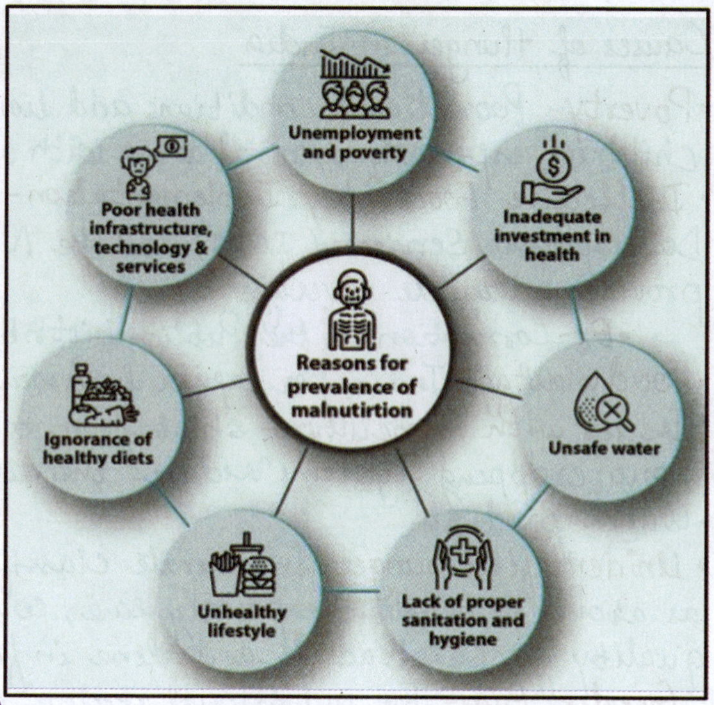

Reasons for prevalence of malnutirtion

Unemployment and poverty

Inadequate investment in health

Unsafe water

Lack of proper sanitation and hygiene

Unhealthy lifestyle

Ignorance of healthy diets

Poor health infrastructure, technology & services

- Demotivation and Despair- Living in poverty can lead to a sense of hopelessness and demotivation, hindering peoples willingness to learn new skills and seek better opportunities.
- Social unrest- Hunger can lead to social unrest and conflict as people may resort to violence to obtain food or other basic needs.
- Manifestation in different spheres:

| | |
|---|---|
| At individual level | • Mentally, cognitive function decreases and physically, starvation substantially affects a person's muscles, bone, skin and internal organs.<br>• A lack of sufficient nutrients also weakens the immune system, making people more susceptible to chronic diseases. |
| On Society | • The impact are multi-generational, as malnourished girls and women often give birth to low birth-weight infants. Thus, Undernourishment being passed on from generation to generation creates a vicious circle.<br>• The reduced physical and mental capacity reduces earnings opportunities, increasing the risk of poverty. |
| On Economy | • Studies reveal that India loses up to 4 percent of its gross domestic product (GDP) and up to 8 percent of its productivity due to child malnutrition.<br>• The bane of child and maternal malnutrition is responsible for 15 percent of India's total disease burden. |

## Initiatives to tackle hunger in India

- National Nutrition Mission (NNM), Poshan Abhiyan- NMH was started in 2018 by the Ministry of Women and Child Development to reduce the level of under nutrition and also enhance the nutritional status of children in the country.
- National Food Security Act, 2013 -The Act legally entitles up to 75% of the rural population and 50% of the urban population to receive subsidized food grains under Targete Public Distribution System.
- Eat Right India Movement- An outreach activity organized by the Food Safety and Standards Authority of India (FSSAI) for citizens to nudge them towards eating right.
- Zero Hunger Program- Launched in October 2017, it aims at eliminating hunger and malnutrition by 2030.
  - It aims to intervene on farms by organizing nutrition foused farming systems, providing zero hunger training, and establishing biofortified plant genetic gardens.
- Pradhan Mantri Matru Vandana Yojana (PMMVY)- PMMVY is a Centrally Sponsored DBT scheme with a cash incentives of ₹5000/- being provided directly in the bank/post office account of Pregnant Women and Lactating Mothers.
- Pradhan Mantri Poshan Shakti Nirman scheme (PM Poshan Scheme)- It is a school meal programme designed with the aim of improving the nutritional status of school-age children across the nation.

## Pathways For Elimination of Hunger in India

- Addressing poverty- Improving economic conditions and reducing poverty levels through job creation and better access to education.
- Improving public distribution systems- Strengthening the public distribution system to ensure that food is distributed equitably and efficiently.
- Increasing agricultural productivity- Enhancing agricultural productivity through better irrigation, improved seeds, and better technology can help increase food production and availability.
- Focusing on maternal and child health- Improving maternal and child health by promoting breastfeeding, adequate nutrition and immunization.
- Addressing gender inequality- Reducing gender inequality and promoting education for girls can help improve their nutrition and reduce malnutrition

- Addressing gender inequality- Reducing gender inequality and promoting education for girls can help improve their nutrition and reduce malnutrition.

- Strengthening monitoring and evaluation systems- Establishing effective monitoring and evaluation mechanisms to ensure that nutritional programs are effective and efficiently implemented.
- Multisectoral Approach- Inclusion of water, education, sanitation, agriculture nutrition etc, should be undertaken by governments
- Diversify Food Basket- Production and distribution of nutrient rich commodities such as millets, leafy vegetables, milk and eggs need to be encouraged under the NFSA.
  - Haryana is providing financial incentives of ₹7000/acre to farmers for shifting from paddy to pulses, oilseeds, and cotton.
- Reduce wastage- Supply chain management reforms including robust transportation infrastructure and cold storage is needed.
- Society activism like the Right to Food Campaign (launched in March 2014) is an informal network of individuals and organisations to persuade State governments to attend to the most pressing demands of society, including proper nutrition.
- Learn from International experience:
  - Thailand reduced child malnutrition (underweight)- rate from 50 percent to 25 percent in the period 1980-1988 → Mix of interventions including intensive growth monitoring and nutrition education, strong supplementary feeding provisions etc.
  - National Plan of Action for Nutrition of Bangladesh- is based on a multi-sectoral convergence strategy involving health, education, fisheries and livestock, environment, social protection, disaster management etc to combact child malnutrition.

## PYQs Corner

*(Write the Answer and Get Free Evaluation)*

1. There is a growing divergence in the relationship between poverty and hunger in India. The shrinking of social expenditure by the government is forcing the poor to spend more on Non- Food essential items squeezing their food - budget. Elucidate. **(2019)**
2. How far do you agree with the view that the focus on lack or availability of food as the main cause of hunger takes the attention away from ineffective human development policies in India? **(2018)**
3. Hunger and Poverty are the biggest challenges for good governance in India still today. Evaluate how far successive governments have progressed in dealing with these humongous problems. Suggest measures for improvement. **(2017)**

# NOTES

# NOTES

# NOTES

# NOTES